Knowledge, Skill and Artificial Intelligence

The Springer Series on

FOUNDATIONS AND APPLICATIONS
OF ARTIFICIAL INTELLIGENCE

Series Editor: KARAMJIT S. GILL

Knowledge, Skill and Artificial Intelligence
Bo Göranzon and Ingela Josefson (Eds.)

Bo Göranzon and Ingela Josefson (Eds.)

Knowledge, Skill and Artificial Intelligence

With 10 Figures

Springer-Verlag
London Berlin Heidelberg New York
Paris Tokyo

Bo Göranzon
Mathematician and Researcher, Swedish Center for Working Life,
Box 5606, S-11486, Sweden

Dr. Ingela Josefson
Linguist and Researcher, Swedish Center for Working Life,
Box 5606, S-11486, Sweden

Cover illustration reproduced by kind permission of
Lennart Mörk, Royal Dramatic Theatre of Sweden

ISBN 3-540-19519-X Springer-Verlag Berlin Heidelberg New York
ISBN 0-387-19519-X Springer-Verlag New York Berlin Heidelberg

British Library Cataloguing in Publication Data
Knowledge, skill and artificial intelligence.—
(Foundations and applications of artificial intelligence)
1. Artificial intelligence
I. Göranzon, Bo   II. Josefson, Ingela III. Series
006.3
ISBN 3-540-19519-X

Library of Congress Cataloging-in-Publication Data
Knowledge, skill and artificial intelligence: tacit knowledge and new technology/
Bo Göranzon and Ingela Josefson, eds.
p. cm.
Proceedings of a conference on the topic of knowledge, skill, and new technology,
held in London in March 1987
Includes bibliographies and index.
ISBN 0-387-19519-X (U.S.)
1. Artificial intelligence. 2. Knowledge, Theory of. I. Göranzon, Bo, 1941–.
II. Josefson, Ingela, 1943–. Q335.K58 1988 006.3–dc19   88-5096 CIP

© Springer-Verlag Berlin Heidelberg 1988
Printed in Great Britain

Filmset by Goodfellow and Egan, French's Mill, French's Road, Cambridge
Printed and bound in Great Britain at The Bath Press, Avon

2128/3916–543210

Preface

This book is a result of a conference held in London in March 1987 on the topic Knowledge, Skill and New Technology. The meeting was an initiative supported by the Swedish Center for Working Life and the project AI-based Systems and the Future of Language, Knowledge and Responsibility in Professions within the COST 13 programme of the European Commission. The project laid the foundations for our visit to Great Britain during the period September 1986 to July 1987 with the aim of establishing long-term research contacts in the area of the impact of technology on professions, between researchers in Great Britain and Sweden.

Our research assistant Satinder P. Gill has given us support in coordinating the editorial work for this book. She has also made the summary of every contribution and the subject index. We are very grateful for her excellent professional work.

Stockholm
31 December 1987

Bo Göranzon
Ingela Josefson

Contents

4. Automation–Skill–Apprenticeship

5. Computerization and Skill in Local Weather Forecasting

6. Tacit Knowledge, Working Life and Scientific Method

SECTION III. Skill and Artificial Intelligence

7. Can Skills be Transferable?

8. Artificial Intelligence and Social Action: Education and Training

SECTION IV. Artificial Intelligence and the Flexible
Craftsman

Contributors

M. Cooley, PhD
Thatcham Lodge, 95 Sussex Place, Slough, Berks SL1 1NN, UK

M. Cross, BSc, PhD
Visiting Fellow, City University Business School, Frobisher
Crescent, Barbican Centre, London EC2 8HB, UK

R. Ennals MA
Staff Development Unit, Kingston College of Further Education,
Kingston Hall Road, Kingston Surrey KT1 2AQ, UK and Exeter
University School of Education, Exeter EX1 2LU, UK

K. S. Gill, DPhil
Director, SEAKE Centre and Principal Lecturer in Artificial
Intelligence, Faculty of Information Technology, Brighton
Polytechnic, Moulsecoomb, Brighton BN2 4GJ, UK

Satinder P. Gill
Research Assistant, Swedish Centre for Working Life,
Box 5606, S-11486, Sweden

B. Göranzon
Mathematician and Researcher, Swedish Center for Working Life,
Box 5606, S-11486, Sweden

P. Gullers
Photographer and Researcher, Swedish Center for Working Life,
Box 5606, S-11486, Sweden

Anna Hart, MA
Lecturer, Cognitive Sciences Group, Faculty of Science, Lancashire
Polytechnic, Preston PR1 2TQ, UK

J. Hilton, MA DPhil
Director, Audio-Visual Centre and Chairman of Drama,
The Audio-Visual Centre, University of East Anglia,
University Plain, Norwich NR4 7TJ, UK

A. Janik, PhD
Professor, Brenner Archive, Innsbruck University, Innrain 52,
A-6020, Innsbruck, Austria

Ingela Josefson, DPhil
Linguist and Researcher, Swedish Center for Working Life,
Box 5605, S-11486, Sweden

T. Karlsen
Director, Trades Union Research Center, Oslo, Fossveien 19,
N-0551 Oslo 5, Norway

Maria Oppen
Researcher, Wissenschaftcentrum, Berlin, Steinplatz 2, D-1000
Berlin 12, Germany

O. Ostberg, PhD
Professor, Testing and Research Laboratories, Swedish
Telecommunications Administration, S-123 86 Farsta, Sweden

Maja-Lisa Perby
Researcher, Research Policy Institute, Box 2017, S-220 02, Lund,
Sweden

P. Pritchard, MA, FRCGP
General Practitioner, Oxfordshire, England, 31 Martin's Lane,
Dorchester on Thames, Oxford OX9 8JF, UK

D.W. Schartum
Norwegian Center for Computer and Law, University of Oslo,
Niels Juels gt 16, N-0272 Oslo 2, Norway

Summaries
Satinder P. Gill

Chapter 2. The Practice of the Use of Computers. A Paradoxical Encounter between Different Traditions of Knowledge

B. Göranzon

Fundamental to the design of knowledge-based systems is the understanding of the nature of knowledge and the problems involved in computerizing it. The paper deals with these issues and draws a distinction between three different categories of knowledge: i propositional knowledge, ii skill or practical knowledge and iii knowledge of familiarity. In the present debate on "Information Society", there is a clear tendency to overemphasize theoretical knowledge at the expense of practical knowledge, thereby completely ignoring the knowledge of familiarity. It is argued that different forms of theoretical knowledge are required for the design of current computer technology and the study of the practice of computer usage. The concept of dialogue and the concept of "To Follow a Rule" are therefore fundamental to the understanding of the practice of computer usage.

Chapter 3. The Nurse as Engineer – the Theory of Knowledge in Research in the Care Sector

Ingela Josefson

The nature of nursing has been the subject of discussion for the last 10–15 years. One reason is that in many countries the education of nurses has moved from teaching hospitals to academic institutions. This move has given rise to the question of the scientific basis for nursing knowledge.

Lately the content of nursing knowledge has become a principal focus in the work on developing expert systems for nursing. Thus theories of knowledge and the nature of new technology are of great concern to the future of the nursing profession. The basic assumptions underlying a chosen theory of knowledge will determine the development and use of advanced technology in the future.

Chapter 4. Automation–Skill–Apprenticeship

P. Gullers

Behind the concept of the automated factory lies the view of knowledge in which all human thought and action can be logically described in a formalized language, and in which all conceivable activities are predictable. So far all attempts to realize this vision have refuted this as being the case. The problem with automating propositional knowledge can be illustrated by analogy to the use of formulae at the expense of practice which means an enormous loss in association material when it comes to tackling problems. It is important to limit use of formalizations to ensure freedom of action through the ability to have a feel for things. Present production techniques do not provide an environment for the development of skills in training hence the retention of an apprenticeship model is fundamental. As Rousseau said: "The experiences of the senses and practical intellect are perhaps both an essential complement and prerequisite of the successful automation of industry" (Emile).

Chapter 5. Computerization and Skill in Local Weather Forecasting

Maja-Lisa Perby

Increased information through computerization does not mean greater reliability in decision making. Consider the case of weather forecasting. Skill here is the ability to select and interpret information. Computer solutions are general and standardized whereas skill is developed through use of concrete, specific examples. Traditionally meteorologists used solely historical material to build up a "comprehensive idea" of the weather situation in their minds. This "comprehensive" idea is the shaping of an inner weather picture which gradually builds up in the minds of meteorologists and leads to understanding and development of skill. Its creation depends on the reflection and digestion of information. Forecasting is a continuous process. The problem with the new methods and information presented by computerization is that there is less importance placed on reflection and therefore understanding through consideration of a variety of knowledge sources, communication between workers, and practical experiences.

Chapter 6. Tacit Knowledge, Working Life and Scientific Method

A. Janik

What is "tacit knowledge"? What role does it play in working life? What implications does it hold for understanding, for example, implications of expert systems for working life? What do philosophers of science have to learn from working life studies?

Certain things defy precise description by their very nature: some non-visual sensory experiences and the procedure involved in following a specific rule, hence what is in the strict sense "tacit" cannot be studied scientifically.

Knowledge entails understanding which makes for creativity. Creativity is therefore linked to the mastery of conventions, that is, rule-following. One can only achieve an element of this creativity through long, intensive sessions with practitioners to gain experience. Armchair speculation is futile. Understanding and grasping the context is fundamental. Western philsophical tradition has failed to take working life seriously. Working-life studies embody an epistemological revolution which philosophers ignore at their peril.

Chapter 7. Can Skills be Transferable?

R. Ennals

When real practical problems need to be solved by people in a particular social and economic context, the technology has no more than an instrumental function. Technology itself is politically, socially, and economically neutral but is political in its use, reflecting and possibly strengthening the value system and the economic and political interests of those who control it. This has implications for concepts entailed in the idea of transferring skills through its use. The preconditions for the transfer of skills are the motivation of the recipient, shared practical context, some common language between those imparting and receiving skills. There are severe limitations as to how far the computer can satisfy these conditions. The issue of the transfer of skills should be of central importance in any political programme. For what future are people to be trained? What skills are to be transferred, and to whom? Who is involved in preparing a solution to perhaps the central problem of our era and who is left to form part of the problem?

Chapter 8. Artificial Intelligence and Social Action: Education and Training

K.S. Gill

One of the central planks of development is the enhancement of peoples' potential for creative participation in the development process by enhancing the provision of basic human needs such as education, health and welfare. If AI technology has any relevance to these developmental issues (as like any other technology it should), then it must also concern itself with the knowledge of human needs and the nature of expert knowledge which contributes to the design of relevant technologies. In order for people to participate in the development process, they must have knowledge and skills to affect such a process. The machine-centred approach of current AI technology restricts its application to those problem-solving domains which can be formalized in logical rational rules. This approach thus takes account of non-intuitive knowledge and ignores the intuitive component which is embedded in the personal experience and in the social and cultural traditions of the user. The human-centred approach, on the other hand, is based on the human-machine symbiosis and provides for creative participation of users in the design of "developmental" systems.

Chapter 9. Skill, Education and Social Value: Some Thoughts on the Metonymy of Skill and Skill Transfer

J. Hilton

Skills are necessarily representative of value systems of which they are a part. Hence the transfer of skill has to be considered as the transfer of a skill and part of a value system without which the intrinsic skill is meaningless. Knowledge transfer is better termed knowledge exchange. At present, training (intrinsic skill acquisition) is being divorced from education as a whole (location of skills in a value system) leading to the danger that skilled groups will lose touch with the social value system within which its skills are located, and probable erosion of skill. The intelligent system can be another powerful tool of the expert or it can be designed to be transparent to the non-professional. To ensure the democratization of knowledge the system must be transparent i.e., the learner is at the centre of this process such that acquisition and personalization of a skill is achieved by transforming what one observes another doing into something of value to oneself.

Chapter 10. Knowledge Acquisition for Expert Systems

Anna Hart

Important issues need raising before detailed knowledge acquisition can take place for designing expert systems. It is futile to try acquiring knowledge and constructing systems unless it is known what it is for.

You need knowledge which is useful for users, where useful means being adequately accurate (as checked by the experts), easily accessible, understandable, relevant. Much of this "useful" knowledge is probable, implicit, tacit, and previously unspoken. There are a variety of methodologies one could use to try and access it but its detailed acquisition will only work if the development team understand why the system is being built and how it should perform.

Chapter 11. Knowledge-Based Computer Decision-Aids for General Practice

P. Pritchard

At present there is a huge growth of medical knowledge with increasing specialization in specific fields. This poses a great problem for the General Medical Practitioner (GP), the sole generalist in medicine, who is unlikely to be able to handle this growth in ten years' time if it continues at this rate. Public expectations and criticisms of doctors have increased as people become better informed through the various types of media. Hence there is pressure for the use of computers in the medical profession to assist the doctor, thereby increasing his/her competence.

Most of the communication between GPs and their patients is informal whereas medical records and computers depend mostly on written text. The challenge is to build computer systems that have this informal know-how in a consistent and generally acceptable form. The application of expert systems will only work if the doctor relies on intuition and loosely-structured knowledge and ignores overall consistency of the knowledge base to ensure the retention of expertise. The pitfalls will be many if the systems are unreliable, seem remote, and do not take account of the real needs of doctors and patients.

Chapter 12. Creativity, Skill and Human-Centred Systems

M. Cooley

We are now at a unique historical turning point. Decisions we make in respect of the new technologies will have a profound effect upon the way we relate to each other, to our work, and to nature itself. Vast computer systems, expert systems, and artificial intelligence systems should not be seen as a technological bolt from the blue. They are in fact part of the historical continuum which is discernable in Europe certainly over the last five hundred years. Scientific and technological change, viewed historically, does seem to embody three predominant historical tendencies. Firstly, there is a change in the organic composition of capital. We tend to render processes capital-intensive rather than labour-intensive. Secondly, it constitutes a shift from the analogical to the digital. The manner in which we perceive our world, analyse it and relate to it is dramatically changed. Thirdly, it is a process in which human beings are rendered passive and the machines become more active. We recall "the more you give to the machines the less there is left of yourself". It is against this historical background that there is an urgent need to view alternative systems, in particular those which may be regarded as human-centred. This chapter describes such human-centred systems.

Chapter 13. Professional Knowledge and the Limits of Automation in Administrations

T.K. Karlsen and Maria Oppen

The aim of this chapter is to consider the limits to rationalization and, therefore, barriers to further devaluation of professional skills. If these limits are not recognized, an erosion in special qualifications acquired through professional training may emerge, thereby adversely affecting the quality of services. It is important to look at how far-reaching are the consequences of using information technologies as a means to distribute tasks and functions of administrative work and to substitute human labour, for the devaluation of skills. Examination of two case-studies leaves little doubt that increased rationalization through automation of various parts of the decision-making process causes erosion of skill and professional knowledge, increased division of labour destroying that element of skill gained from the organizational culture, and hence limits the scope for action (inflexibility as technology does not accept the contradictions of social reality) and the ability to act with competence in a context. Only through "careful" strategies of rationalization can flexibility and effectiveness of administrative action be maintained or improved in an increasingly complex environment.

Chapter 14. The Changing Nature of the Engineering Craft Apprenticeship System in the United Kingdom

M. Cross

This chapter discusses the changing nature of apprenticeship training and describes some of the principles and weaknesses of the system of supplying engineering craftsmen in the UK. The "new" approach to craft training in the UK focusses on aspects such as duration, contents, standards, assessment, relevance, and openness. For example, training needs are increasingly seen in terms of mending and mental rather than making and manual skills and knowledge. This development requires that job structures should transcend existing rigid job boundaries and take into account such features as versatility, adaptability, and diagnostic ability. While there is a move to create a high degree of common skilling amongst engineering craftsmen there is also the recognition of a need to produce both "skill" and "process system" specialists. New apprenticeship in the UK is being developed with three recognizable streams: specialist craftsmen; operator craftsmen; and process systems craftsmen.

Chapter 15. Delegation and Decentralization – Computer Systems as Tools for Instruction and Improved Service to Clients

D. Schartum

This chapter deals with issues such as those of delegation of decision making, quality of service and competence, arising from the application of Information Technology in the domain of the Norwegian National Insurance Administration system. For example, within the context of "national conformity" of practice, the quality of service will demand uniformity in interpretation regardless of the individual insured person's particular circumstances. The emphasis on efficiency and time, and a degree of "tailor-made" information may lead to reduced access and communication between the people who want to use the system and the service itself. Rationalization in complex domains (cases) of decision-making may cause the case-handler either simply to ignore the problematic aspects of a case, or to make an intuitive choice instead of conferring with the relevant legal sources. There is empirical evidence from the Norwegian case that in a large number of cases the use of data systems may have a positive effect as they can weed out elementary errors and omissions in calculations, but at a more complex level where legal expertise and judgement is required, such systems may give no insight and support. It is important, therefore, to develop criteria for evaluating the non-time-related aspects of the quality of service, and thereby define aims for, and evaluate public-oriented activities.

Chapter 16. Applying Expert Systems Technology: Division of Labour and Division of Knowledge

O. Ostberg

This chapter reviews work on expert systems and points out that there are two main streams of development. In what is described as the "laboratory environment", research focusses on providing cloned expertise, that is, highly complex "high-road" emulation of experts' heuristic knowledge. However in the world of business the focus is on transactional or teaching applications, that is, less complex "low-road" algorithms of specified task functions. Very few expert systems are actually in operation outside the laboratory environment, and there is a serious gap between claims and reality of their applications. "Knowledge engineering" is a modern form of "work study engineering", and yet job and organizational design issues are rarely addressed in the literature on designing expert systems. This serious gap is discussed. Another problem for concern arises when regular domain workers are excluded from both the design and continuous improvement of the tools/methods used in the work process, and when the systems lack interpretable information i.e., lack sufficient explanation facilities for dealing with uncertain knowledge. The workers become alienated from their own knowledge and their creative ability is seriously diminished, and the division of labour between humans and machines grows into an unwanted division of knowledge. These and other important issues for both the design and application of expert systems are discussed in this paper.

Section I:

Introduction

Chapter 1

Introduction

B. Göranzon and Ingela Josefson

The term "information society" was first used in a 1972 Japanese futurologi-cal study (Japanese Computer Usage Development Institute 1972), in which the time perspective was limited to the year 2000. If the visions of this study were to become reality, a "computer mind" should have been established through education by the year 1985. A different perspective emerges from a new Japanese futurological study from 1985 (National Institute for Research Development 1985), which contains an example that illustrates the effects of a longer period of computer usage on one's confidence in one's actions.

I don't know why, but I feel depressed and lose my self-confidence. Human beings should use computers, but the machines are gradually taking over, and we are having to accommodate ourselves to their ways of working. Computers are like babies, they lack adaptability: they refuse to understand very human concepts like "this is acceptable; let it pass". They prefer black and white; I prefer grey.

The term "functional autism" is used in the Japanese study to describe the phenomenon of people who work for a long time in a computer technology environment, with its characteristic view of reality as falling into categories of black/white or right/wrong, experiencing difficulties in confronting reality; a reality which is in essence the ability to cultivate social relation-ships. In developing this line of reasoning, the educational issues become important.

This does not automatically mean that in the first Japanese study from 1972 the education referred to is education in computer technology. Japanese culture is based on a long tradition of apprenticeship training which they are unwilling to abandon when moving into the information society. There is a limit beyond which we must be reminded not to go.

In this book there is a meeting of British and Scandinavian research. Research in Great Britain on the development of expert systems, for example, is well advanced. Scandinavia's research traditions have, for rather more than a decade, attempted to develop theoretical reflections on the effects of new technology through working life case-studies. This diversity of experi-ence is reflected in the articles in this book. In both these perspectives, great weight is given to the conditions in which the skills and knowledge of craftsmen are transferred to machines. Where are the difficulties to be found?

All the contributions reflect the realization that there are different aspects of knowledge and that knowledge is developed in different ways.

The writings from Great Britain emphasize the importance of taking human conditions as the basis for research on developing and using new technology. Consideration must be given to the set of values of which the craft knowledge is a part and, if they are to be usable and democratic, the systems allow user insight. Peoples' educational backgrounds must be taken into consideration and it will become more important to give thought to future educational requirements.

The Scandinavian examples derive from a research tradition that is influenced by the work of Ludwig Wittgenstein, the philosopher. In his work he gives considerable attention to the phenomenon of tacit knowledge, the knowledge that resists formulation in scientific terms, but which shows itself "in the carefully chosen examples". Interest is focussed less on the type of tacit knowledge that can be formulated, but which, because of its familiarity, for example, cannot be perceived other than against the background of genuine tacit knowledge, and more interest is focussed on knowledge that cannot be generalized; the type of knowledge that makes a skilled person able to make assessments and take action in unique situations. This is a question of the complicated interweaving of theoretical knowledge – factual knowledge – and knowledge gained through experience. The knowledge of experience bestows viability on theoretical knowledge. On the other hand, theoretical knowledge is essential to provide a direction for experience. Many of these complicated problems have previously been overcome through apprenticeship. What sort of masters will expert systems prove to be?

The debate deals with complicated epistemological issues, and this book is intended as a contribution to this debate. In recent years, the term "tacit knowledge" has occurred in various forms in the debate on computers and knowledge. There is a risk, because of some of the serious distortions that have been introduced into the concept of tacit knowledge, that it will become unusable. There is good cause to include in this book, for its clarifying effect, the article by Allan Janik, the philosopher.

The import of a crucial concept such as tacit knowledge will mould the future structure of education. It dictates the limits of what we conceive as possible to computerize before feeling what are known as the long-term contra-effects. Things that initially appear to be beneficial often turn out to be the product of a process of erosion, a process which leads to losses that, in the long run, outweigh the gains.

The cognitive science on which rests the theoretic basis of research on artificial intelligence draws parallels between the way information is processed by the brain and by a computer. Comparisons have always been made between the human brain and the technology of the day. The brain has been likened to a telephone network, a telegraph system, and today, to a computer. What else can it be? Cognitivism is based on the notion that we should, by studying computers, be able to learn something about ourselves as human beings.

When reality kicks back and demands results from the financial investments that have been made, cognitivism finds itself being chased up a blind alley. At this point a resurgent interest in philosophy, particularly in epistemological matters, is natural. Ludwig Wittgenstein's philosophy of language is now the height of fashion. In a growing number of contexts it is placed in a cognitivist Procrustes' bed. Here there is a risk in using Wittgenstein as varnish and polish.

A central theme in Wittgenstein's philosophy of language is his desire to remind us of the inner relationship between understanding human actions and understanding forms of artistic expression. Art has an ability to portray indirectly the phenomenon of the "unsayable", to use Wittgenstein's own term. The most important features in human actions cannot be understood analytically as, for example, can a problem in physics, but must be considered in an aesthetic perspective if we wish to capture their human dimension.

In his *Dialogues*, Plato expresses his admiration for mathematics as a pattern for pure abstract thought which leads the mind away from concrete, earthly issues, to the higher sphere of thinking. In this, it is different from the language of poetry, he means, because it devotes itself to the ambiguous.

Plato's ideas are based on the basic concept that it is possible to reduce all knowledge to a mathematical language. The same issue is taken to its extreme in the debates of our time on artificial intelligence and its applications, for instance in expert systems.

To what extent is it possible in a logical, mathematic language to express human knowledge, so that it can be transferred to a machine? What will the consequences be of attempting, in the spirit of Plato, to reduce multiplicity and ambiguity in a mathematical language? Today, we have the opportunity to reflect on some of the experiences gained from this work.

An information technology programme must put the basic question of what can be considered to be development. It becomes increasingly important to emphasize cultural, political and epistemological issues in the ongoing debate on expert systems and their application in working life: these issues are discussed at an international conference in Stockholm in May 1988 on this theme. Our connections with information technology programmes the world over have strengthened our intention to make a more active contribution towards focussing the debate on the issues of cultural and educational policy. The increase in interest in apprenticeship training and the humanities' position as a force to counterbalance technological change are two themes that require deeper debate.

References

Japanese Computer Usage Development Institute (1972) The plan for information society – a national goal toward the year 2000. Japanese Computer Usage Development Institute, Tokyo
National Institute for Research Development (1985) A comprehensive study of micro-electronics. National Institute for Research Development, Tokyo

Section II:

Tacit Knowledge and Apprenticeship

Chapter 2

The Practice of the Use of Computers.
A Paradoxical Encounter between Different
Traditions of Knowledge

B. Göranzon

Fundamental to the design of knowledge-based systems is the understanding of the nature of knowledge and the problems involved in computerizing it. This chapter deals with these issues and draws a distinction between three different categories of knowledge: propositional knowledge, skill or practical knowledge and knowledge of familiarity. In the present debate on "Information Society", there is a clear tendency to overemphasize the theoretical knowledge at the expense of practical knowledge thereby completely ignoring the knowledge of familiarity. It is argued that different forms of theoretical knowledge are required for the design of current computer technology and the study of the practice of computer usage. The concept of dialogue and the concept of "To Follow a Rule" are therefore fundamental to the understanding of the practice of computer usage.

Paradoxical Views of Knowledge in the Age of Enlightenment

In the modern sense, applied mathematics was the creation of René Descartes. In 1637, Descartes presented a study in which he showed how, by applying abstract algebraic concepts, it is possible to formulate geometry's concrete points, lines, surfaces and volumes. He demonstrated a link between our three-dimensional world and a mathematical–logical way of thinking.

In Descartes' work *Discourse on Methods, Optics, Geometry and Meteorology* (Descartes 1637) in which he presented his revolutionary mathematical theory, the word "machine" is applied to the human body for the first time in history:

And this will not seem strange to those, who knowing how many different automata or moving machines can be made by the industry of man without employing in so doing more than a very few parts in comparison with the great multitude of bones, muscles, nerves, arteries, veins, or other parts that are found in the body of each animal. From this aspect the body is regarded as a machine which, having been made by the hands of God, is incomparably better arranged, and possesses in itself movements which are much more admirable, than any of those which can be invented by man.

Descartes continues with an important argument:

Here I specially stopped to show that if there had been such machines, possessing the organs and outward form of a monkey or some other animal without reason, we should not have had any means of ascertaining that they were not of the same nature as those animals. On the other hand, if there were machines which bore a resemblance to our body and imitated our actions as far as it was morally possible to do so, we should always have two very certain tests by which to recognise that, for all that, they were not real men. The first is, that they could never use speech or other signs as we do when placing our thoughts on record for the benefit of others. For we can easily understand a machine's being constituted so that it can utter words, and even emit some responses to action on it of a corporeal kind, which brings about a change in its organs; for instance if it is touched in a particular part it may ask what we wish to say to it; if in another part it may exclaim that it is being hurt, and so on. But it never happens that it arranges its speech in various ways, in order to reply appropriately to everything that may be said in its presence, as even the lowest type of man can do. And the second difference is, that although machines can perform certain things as well as or perhaps better than any of us can do, they infallibly fall short in others, by the which means we may discover that they did not act from knowledge, but only from the disposition of their organs. For while reason is the universal instrument which can serve for all contingencies, these organs have need of some special adaptation for every particular action.

The notion that "animals are machines" lies at the core of the cartesian view. Descartes coined a phrase to express this opinion: Bete machine. There is a reference to this phrase in one of the earliest documents produced in the French Age of Enlightenment: *Man a Machine*, published in 1748 by Dr de La Mettrie. To La Mettrie, learning to understand a language – i.e. learning to use symbols – is to become a human being. Culture is what separates man from the animals. La Mettrie means that thinking should turn from general abstractions to consider the concrete, the details. It is the models to be found in the concrete examples we meet that nurture us in a culture. According to La Mettrie, a mind that has received poor guidance is as an actor who has been spoiled by provincial theatres; he goes on to say that the separate states of the soul are in constant interaction with the body. La Mettrie struck a chord that was to characterize the contradictory views of knowledge during the French Age of Enlightenment (Lindborg 1984).

Denis Diderot, leader of the French Encyclopedia project in the Age of Enlightenment attempted to track down the paradox inherent in the perception of the way knowledge and competence is developed and maintained. On the one hand there is the belief that everything can be systematized and formalized in a symbolic logical notation. On the other hand there is Minerva's owl which, although it first appears on the periphery of the project, when seen as a link with the current debate on technical change becomes vitally important to develop further.

Denis Diderot says this: "If I knew how to speak as I think! But as it is now, I have ideas in my head but I cannot find words for them." (Josephs 1969).

To be at once within and standing apart from oneself. To observe and be the person who is observed. But thought is like the eye: it cannot see itself. How do we shape the rhythmic gestures of our thoughts? Here we can establish a link with Ludwig Wittgenstein's philosophy of language, which is currently becoming more prominent in the international debate on technical advance.

On Following Rules

Ludwig Wittgenstein's philosophy focusses attention on the particular concrete case or example. He wishes to remind us of the complex and many-faceted logic of the example:

It is not only a question of the errors in thinking we make when we focus only on the universal. It is also a question of the values that are lost through this intellectual attitude (Kjell S. Johannesen 1987).

The multiplicity of disparate activities or *practices* – following a rule in one's activities is what Wittgenstein refers to as a practice – is the focal point of his interest.

Wittgenstein perceives a concept as a *set of activities that follow a rule*, in contrast to regarding the concept as a rule, a view that characterizes the earlier scientific traditions to which we have referred. In this way, the concept becomes related to its usage. The use of the concept determines its content. It is our usage or *practice* that shows the way in which we understand something.

The rule is built into the action. The concept of practice brings out this fundamental relationship. To master and coordinate actions implies an ability to be part of a practice: " . . . But if a person has not yet got the concepts, I should teach him to use the words by means of examples and by practice . . . (p.201, *Philosophical Investigations*) . . . If language is to be a means of communication there must be agreement not only in definitions but also (queer as this may sound) in judgments. (p.242, *Philosophical Investigations*)

We are taught a practice through examples, through models. The ability to formulate examples is vitally important. There are good examples which lead our thoughts in the "right" direction and which refresh our minds, and there are examples that make it impossible to understand the sense of a practice. This cannot be made explicit by means of a formal description. It requires the ability to put forward the essence of a practice through examples that are followed by teaching, by practice. We acquire a deeper understanding of the concept "tool" by using tools in different activities. Taking part in different practices, when, for example, using computers, can give different opinions about the way computer usage affects the activity, while people sharing in a common practice may have varying opinions about the use of computers in this practice.

What is a Computer?

At an international conference in Sigtuna, Sweden in June 1979 on the theme "Is the computer a tool?", Allan Janik (Janik 1980) the philosopher, discussed *"essentially contested concepts"* and the part played by these concepts in our attempts to describe reality:

Basically, the most vexed issues which humans face involve conflicts about how we are to describe the situation we confront . . . Our evidence may be the wrong sort of evidence and our tradition may lead us to ask the wrong questions. We must be at one and the same time guided by what we take to be the substance of the issues at hand and also prepared to reconsider precisely what the substance of the issue actually is. It is always necessary to bear in mind that the most serious issues we confront concern "essentially contested concepts", i.e. disagreement over just what the substantive issues are. To prevail in the conflict is to be prepared to follow the discussion, even when it leads us into unfamiliar terrain.

The content of the concept "tool" is not self-evident in the same way as understanding what a computer is. There is a profusion of metaphors and parallels about computers in analogies with steam engines, electricity, the motor car, typewriters etc. In the same way there are numerous analogies of what a human being is in connection with the debate on technological development: man as a clockwork machine, an ant, a piano etc. A usual starting point in the debate on computers is to compare the memory capacity of the brain to that of a computer. Here, the main function is information processing. A different starting point is the comparison between human language and the "language of machines". The point of this comment is to interpret Allan Janik's attention to "essentially contested concepts", namely that our perception of the man–machine relationship plays a decisive part in controlling our questions on the use of computers.

A Boat Builder on the West Coast of Sweden

The conference on "Is the computer a tool?" was also attended by Thomas Tempte, a carpenter and craftsman who for his part could see no striking similarities between computers and what he in his own "profession" was used to calling "tools".

Thomas Tempte (1981) described Gösta, a boat builder on Sweden's west coast:

Gösta is a product of the old master-journeyman-apprentice training system in which sophisticated and complex knowledge was passed on without using words. This is not because of any aversion to transferring knowledge by means of the spoken word, but because no such tradition had been developed.

Putting a question to Gösta elicits very precise information, often after a pause for thought. His knowledge is neither unconscious or unrefined, but he is not used to passing it on in words. He demonstrates by doing the job, supplementing his example with a few words of commentary. This often takes the form of a story about a craftsman who did not do the job in a certain way, which caused him to make a mistake. One gets the feeling that he has all the answers, and this allows him to disassociate himself from the ill-judged behaviour of the offending craftsman. All this is related in the form of an anecdote.

Here, Tempte gives an unusually penetrating description of his professional work. None-the-less, it contains an unacceptable assumption on the nature of knowledge and how it is transferred. Tempte expresses himself from within a tradition which more or less tacitly presupposes that it is possible to express everything in words. At the same time, he describes the master craftsman as "demonstrating, with a few words of commentary". This is as far as one can go – providing examples and stimulating practice.

One consequence of the essential operation of following a rule is that special emphasis is placed on practice/learning. Previous experience and problem-solving – so-called sediment – is turned into a process of following rules that form the basis of the practice that we are being taught: "Is it that rule and empirical proposition merge into one another?" (*On Certainty*, §309) Wittgenstein asks, and goes on to say: "If experience is the ground of our certainty, then naturally it is past experience and it isn't for example just my experience but other people's, that I get knowledge from." (*On Certainty*, §275)

There are many ways of following a rule. In Wittgenstein's view, guessing is of central importance to a rule system and to all forms of learning. Applying a rule is a matter of knowing what to do at the next stage. Guessing is done on the basis of examples we have been presented with and continues until we have the talent to do it correctly.

As we grow more sure – i.e., have met a large number of examples through our experience – our competence increases, and we master a practice.

Judging Light in Photography

Peter Gullers (1984), a photographer, has reflected upon his professional work and made a penetrating description of the essential aspects of judging light in photography:

The text of a recent advertisement for cameras said: "Instructions for taking good pictures – just press the button". Thanks to new technology we no longer need to know a lot about the technique of photography before we can take good pictures. The manufacturer had built a program into the camera, a program which made all the important decisions and all the assessments needed to produce a satisfactory result.

New technology has made it easier to take photographs and photography has become very reliable and accurate in most normal conditions. When there is not enough light, the exposure is blocked or a built-in flash is activated to ensure satisfactory results.

The program cannot be modified and no opinion can be passed on the results until later. The underlying principles are invisible – the process is soundless. Neither does the manufacturer describe how the program makes these assessments. In retrospect, when the picture has been developed, even the uninitiated judge can say that the picture is too dark, too light or blurred. On the other hand the cause of the fault is difficult to establish without a thorough knowledge of technology, or of the conditions under which the photograph was taken.

There are numerous problem areas and the causes of these problems tend to merge with each other.

Physiologists claim that the eye is a poor light-meter because the pupil automatically adapts to changes in the intensity of light. This may be so. When faced with a concrete situation that I have to assess, I observe a number of different factors that affect the quality of the light and thus the results of my photography. Is it summer or winter, is it morning or evening? Is the sun breaking through a screen of cloud or am I in semi-shadow under a leafy tree? Are parts of the subject in deep shadow and the rest in strong sunlight? Then I have to strike a balance between light and darkness. If I am in a smithy or in a rolling mill shop, I note how the light coming through the sloping skylights contrasts with the sooty heat of the air in the brick building. The vibrations from hammers and mills make the floor and the camera tremble, which makes photography more difficult and affects the light-metering. The daylight is enhanced by the red glow of the steel billets.

In the same way I gather impressions from other situations and environments. In a new situation, I recall similar situations and environments that I have encountered earlier. They act as comparisons and as association material and my previous perceptions, mistakes and experiences provide the basis for my judgement.

It is not only the memories of the actual process of photography that play a part. The hours spent in the darkroom developing the film, my curiosity about the results, the arduous work of re-creating reality and the graphic world of the picture are also among my memories. A faulty assessment of the strength of the light and the contrast of the subject, the vibrations and tremors become important experience to be called upon next time I face a similar situation. All of these earlier memories and experiences that are stored away over the years only partly penetrate my consciousness when I make a judgement on the light conditions. The thumb and index finger of my right hand turn the camera's exposure knob to a setting that "feels right", while my left hand adjusts the filter ring. This process is almost automatic.

The problem with automatic computer-aided light-metering is that after a long period of use one tends to lose one's ability to judge light conditions. Few people can manage without mechanical or electronic light-meters today.

But it is not simply the ability to judge the light value that is disappearing. Unless one regularly makes a manual judgement of light, one's sensitivity to shades of light tends to become blunted. Our pictorial memories of past experiences are not activated in the same way unless they have been connected with similar assessments. Unless one regularly performs the actual work of producing pictures, the ability to make the best use of composition and light-modifying techniques when printing will wither too.

The problem with the automatic meter is not only that its program does not consider whether it is day or night, or the nature of the subject, or the inexperience of the user. The most important point is that it denies me access to my memories and blunts my perceptions and my ability to discern shades of light. This intimate knowledge is not linked to what I do when I photograph, i.e. the operations I perform, but to actual memories and experiences when I take photographs and when I develop and print pictures.

Technology and Culture

Gullers' example contains a cultural–critical perspective. The type of change in professional competence that Gullers points to, "the sensitivity to shades of light tending to become blunted" is a phenomenon that takes a long time to occur. It is one of the reasons for calling attention to links with the past. Without a link with the past through epistemology and the history of ideas, a debate on the future of technological development will lack any contact with reality. It will be devoid of content and full of cliches and vague rhetoric such as "placing the human being in the centre".

The cultural–critical element is constantly present in Wittgenstein's thinking.

Describing a practice involves adopting a standpoint on the description of a culture. "A whole culture belongs to a language-game." A practice is thus at one and the same time both fundamental and relative to the culture and the epoch.

In a study carried out by the International Labour Organization in Geneva comparing 13 industrial countries and their experiences of technical change in the 1970s, a common factor emerged, namely the attention given to changes in professional qualifications. When discussing solutions to the problem of changing professional qualifications, it becomes evident that individual cultural and national characteristics become involved. The problem is a common one, but *culture and tradition* become decisive factors in the way different solutions are debated. There are culture–specific characteristics that must be observed when making international comparative studies. Why, for example, are "isolation" and "lack of identity" emphasized in West

German studies of the use of computers? Has the computer any decisive significance in terms of the occurrence of these phenomena or are they culture–specific and can they be discussed separately from the issue of computers?

Routine Practice and Development Practice

We call an activity that can be described exhaustively in stated rules a *routine practice*. Here, the rules are closed; they can be described in a set of essential and sufficient conditions. There is an obvious relationship to a set of rules adapted for computer technology.

An activity that is characterized by *open rules*, meaning that their expression admits of a variety of meanings, we shall call a *development practice*. It is this kind of practice that we are primarily interested in. The rules that form a development practice cannot be entirely expressed in words. As we pointed out earlier, it is essential to have good examples and to learn a practice by training. It is the following of the rules rather than the rules themselves that is the prism in this perspective.

At the same time, it is important to emphasize the intersubjective aspects of following rules in a practice. It is logically impossible to be the only person following a rule. A single practice can therefore not be seen as a logical place for dialogue and shared action.

Error-Location in a Computer Program

Per Svensson (1983) who is responsible for developing a computer system for forest valuation, makes the following remarks on error–location in a computer program:

In the routines at the Agricultural Administration for valuing forests using EDP, error-location and the correction if input data is one of the most important jobs. Programs have been written that search through input data and report any errors, controlled by given rules that are part of the program. It is impossible to make programs to locate and make a perfectly clear report on every kind of error. The input data varies far too much for this to be a practical possibility. Instead, the users must learn this work through experience. After having worked with this application for a long time, the speed with which most experienced users now locate these errors is incomprehensible to new employees. When asked: "How do you locate this error?", they answer: "I see that it is an error". One explanation of why experienced users recognize errors when inexperienced users do not discover them is that their experience contains memories from earlier, similar cases, even if one cannot with certainty report when they occurred. This is a form of knowledge that is extremely difficult to document, but which none-the-less exists and works in practice.

Attempts have been made to document this particular work operation. The experience gained from these attempts is daunting. The result of the documentation was a very comprehensive catalogue of every imaginable error, how they were reported by the program and what action should be taken on them. For new users, this catalogue was both frightening and of little use, while experienced users worked quicker and more surely if they trusted their own experience and did not use the error-location catalogue. Experience cannot always be documented in a usable way.

This knowledge cannot be taught directly to others, but can be transferred to some people by using analogies and concrete examples. At the same time the individual must strive to win a deeper insight into a practice and become proficient in its use. There are different practices for error-location, for example the skills mastered by flight mechanics, and in the medical care sector in professional groups such as physicians and nurses in order to make diagnoses. To be skilled in one of these practices does not mean that one can transfer this ability to another practice. Error-location on aeroplanes and error-location in a computer program for forest valuation are not inter-changeable skills. At this level analogies and examples are not transferrable between different practices. Today, because these different activities use computer technology, there is growing interest in the possibility of moving from one activity to another if one has mastered the technology. It is this perspective that, for example, André Gorz expresses when he claims that less emphasis need be placed upon professional skills and that computer technol-ogy skills must be given pride of place. It is important to emphasize the activity-specific aspect of mastering a practice and that analogies and examples must be taken from within a practice. Of course, there may be striking examples that can be used to illustrate a number of different activities. A special talent is needed to formulate and present these good examples. There is a continuity in the mastery of error-location in an activity that is accentuated in the conversion from old to new technology.

Three Categories of Knowledge

The exercise of error-location involves the application of what we may call *practical knowledge*, knowledge which contains experiences obtained from having been active in a practice. At the same time there is a great deal of knowledge within this practice that we learn by examining the examples we are given by others who have been working within the practice. It is from this aggregate experience that we also build up our competence and learn from first-hand experience. The interaction between people in the same professional group is of decisive importance here. This latter kind of knowledge, knowledge that we acquire from learning a practice by examin-ing the examples of tradition, we can call the *knowledge of familiarity*.

That part of a professional tradition that has been expressed in general traditions, theories, methods and regulations and that we can assimilate from a theoretical study of an activity, we can call *propositional knowledge*. There is a close relationship between propositional knowledge, practical knowledge and the knowledge of familiarity. We interpret theories, methods and regulations through the familiarity and skills we have gained by taking part in a practice. Allan Janik's attention to the inconsistencies in the content of these concepts is of central importance here. The dialogue between the members of a group involved in a practice contains an aspect of friction between different perceptions based on their different experiences – exam-ples in familiarity and practical skills. Being a member of a practice and at the same time acquiring greater competence involves participation in an ongoing dialogue. Being professional implies extending one's perspective towards a broader overview of one's own skills. Being aware of anomalies – failure – is of particular importance in terms of accepting professional responsibility. The historical perspective is a central factor in the knowledge of familiarity. The paradox in this argument is that if we remove all practical knowledge and knowledge of familiarity from an activity we will also empty it of propositional knowledge. These are interpretive actions that are crucial to a pragmatic perspective. What can be stored in a computer, processed in algorithms, propositional logic etc., and reported as a result in the form of a print-out is raw material that has to be interpreted by the actions of a person qualified in a practice. If attention is focussed on the raw material and the action of interpretation disappears, an activity will move towards chaos – disorder – death, according to the second main law of thermodynamics.

We get a division of the different kinds of knowledge into three categories:

1. Propositional or theoretical knowledge
2. Skills, or practical knowledge
3. Knowledge of familiarity

There is a clear tendency to overemphasize theoretical knowledge at the expense of practical knowledge and we tend to forget completely the knowledge of familiarity when discussing the nature of knowledge in a philosophical context. One effect of tending to ignore skills and familiarity when discussing knowledge is that one tends to assume that people who lack theoretical knowledge in given areas also lack any knowledge whatsoever of that area.

An Epistemological Error

In a postscript to this book *The Structure of Scientific Revolution* which is focussed on his rejection of explicit rules and his referral to tacit knowledge for the comprehension of scientific practices, Kuhn (1970) says that when he talks about intuitions he is not discussing individual intuitions. Instead, intuitions are the tested and shared possessions of the members of a successful group and the novice acquires them through training as part of his preparation for group membership.

When I speak of the knowledge embedded in shared exemplars, I am not referring to a mode of knowledge that is less systematic or less analyzable than knowledge embedded in rules, laws, or criteria of identification. Instead I have in mind a manner of knowing which is misconstrued if reconstructed in terms of rules that are first abstracted from exemplars and thereafter function in their stead.

In the introduction to the Encyclopedia of 1751 J. R. d'Alembert wonders how many questions and problems would be avoided if one finally established a clear and exact definition of words. This conception of an exact definition that removes all ambiguity contains the hope that in the definition there would reside a power to make our knowledge clear and explicit.

This perspective on the basis of the theory of knowledge can be used in the construction of designs in computer technology. To adopt a total view to include the use of computers is an epistemological error. The development of the practice of computer usage requires an openness to the paradoxical encounter between different traditions of knowledge during earlier epochs in the history of ideas. This requires a development of interest in the concept of education. Within the framework of the theme of Education–Work–Technology, it is my judgement that this will be a significant factor in the debate on technology, science and culture during the coming ten years.

References and Further Reading

d'Alembert JR (1751) Discours préliminaire des editeurs, in Encyclopedia au Dictionnaire raisonné des sciences, des arts etc Paris. In: d'Alembert, Inledning till Encyklopedin, Carmina klassiker, Uppsala, 1981

Bergendal B (1985) Bildningsens Villkor. Studentlitteratur

Descartes R (1637) Discourse on Method, Meditations and Principles. J. M. Dent and Sons Ltd, London (1981)

Frangsmyr T (1974) Drommen om det exakta spraket. Vetenskapens Trad, Stockholm

Göranzon B (1983) Datorn som Verktyg. Studentlitteratur

Göranzon B (1984) Datautvecklingsens Filosofi. Carlssons Bokdorlag (reference for the example of light metering in photography)

Göranzon B (1986) Artificial intelligence or the dream of the exact language. Dialoger magazine, no. 2 (an introduction to the Age of Enlightenment's paradoxical view of knowledge)

Göranzon B et al. (1982) Job design and automation in Sweden. The Swedish Working Life Centre (the perspective in the section on technology and culture is from this study. It is a research report produced within the framework of the ILO project and compares the experience of the use of computers in thirteen industrial countries)

Gullers P (1984) In: Göranzon B (ed) Datautvecklingsens Filosofi. Carlssons Bokforlag, pp. 31–35

Janik A (1980) Breaking the ground. In Sundin B (ed) Is the computer a tool? Almqvist and Wiksell, Stockholm

Josephs H (1969) Diderot's Dialogue of Language and Gesture. Ohio State University Press, Dayton

Johannesen KS (1988) Tyst Kunskap: om regel och begrepp. Research Report, Swedish Center for Working Life, Stockholm

Kuhn T (1970) The structure of scientific revolutions. University of Chicago Press, Chicago Illinois

Lindborg R (1984) Maskinen, Manniskan och doktor La Mettrie. Doxa,

Lindstrom L (1986) Bildningsbegreppets rotter. Det polyteknisks bildingsidealet. Education–work–technology project at the Swedish Life Center

Runeby N (1978) Teknikerna, Vetenskapen och Kulturen.

Uppsala University Press, Uppsala, Sweden (Runeby's study covers the period from 1860 to 1890 and includes a documentation of the restructuring of the educational system in relation to the breakthrough of industrialism. There is a fruitful connection to the current debate on technological change and the demand on the educational system)

Svenssen P (1983) Felsökning i ett datorprogram. In: Göranzon B (ed) Datautvecklingens Filosofi. Carlssons Bokförlag, Stockholm p. 29

Tempte T (1981) Arbets Ara. The Swedish Working Life Center, Stockholm

Wittgenstein L (1953) Philosophical investigations. Blackwell, Oxford

Wittgenstein L (1969) On Certainty. Blackwell, Oxford

Chapter 3

The Nurse as Engineer – the Theory of Knowledge in Research in the Care Sector

Ingela Josefson

The nature of nursing has been the subject of discussion for the last 10–15 years. One reason is that in many countries the education of nurses has moved from teaching hospitals to academic institutions. This move has given rise to the question of the scientific basis for nursing knowledge.

Recently the content of nursing knowledge has become a principal focus in the work on developing expert systems for nursing. Thus theories of knowledge and the nature of new technology are of great concern to the future of the nursing profession. The basic assumptions underlying a chosen theory of knowledge will determine the development and use of advanced technology in the future.

Two Irreconcilable Traditions

In 1984, Professor Herbert Simon gave a lecture at the 20th Nobel conference. In his address *Some computer models of human learning* he describes the current position of research into theories of learning on the basis of cognitive science (Simon 1985).

Simon discusses what he calls the hypothesis of "the physical symbol system". Put simply, it deals with the ability to recognize patterns: a human face is a recognizable pattern for us. A pattern consists of a collection of configurations which we can learn to discern from one another and in which we can see similarities. They may be set in relation to each other and they may be compared with each other. Simon emphasizes that a system must have this symbolic capacity if it is to function intelligently. Computers have this capacity, he says: "We can find that out by opening the box, so to speak".

In his lecture, Simon gives an example of mankind's ability to recognize patterns; man has a limited short-term memory. If I give you a list of six words, you can keep them in your mind long enough to allow you to repeat them back to me. But, as a rule, if I give you nine words, you cannot. In cognitive science today, the prevailing opinion is that the structure of short-term memory is of decisive importance in the way experts store knowledge. The ability of experts to recognize "cues" in a familiar situation gives them access to relevant information in their long-term memory. Simon points out that an expert's long-term memory comprises some 50 000 "chunks", and gives an example from the world of chess.

You set up a chess board with the pieces at, for example, the twentieth move of a well-known game. You let the subject of the test study the chess board for between 5 and 10 seconds and then remove the pieces.

A chess master will succeed in replacing the pieces with 90% or more accuracy. If I repeat the procedure, but position the pieces at random, the master will only manage to position six of the pieces correctly. The chess master achieves a better result in the first test because of the patterns that he knows and that are stored in his long-term memory, and because of the information he recalls through association when he sees the pattern on the chess board. According to Simon, it is this ability, this expert intuition, that "can be given a perfectly reasonable explanation in information-processing terms, in terms of recognition processes".

In the subsequent discussion, Simon was asked the following question from the audience:

Dr Simon, Descartes said that science has the perspective of studying the uniquely simple problems in material nature. Repetitive processes yield nicely to science and maths. However, unique processes, heroism, love, mercy diverge from this adaptive model, from repetitive processes. They also seem rather non-material. How do you relate these characteristics to perfection of the non-uniqueness of human beings in nature?

Simon answered:

Of course, I relied on the fact that this conference is dealing with cognitive science, not with human beings in general, and I tried to be very careful in introducing physical symbol systems to say that a human being is at least a physical symbol system. Now the human brain resides in the head, and the head, of course, is connected with the body, and the connection is thought to be important – important enough so that most people are reluctant to have the two separated from each other. In order to introduce any of the concepts of human motivation and effect, we would have to have a much more elaborate and comprehensive theory than any of us are discussing or proposing at this conference. . . . One of the reasons that it's hard to talk about things like love or heroism in connection with a computer is that a computer has none of those connections with the body and that computers, or at least computers of our generation, have almost none of the experiences that human beings store away and that are relevant to those aspects of our lives.

A reasonable interpretation of Simon's response is that he does not regard ethics, for example, as an aspect of experts' knowledge.

This is my point of departure in introducing the philosopher Ludwig Wittgenstein, whose works are characterized by precisely the ethical dimension of knowledge.

Wittgenstein's work, *Tractatus logico-philosophicus*, was published in England in 1922. It immediately attracted a great deal of attention, with the philosopher Bertrand Russell as its main proponent. In the foreword, Wittgenstein describes what he regards as the aim of the book; "What can be said at all can be said clearly, and what we cannot talk about we must pass over in silence".

In the *Tractatus*, Wittgenstein develops a formalized, ideal language whose structure, he says, reflects precisely the structure of expressed thought. He sees language as an instrument for making statements on material conditions. I quote again from the foreword:

Thus the aim of the book is to draw a limit to thought or, rather – not to thought, but to the expression of thought: for in order to be able to draw a limit to thought, we should have to find both sides of the limit thinkable (i.e. we should have to be able to think what cannot be thought).

It will therefore only be in language that the limit can be drawn, and what lies on the other side of the limit will simply be nonsense.

At the end of the book, Wittgenstein develops the ideas to which he will subsequently devote all his attention for a period of 25 years. He says: "We feel that even when all possible scientific questions have been answered, the problems of life remain completely untouched. Of course, there are then no questions left, and this itself is the answer."

This is the only book that Wittgenstein published. The other works are compilations of the very large volume of his work, the best-known being *Philosophical Investigations,* published posthumously in 1953.

Wittgenstein's later philosophical work is characterized by his strong emphasis on the use of language instead of thinking in terms of the meaning of words that can be described in definitions. In the first paragraph of the book he writes: "But what is the meaning of the word 'five'? – No such thing was in question here, only how the word 'five' is used."

Thus the aspect of action in language occupies a prominent place in Wittgenstein's philosophy: "I shall also call the whole, consisting of language and the actions into which it is woven, the 'language-game'."

On the basis of this approach, examples naturally play a crucial part in Wittgenstein's theory of knowledge. In fact, Herbert Simon also has examples in mind when he talks about "patterns" as being essential to the development of expert knowledge. But that is the full extent of any similarity between the two. They have divergent views of the part played by the example.

When Simon expresses his conviction that the way in which experts associate to earlier encounters with patterns can be described in the form of rules, Wittgenstein attributes this to that which cannot be expressed in language itself. Knowledge is expressed in examples. While you can point to an example, knowledge does not allow itself to be formulated in general rules.

Simon and Wittgenstein represent two disparate approaches. They are to serve as the background to a discussion on the nursing profession, a discussion which is motivated not least by developments in nursing science and in computer technology.

Systems Theory in Medical Care

"We would like to place the current issue of nurses on a different, I venture to say, higher level. It is an indisputable and purely woman's issue. Au fond, it is based on one of women's purest and deepest attributes; that of motherliness." (Dr Professor John Berg in an address to nurses, 1926)

These are the roots of the nursing profession; the vocation and the self-sacrificing acts of love, the value of which could not be expressed in financial terms. There is a different view of the nursing profession today, in 1987, but the financial rewards are still meagre.

In Sweden and in many other countries, nursing training has taken the form of a college education in recent years. One of the reasons has certainly been that an academic training would upgrade the profession. Nursing training in Sweden used to be carried out at a number of the large hospitals. Today, trainee nurses have become nursing students and colleges have been established for the medical-care sector. Whereas nurses' training used to be largely on an apprenticeship basis, today the scientific content of the training is emphasized. The training must be based on science.

What is the content of the discipline that is known as nursing science? This has been the subject of lively debate in the last decade. However, there seems to be a consensus that the task of a nurse is "care", and the task of a doctor is "cure". These tasks require different types of knowledge. For example, it is the nurse who has the most intimate contact with the patients. Nursing science is yet another science whose direction is obscure. What research there is, is modelled on research in medicine or behavioural science.

I would like to discuss some aspects of nursing research on the basis of a seminal work in nursing science; Katie Eriksson's book *Introduktion till vårdvetenskap* (*An introduction to nursing science*), published in 1983. Katie Eriksson is principal of the Swedish Nursing Institute in Helsinki, and in 1982 presented a doctoral dissertation on the nursing process. Her ideas have attracted a great deal of attention in the debate on research in this area.

According to Eriksson, it is of greatest importance that a theoretical basis is developed for nurses. This will allow nurses to become professionals, which is a pre-requisite for raising the status of their occupation. A scientific approach in the profession means that nurses can develop self-criticism. She sees this as indispensable in an occupation with long traditions in which training has, for long periods, been based on the apprenticeship model. With such a historical background there is considerable risk that people develop a "fixation with habitual and hidebound behaviour", and this is often expressed in an aversion to progress. Eriksson says that a scientific attitude means that "applying a scientific model in solving problems becomes a challenge". Knowledge should be developed towards a high degree of organization and general validity, and precision must be developed in forming concepts. For "a person who is at a higher logical level is better equipped to take responsibility, structure her working method, adapt to changes in her surroundings, be creative in her work and be less dependent on external authority".

According to Ericksson, it is primarily the role of the theoretician that is needed in nursing science, in the absence of a basic research paradigm, this being the reason why the discipline has not succeeded in acquiring much status in the scientific world. The nurse of tomorrow should, in addition to her nursing assignments, be involved in research and development work.

In order to achieve these goals, nursing science must find models for care. The care process must be formalized in order to develop such a model. This requires the concepts to be well-defined – there is a considerable confusion of concepts in the medical-care sector today. This is rooted in a lack of precision when analysing these concepts. But the theoretical concepts are important; "They have a greater power of explanation than the observable, and therefore have a wider area of use".

Eriksson's model is taken from systems theory. The central concepts are the system, components, relations, structure, function and information. Nursing care is the system, the components are the objective, the nursing staff, patients, patient analysis, the priority of areas of nursing care, the choice of nursing intervention, and process factors.

When making changes in the care system, the change that one wants to bring about is "a change between the input and output status of the components or elements".

In contrast to this systems model, earlier models in nursing care were largely practical, concrete and detailed. The knowledge is of the "know-how" type. Practical nursing interventions in care are not the primary aim of a systems-theoretical model.

Eriksson summarizes her care plan in four points:

1. It must specify the care ideal, the objective, i.e. the integrated person affected by nursing interventions
2. It must contain a description of the methods that will lead to this goal
3. It must describe how different nursing contexts affect the process of medical care
4. A care plan must explain the assessments on which nursing interventions are based

Expert Systems

Before I discuss Katie Eriksson's model of nursing care and the view of nurses' knowledge that it expresses, I would like to give a summary of a research project whose theory is close to that of Eriksson. The research work is on the development of expert systems for nurses. The researcher is Judy Ozbolt, a professor at the Center for Nursing Research at Ann Arbor, Michigan. In a series of essays, Ozbolt (1985), who used to be a nurse, has developed her views on ways in which methods could be developed to reach the objective of expert systems for nurses. My summary is largely based on the essay entitled *A proposed expert system for nursing practice. A springboard to nursing science.*

Like Eriksson, Ozbolt emphasizes that, until now, nurses' knowledge has been largely developed from an apprentice model. The knowledge acquired by a nurse through practical experience made her an expert. The expert passes on her knowledge to the novice. According to Ozbolt, a regrettable result of this is that knowledge "is often idiosyncratic in conceptualization and untested in validity and reliability". Current information systems for nurses reflect this fact, "the largely unsystematic nature of nursing knowledge."

If the next generation of technology is to be an improvement, it is necessary that "nursing knowledge be codified for incorporation into the systems". In return, this will lead to major advances for the profession. Such systems would offer a mechanism for systematically testing existing knowledge and returning new knowledge to practical nursing. Today, nursing faces the problem of the lack of a well-developed theory of knowledge, which is an obstacle to the development of data systems that can facilitate the cognitive tasks of nursing care.

Nurses' knowledge is "personal and idiosyncratic". It is fragmentary and lacks cohesion, and will continue to do so until nurses find principles that permit the systematic testing of their knowledge, and a way of synthesizing and codifying this knowledge.

The problem is that nurses have difficulties in describing what they know. Even if they agree that they work on the basis of a problem-solving process, it is difficult for them to "implement" the process, in spite of the existence of information systems that support this work.

Ozbolt asks which methods nurses use to collect "data". She says that four main methods are used, and refers to a major inquiry on these methods. The first two methods, *tenacity* and *authority* are of the least value. The tenacity method perpetuates old truths and traditions; "we've always done it this way", with the attendant risk that because there is suspicion of less traditional knowledge, false knowledge will be passed on. In its turn, the authority method implies a tendency simply to accept the knowledge of recognized authorities. This may persuade the nurse to accept invalid knowledge and be ignorant of valid knowledge.

The two foremost methods are the method based on intuition on the one hand, and scientific knowledge on the other. The nurse uses the intuitive method when she, as Ozbolt puts it, "reviews a mass of patient data and makes an intellectual leap to diagnoses". There is a risk that nurses, even if they are well-qualified, may disagree in their assessment, and the method in itself cannot resolve such a dispute.

Nurses' use of the scientific method is finally becoming more widespread today. It is characterized by objectivity, when assertions can be subjected to empirical tests. But even this method is problematic, because researchers bring different perspectives to their work. Their knowledge cannot be synthesized in "the growing body of knowledge". For that reason, it is difficult to introduce knowledge from research into nursing practice. If the scientific method is to work, then nurses must find suitable and applicable ways of classifying their data and diagnoses.

The chief drawbacks in the information systems for nurses today are, according to Ozbolt, that they do not provide an individualized care plan. This must be done by the nurse. Individualization is one of the greatest advantages in using expert systems. They have "a much richer and more complex knowledge base, one that can be used by the computer for artificially intelligent reasoning, and one that will grow with experience".

Expert systems may, in the future, serve as a springboard for nursing science, according to Ozbolt. The expert systems that she works with herself are based on a multivariate mathematical approach to clinical decision-making. It "permits the incorporation of information-processing strategies experts typically used while maintaining the statistical rigour of data-based systems". Both factual knowledge and associative information are used for drawing clinical inferences. In a later essay, *Designing information systems for nursing practice: database and knowledge base requirements of different organizational technologies.* Ozbolt (1986) describes a model for nurses to apply in developing their work. The model deals with what nurses do when confronted with "stimulus". I do not intend to discuss in detail the argument she puts forward in the article, but I would like to highlight what I perceive as the core of her view of the future knowledge of nurses. Ozbolt applies four categories in her work. The nurse can act as a *craftsman*, as a potter works with clay. She can practise her profession as an art and be very innovative. The problem is that "the innovations are not designed to adapt care to a unique person, since in this model the stimuli are considered to be mostly alike". The same problems are to be found in the *routine method*, because "clients who share a common diagnosis are expected to be more alike than different".

Individualization is best achieved in the *engineering* model, in which each patient is seen as a unique case. The nurse collects and analyses the patients' data to arrive at a diagnosis, which includes, but is not limited to, issues that concern medical diagnosis and treatment. "The nurse sets objectives based on knowledge and experience of what is desirable and achievable and designs an individualized care plan by selecting from a known repertoire of nursing interventions those most likely to lead to achievement of the objectives. After implementing the interventions, the nurse evaluates their effectiveness by comparing the client's subsequent condition with previous diagnoses and objectives."

In the last model – the *non-routine* model, which is a research model – the patient is still seen as unique. The problem is that the search procedures cannot be analysed because more judgement and intuition is required in making decisions.

The Theory of Knowledge for Practitioners

A recurring theme in both Eriksson's and Ozbolt's work is the inability of nurses to articulate their knowledge. Ozbolt also points out that the absence of studies of the theory of knowledge is a problem for nursing practice today.

The question is: what theories of knowledge are most likely to capture the versatility of the nursing profession?

My argument is based on eight years' experience in working life research. The essence of this work has been to interpret case-studies as to the changes in professional knowledge as a consequence of the computerization of different workplaces. One of these studies is of computerization in social insurance offices. Over the past three years, I have concentrated on medical care, most of the interviews having been with nurses on the subject of their professional knowledge. An exhaustive discussion on what experienced nurses perceive as the core of their professional knowledge should be an obvious starting point for subsequent discussions on which applications of technology are suitable. In the field of medical care it is often emphasized that technology should contribute to the improvement of care, and this view places central importance on the theory of knowledge issues.

Half of the group of about ten nurses that I meet on a regular basis have either administrative or trade-union duties. These nurses feel the greatest problem in their profession is that nurses have a very poor ability to formulate and articulate the knowledge they possess. "A language that captures the real knowledge of nurses must be developed" has been a recurrent theme in the group's discussions over the last three years. This is an understandable viewpoint. As long as nurses are unable to describe in explicit terms what they know, they will not succeed in putting forward convincing arguments for upgrading their occupation.

Several of the people in the group felt that upgrading the theoretical training may help to improve nurses' ability to express themselves. Basically, Eriksson is also a proponent of this approach.

Let us consider the question: why are nurses so bad at formulating their knowledge?

If, unlike the physician's profession, the basis of the nursing profession is care, then a different kind of knowledge needs to be developed in the nursing profession than in the doctor's profession. Theoretical training inculcates important medical facts; information that is essential to the nurse. But it does not entirely prepare her for dealing with unexpected events in the care of patients. Newly-qualified nurses usually report that a large part of their time is spent remembering the rules for practical actions such as setting up a drip feed. This gives rise to problems in situations when nurses must act quickly. These actions must be second nature to them before nurses can focus their attention on the patient. Work in the medical-care sector is full of unexpected complications. To deal with this degree of complexity nurses must have the ability to make a reasonable interpretation of events not covered by the descriptions in the rule book. This requires multi-faceted practical experience, through which the information acquired through formal training can be developed into knowledge. That knowledge is built up from a long series of examples which give different perspectives on an illness. Different kinds of knowledge are acquired, some of which can be described explicitly in generally applicable rules. We can call this "propositional knowledge", a term which reflects the nature of the knowledge. Another equally important type of knowledge is the knowledge that becomes apparent in encounters with unforseen complications in everyday care. This "knowledge of familiarity" cannot be described in a meaningful way in general rules because its core is the ability to act with good judgment in unique situations. Propositional knowledge and the knowledge of familiarity presuppose each other and affect each other; they require many-sided, practical experience in order to develop.

When considering in their interviews what they perceive as important in their professional knowledge, the nurses mainly describe examples of a well-developed knowledge of familiarity.

I have chosen to illustrate this with two examples from the interviews:

A nurse of around 50 describes her work in a post-operational ward where she has had 30 years' experience. One day a patient was admitted to her ward: he was a middle-aged man who had just undergone surgery. After a short conversation with him the nurse quickly realized that his condition was not normal, although the man said he felt surprisingly well.

She called out the physician on duty, a young doctor with little experience who, seeing that the patient's vital signs were normal, reproached the nurse for calling him out unnecessarily. Later in the day, the patient died, and the post mortem uncovered a complication that could not have been diagnosed by an examination of his vital signs. The nurse's comment was that she noticed that something was out of the ordinary, but could not explain how she had arrived at this conclusion. Previous experience, of course, she pointed out, was a decisive factor.

A middle-aged psychiatric nurse describes how, shortly after qualifying, she found herself working at a hospital where the view of mental illness differed from the view inculcated by her training. Her training has given her a perception of mental illness rooted in the natural sciences. When patients became violent, they were given heavy doses of medicine and were physically restrained. Psychotherapeutic principles were applied at this, her first place of work, so the patients were not bound when they became aggressive. At first she was constantly afraid of what the patients might do, but having worked in fear for a while, she began to notice that an older woman, a nursing auxiliary, was better able than others to induce calm in those around her, even in the most tense and threatening situations. Our young nurse kept as close as possible to this woman, from whom she learnt how to deal with many of the situations that she had previously found terrifying. But, the nurse told us, she never discussed this with the older auxiliary, and she commented that it was remarkable that she could learn so much from someone who had so little formal education.

Both of these examples provide an indication of the content of what we call the knowledge of familiarity. The multi-faceted, reflected experience hones the ability to notice things that are out of the ordinary, and to apply experience won from previous examples as a starting point in interpreting the unique case. The ability to deal with what are often conflicting amanuenses cannot be acquired through formal book learning, but is often developed through "tips" given by more experienced colleagues. This requires both maturity and a knowledge of mankind.

The dilemma for nurses is that they are aware that a "good" nurse has a wealth of knowledge of familiarity. On the other hand, this knowledge is not scientific knowledge in the sense that it can be formalized in general descriptions. It can, however, be expressed in the form of descriptive examples, but this is a different type of description from that found in the domain of propositional knowledge. In my conversations with nurses, they often emphasize that they know no-one who has been better able to give expression to the knowledge that they themselves find important than Ludwig Wittgenstein, the philosopher. The following is a much-quoted passage from his *Philosophical Investigations* that has been the subject of repeated discussions:

Is there such a thing as "expert judgment" about the genuineness of expressions of feeling? – Even here, there are those whose judgement is "better", and those whose judgement is "worse".

Correcter prognoses will generally issue from the judgements of those with better knowledge of mankind.

Can one learn this knowledge? Yes; some can. Not, however, by taking a course in it, but through "experience". – Can someone else be a man's teacher in this? Certainly. From time to time he gives him the right tip. –This is what "learning" and "teaching" are like here. –What one acquires here is not a technique; one learns correct judgments. There are also rules, but they do not form a system, and only experienced people can apply them right. Unlike calculating-rules.

What is most difficult here is to put this indefiniteness, correctly and unfalsified, into words.
(*Philosophical Investigations*, §277)

The Concept of Practice

As I have understood it, nurses' appreciation of Wittgenstein's paragraph on
the knowledge of humanity has its basis in his realization that this is a type
of knowledge that is not taught from the handbook. Nurses' personal
experience has brought home to them the fact that knowledge of mankind is
not easily gained. Nurses who are involved in nursing training know that
courses on the knowledge of human nature generate the least interest among
students. Instead, the students would like to have more training in, for
example, anatomy, a subject based on factual knowledge. Wittgenstein's
reflections on teaching and learning would, if transposed to work in the care
sector, focus attention on apprenticeship. The experienced give tips to the
less experienced. In another part of his *Philosophical Investigations* (1953)
Wittgenstein says this:

But if a person has not yet got the concepts, I should teach him to use the words by means of
examples and by practice. –And when I do this I do not communicate less to him than I know
myself. I do it, he does it after me; and I influence him by expressions of agreement, rejection,
expectation, encouragement. I let him go his way, or hold him back and so on. (§208)

How are these different types of knowledge to be reconciled? It is self-
evident that nurses require factual knowledge. However, what must be
discussed is how the information contained in their training is to become
knowledge for the nurse.

There is a difference between acquiring information, that is to say facts,
and having knowledge that is rooted in a many-faceted practical experience.
In the latter case, knowledge has been tested and validated through encounters with unique events, and one's assessment of it is based upon similarities
and disparities in comparison with previous examples. One must take an
active part in work in order to acquire propositional knowledge. But the rules
of propositional knowledge are not enough. Wittgenstein says: (1969) "Not
only rules, but also examples are needed for establishing a practice. Our rules
leave loopholes open and the practice has to speak for itself." (§139)

A practice constitutes a whole of rules and examples, and in the practice
both propositional knowledge and the knowledge of familiarity are
developed.

Who Draws the Boundary between Man and Machine?

Let us use this basis of the theory of knowledge in reflecting upon Katie
Eriksson's and Judy Ozbolt's view of knowledge. Their work aims to make
nurses' knowledge more explicit than it is today. To reach this goal, the nurse
must be able to develop a scientific attitude to care. This is emphasized by
both Eriksson and Ozbolt. The scientific model should be a lodestar in
problem solving. Knowledge should be developed towards a high degree of

general application, and nurses must be more precise in defining concepts. They must have a higher abstraction level. The nurse as a theoretician is, according to Eriksson, what we need most today. Seen from my arguments related to Wittgenstein's philosophy of language, it would appear that Eriksson is referring to the nurse as a better collector of information. Knowledge of mankind, the precondition to developing the ability to provide nursing care, can hardly be found in Eriksson's model. Neither is it a mark of the system's theoretical approach. This is probably the price that must be paid for choosing this type of model to improve the status of the nursing occupation. The knowledge of familiarity is not developed at a high abstraction level separated from practice. But then neither is propositional knowledge. What remains is the nurse as a carrier of information.

Both Eriksson and Ozbolt attempt to renounce the apprenticeship model that has been accepted as self-evident in the care sector for so long. It is perceived as irrevocably out-of-date and is regarded as one of the reasons for nurses' knowledge being "idiosyncratic and impossible to validate and test". The conclusion is that new models are needed. The strongest criticism Ozbolt makes of the traditional nurse is, however, her inability to see the patient as unique. In her opinion, this is something that the expert systems of the future can help to remedy. The traditional nurses tend to regard "clients who share a common diagnosis . . . as more alike than different". The systematic analysis of the patient's condition by an expert system provides a different basis for interpreting it in a unique way. This requires a comprehensive knowledge base.

I began this essay by setting two views of the theory of knowledge against each other. Where Herbert Simon develops a natural sciences model to describe mankind's ability to build up knowledge. Wittgenstein emphasizes the context within which knowledge develops. The actions that are carried out in an organization are permeated by the culture and the values that mould a practice. People serving as role models and examples give knowledge its deeper content, since (as Wittgenstein expresses it in a passage I have already quoted): "Not only rules, but also examples are needed for establishing a practice. Our rules leave loopholes open and the practice has to speak for itself."

Seen from this perspective, it is apparent that Wittgenstein's theories of knowledge capture much more of the knowledge of mankind than Simon manages to do with his model. It is possible that what Wittgenstein develops is precisely what Simon is searching for in the discussion that followed his speech: "In order to introduce any of the concepts of human motivation and affect, we would have to have a much more elaborate and comprehensive theory than any of us are discussing or proposing at this conference . . .".

The theories behind the works of Eriksson and Ozbolt are close to Simon. However, faced with the future technical advances that await in the field of medical care, I believe that it is both important and fruitful to allow different theoretical approaches to focus on the same reality. If one objective of technology is to improve the quality of care, we must first have a conception of where the boundary between man and machine lies. It is the people who have many-sided experience from practice who are in the best position to determine which theories are best able to capture the knowledge that they consider to be important in order to do good work.

Conclusion

In the predominant nursing science the scientific model for developing nursing is pleaded for. The model of apprenticeship in learning is heavily attacked.

But science is concerned with universal, general knowledge. Nurses have until today usually seen the practical knowledge directed towards the unique patient as the main point of their knowledge. "The most important thing in caring is to see every person as unique, but it is also the most difficult thing to cope with when you are young and lack experience," a young British nurse said whom I interviewed some weeks ago.

These are two different approaches.

There is a risk when models from, for instance, natural sciences are transferred to areas which have another character. The scientification of knowledge does not improve the quality of caring if it deteriorates the conditions for developing knowledge by familiarity.

Regarding the high esteem of scientific knowledge in our culture at the expense of practical knowledge it is hardly surprising that nursing science aims at giving "caring" scientific status. But if unjustified models for "caring" serve as a basis for developing advanced technology in nursing, it might have unfortunate consequences for the profession.

A thorough discussion of nursing knowledge from different theoretical points of views should precede the development of, for instance, expert systems in caring.

References

Eriksson K (1983) Introduktion Till Vårdvenskap. Almqvist & Wiksell, Stockholm
Ozbolt J (1985) A proposed expert system for nursing practice. A springboard to nursing science. J. Med Syst 9
Ozbolt J (1986) Designing information systems for nursing practice: database and knowledge base requirements of different organizational technologies. Comput Methods Programs Biomed 22 61–65
Simon H (1985) Some computer models of human learning. In: Shafto M (ed) How we know. Nobel Conference XX. Harper and Row, New York
Wittgenstein L (1922) Tractatus Logico-Philosophicus. Routledge & Kegan Paul, London (1961)
Wittgenstein L (1953) Philosophical Investigations. Blackwell, Oxford
Wittgenstein L (1969) On certainty. Blackwell, Oxford

Chapter 4

Automation – Skill – Apprenticeship
P. Gullers

Behind the concept of the automated factory lies the view of knowledge in which all human thought and action can be logically described in a formalized language, and in which all conceivable activities are predictable. So far all attempts to realize this vision have refuted this as being the case. The problem with automating propositional knowledge can be illustrated in analogy to the use of formulae at the expense of practice which means an enormous loss in association material when it comes to tackling problems. It is important to limit use of formalizations to ensure freedom of action through the ability to have a feel for things. Present production techniques do not provide an environment for the development of skills in training hence the retention of an apprenticeship model is fundamental as "The experiences of the senses and practical intellect are perhaps both an essential complement and prerequisite of the successful automation of industry". (Emile, Rousseau)

The Dream of the Automated Factory

"The Automated Factory" was a large headline in the November 1946 issue of *Fortune* magazine. The threat and the promise of a machine without workers was closer than ever before. All the components already existed. The model for the automatic factory came from the processing industry. Continuous manufacture by a self-monitoring closed system using steering and control technology. This dream is of a far earlier date. In 1825 and 1830 Babbage and Uhre had, in *On the economy of machinery and manufactures*, and *Philosophy of manufactures*, described the factory as the physical expression of mathematical principles – a gigantic automatic machine.

The principle for numerically controlled machines was developed at the end of the 1940s at the MIT servolab, which produced flight simulators for combat pilots. As a logical extension of being able to simulate the way a real aeroplane behaved in the air, the idea emerged of predicting an aircraft's characteristics in a strictly mathematical way before it had been built. Design and production would then be carried out on the basis of these mathematical models.

Thanks to almost unlimited state funding, the development work was continued, even though numerically controlled (NC) machines could not be made commercially attractive, largely because of the programming costs but also due to a lack of real experience of actual industrial production.

General Electric was one of the first companies to introduce NC machines in normal production. At the beginning of the 1960s NC technology was to attain two important goals. Firstly, it was a way of meeting the air force's increasingly stringent accuracy and tolerance specifications. Secondly, it was seen as a way of becoming less dependent on bench-hands, who were commanding higher and higher wages. Because the NC machine was self-steering, it could be run by button-pushers with no real skills. After five arduous years spent introducing the system, the company was forced to accept that it was difficult to bring down production costs, it was difficult to reach a sufficiently high degree of availability and it was difficult to manage without the craft skills possessed by the engineering workers who did more manual kinds of work.

David Noble (1977) a technology historian who has described the General Electric case, summarizes their experience like this. "The paradox was that the NC technology introduced in part to make the company independent of the skilled craft worker needed precisely that skill in order to succeed."

Instead of reducing the operators' wages, responsibilities and powers, a "pilot project" was started, where machine operators became machine controllers. Their traditional job skills were extended to include training in programming and mathematics.

Fifteen years after the General Electric pilot project, Eric Gierz in *Det framtida verkstadsarbetet* (*The future of engineering work*) described the situation in some of Sweden's large engineering companies. His conclusion was that the fragmented work of traditional Taylorism (Taylor 1906) had outlived its usefulness: new technology makes it more important that workers on the shop floor can master the machines and control systems. Work organization must be characterized by far-reaching horizontal and vertical integration, so that new technology can meet the efficiency goals set for production. In case-studies from a number of large engineering companies with sophisticated production methods and a considerable amount of new technology, Gierz observes that "the traditional craft skills possessed by engineering workers are still important" and that new production systems still suffer from major shortcomings.

Gierz cites examples:

1. Sandvik: "The operator sets the tools, feeds new figures into the computer and corrects for simple deficiencies in the program. Retooling is often a source of trouble. Changeover times are often longer than planned and the scrapping frequency is high."

2. Stal: "The situation seems to be a somewhat different in heavy engineering. It is difficult to automate materials handling processes, small batches and high-cost workpieces. There must be practically speaking no scrapping. Although programming costs are high, there are running-in problems, usually with the first workpiece. Unforeseen vibrations and similar problems require modifications to the tool, the tool runners, the cutting data, etc. . . . The programmers often have to consult with the operator in order to produce usable programmes."

3. ASEA on the future: In ten years' time engineers should be able to produce NC programmes straight from product models. But the path to this goal is long and hard. One of the greatest obstacles is that many engineers lack sufficient knowledge of production and production economics.

The examples given by Gierz bear a marked similarity to the experiences reported by General Electric in the 1960s. Since then, there have been great advances in technology, chiefly in terms of data capacity and programming costs. Yet some problems still remain. It is difficult to get technology to work economically, reliably and with a high degree of availability.

A review of the history of technology highlights the main problems even more clearly. Gierz describes how Taylor's principles worked in practice. His description is worth quoting:

> The vertical division of labour involved a certain amount of deskilling in engineering work. But it was still the workers who carried out the toolsetting and set up the machines. It also appeared to be an exception that they used the cutting data supplied by the production engineers. The payment-by-results system put a premium on high cutting speeds and the price to be paid was greater wear and tear on machine tools. Inconsistencies in the workpieces to be processed, problems caused by the machine's instability, unforseen vibrations etc. made it necessary to modify the theoretical values.
>
> The production engineers' instructions served as some kind of *basic values that were informally changed by the skilled workers.* (Gierz, 1986 p. 63)

According to Gierz, NC technology changed the rules of the game. Now the process engineers no longer produced working instructions, their work resulted in a punched tape that automatically controlled the position, revolutions and cutting depth of the machine tool. But production management soon discovered that the process engineers' basic data were far too incomplete to be translated directly into control information. "The fact that skilled workers previously made informal modifications to their working instructions to correct the greatest shortcomings became apparent when these workers were no longer there to form the final link in the chain between design and manufacture. . . . As a result it became increasingly common for the company to involve skilled workers in process engineering and programming." (Gierz, 1986, p. 62)

Gierz's conclusion is that work organization must be changed and that greater demands must be made for training. As Gierz writes: "It may appear that traditional experience-based craft skills are enjoying a renaissance", which he sees as paradoxical. He indicates that the demands of new technology are to be met chiefly through new theoretical knowledge.

Before continuing to discuss the issue of the direction of training, I shall digress for a moment. Gierz brings forward the problems that have been present throughout the 1900s, when attempts have been made to describe a production sequence on the basis of theory and mathematical models. He expresses these problems as unforseen events – vibrations, inconsistencies in the raw materials, incomplete process engineering data, program errors, imbalance or the properties of the production plant. Skilled workers have, over time, learned to interpret these shortcomings and make predictions or compensate for errors during the work process. They do this informally, intuitively, or through documented experience.

This skill, then, has been and still is essential in spite of automatic technology, or perhaps it is, paradoxically enough, even more essential now since without it the machine will automatically repeat its mistakes.

At an early stage, new technology had its sceptics. Norbert Wiener (1948, 1961) the father of cybernetics, warned against taking parallels between closed logical systems and living systems too far. In the human system, the controller, the self-correcting mechanism, is not steered by formal logic but uses his skill, experience and his sense of appropriateness as controls. The system must permit constant feedback to allow the individual to stop a process and permit "second thoughts" in response to unforseen developments.

Is not this exactly what the experienced engineering worker does? The inherent problem in the closed automation system is that the option to stop or correct is reduced or disappears entirely.

Gierz writes that there are shortcomings in the production engineering data. They do not give an exhaustive description of all essential operations. Gierz does not discuss the causes for this in any more detail. He appears to consider that it should, in principle, be possible to get around them. However, Gustaf Östberg (1982), a professor in construction materials science, has done a great deal of work on this particular phenomenon. How can the gap between the materials technicians and the design engineer be bridged? One cannot expect the concepts developed by materials science to describe and explain the internal structures of materials to have much in common with the concepts related to form and dimension used in engineering science. But, notes Östberg, mechanical engineers generally appear to select suitable materials for their designs. There seems to be, therefore, something that bridges this gap, but unfortunately neither pedagogues, psychologists, scientific nor systems theoreticians can give us any idea of the content of whatever it is that bridges this gap.

Östberg does not discuss the gap between programmers or design engineers and the machine operators on the workshop floor. The programmer presupposes that the material will behave according to the ideal description of its properties, while the engineering worker has learned to bridge the gap between this ideal model and reality. He has learned to navigate in what are partly-unknown waters. The critical question is how this is done, and how one learns to do it. Recommendations on the direction and content of training are totally controlled by the perception of this "something", which may be called "the knowledge of familiarity", "skill," "tacit knowledge".

Gierz makes an unexpressed determination of traditional craft skills as being practical knowledge; knowledge on the craftsman model and experienced-based knowledge that should, in theory, be possible to supplant with better formal descriptions, and more reliable technical systems. But both Östberg and Wiener indicate a different approach.

The conclusion of Östberg's argument is that we *cannot* replace the knowledge of familiarity for the simple reason that we lack a language that bridges the gap between, for example, the conceptual worlds of the materials technician and the engineer.

Gierz defines the problems that ASEA met in their efforts to introduce automatic processes as being that the design engineers lacked production experience and workshop floor skills. In an interview, Torsten Hägerstrand described this as follows: "If you talk to an engineer of my age, you will find he has a practical feeling for things. The new generation mostly write formulae, and that is a good thing in some contexts, but it means an enormous loss in association material when it comes to tackling problems." (Abrahamsson, 1982 p. 200)

The conclusion from Wiener's words of warning (1948, 1961) is that we *should not* go too far in our formalizations, even if this is theoretically possible. We should set a limit in order to retain freedom of action. To quote Hägerstrand: "to maintain a practical feeling for things. Being able to deal with problems requires a wealth of association material, i.e. experience or the knowledge of familiarity."

If this cannot be fully reproduced in a formal way, it means that it only exists in a human carrier as a skill that is handed down in a group. If everything could be learnt from books, then why would we need teachers? The problem of identifying the knowledge of familiarity is that it does not need to be expressed in practical action. Error-location in computer programs or medical diagnoses *demonstrate* whether a person is competent by the fact that the error is corrected or that the patient is given the correct treatment. The exact way that this is done cannot always be described, even by the person who has made the diagnosis. It is sometimes interpreted as the person in question not actually knowing what he is doing or not *wanting* to share his secrets with others.

If we accept this argument, then there are two conditions that can be stated for the transfer of the knowledge of familiarity. The knowledge of familiarity must be taught by someone who has a wealth of personal experience. Since this knowledge cannot be formally taught, it must be transferred with the aid of examples from real life. Through his own actions, the instructor or the teacher himself becomes a model. This teaching takes place in the present, in a social context, but the actions also have a background, by contrast to, for example, an industrial robot.

Practical Knowledge

More than anything else, it is practical actions that we associate with traditional craft skills. To forge, grind and file a piece of metal to make a usable object, to build a guitar, blow glass or throw a pot is tangible and, for the uninitiated, something that is incredibly difficult and that we admire. It is a manual skill, by contrast to physical labour or abstract thinking. It is a manual skill that we know takes many years to master completely. Industrial and artistic skills evoke a feeling of respect.

Many people would like to acquire these skills, but the long and arduous years of apprenticeship are a deterrent. To file pieces of metal day-in and day-out as engineering apprentices had to do, or to devote several hours a day to practising the movements of classical dance, may be compared to equestrian dressage. Both self-control and, to some extent, physical and intellectual subjection are needed. Many occupations require the practical training of skills in order to master the essentials of a tradition and then to be able to progress beyond the limitations of accepted practice.

Some skills, such as learning to write, to ride a bicycle or to read, stay with us even without regular training. Our strength, speed and precision may deteriorate in some cases, although we still *know how* to perform these actions. Even an old, retired craftsman can act as an instructor, that is to say he can still make assessments, demonstrate and correct faulty technique and methods. He retains his eye for the job, his feeling for form and his knowledge of the materials used.

Two things are important here in maintaining our knowledge levels. Practical knowledge and the knowledge of familiarity are closely interrelated. They are mutually interdependent. It may be difficult to make a general definition of the extent to which the knowledge of familiarity can be maintained without maintaining our ability to carry out the practical action. If modern production technology works today thanks to the fact that older craftsmen with a broad and deep knowledge of familiarity are still to be found in our workshops, then the problem remains of whether it is possible to pass on this knowledge when production technology has become so abstract and automated that there is no longer any scope for training practical skills. If this is an essential relationship, then the old production methods must be maintained in our workshops or in other special environments such as occupational training colleges. Then the question is, what may be lost? Can the reality of a production environment be transferred or reconstructed in a training environment?

A survey commissioned by the Swedish National Industrial Board claims that our school system is on the verge of a crisis as a system for transferring knowledge. The gap between industry and schools is widening because a great deal of the knowledge in industry is tacit knowledge. The knowledge is there, but it cannot be coded, stored and taught in our schools.

Propositional Knowledge

A third category of knowledge that is part of professional competence is formal knowledge. It is the knowledge that one learns from books, for example the theories, models and concepts of a given subject. In the debate on occupational training the importance of having more theoretical knowledge to meet the demands of new technology is emphasized. We can call this kind of knowledge "propositional knowledge". By virtue of the fact that it can be formulated in language it is, by contrast to the knowledge of familiarity and practical knowledge, explicit.

Hägerstrand, Östberg and the research institute that compiled the report for the Swedish National Industrial Board all emphasize how dependent theoretical knowledge is on knowledge that cannot be formalized, the kind of knowledge that we refer to here as the knowledge of familiarity and practical knowledge.

Thomas Kuhn (1970) has looked into how scientific work and learning actually take place. A verbalized statement of scientific law is in itself "virtually impotent". One does not learn science solely by verbal means, but the result of the learning process is tacit knowledge, which is attained by *practising* science rather than learning the rules of how to practice it. At the end of his book Kuhn says that like language, scientific knowledge is the common property of a group or it is nothing at all, and if we are to understand it we must become familiar with the particular characteristics of the group that creates and uses it.

If this is true, an *understanding* of propositional knowledge cannot be attained solely through formal teaching. If one wishes to claim that more theory is required in order to understand sophisticated computerized processes, then one must, if the above is true, add that computers cannot teach their own "knowledge" in formal programmes for teaching. In this case there are no short cuts to real knowledge. Even propositional knowledge is based on experience. It must be handed down in the form of actions. Even propositional knowledge presupposes the training of skills. The conclusion of this argument is that propositional knowledge, practical knowledge, and the knowledge of familiarity are interdependent. One kind of knowledge cannot be separated from the other two kinds. Formal expert systems can therefore neither replace nor compensate for shortcomings in propositional knowledge, the knowledge of familiarity or practical knowledge. Professional skills cannot be completely formalized. This is what lies behind the current resurgence of interest in the apprenticeship model.

Today, it is primarily formal propositional knowledge that is emphasized, but it is devoid of skill and familiarity. It is a kind of knowledge that is deliberately devoid of subject.

Practical knowledge is deprived of its intellectual content and is perceived as being purely instrumental. The knowledge of familiarity is excluded. Experience is perceived primarily as counter to development, and as being irrational and conservatively prejudiced.

The emphasis on abstract knowledge has traditions that have Descartes as their first major interpreter. He was attempting to find what is absolute certainty beyond the illusive impressions of our senses and established conceptions. Descartes' world becomes a space without time, i.e., a reality without history.

Conclusions

Behind the dream of automated factories we find a view of knowledge in which all human thought and action can be logically described in a formalized language, and in which all conceivable activities are predictable.

So far, every attempt to realize this rejects the notion that this is the case. Professional knowledge and skills are still required in our workshops.

So-called traditional professional knowledge is often seen as being the same as having a manual skill. It has therefore been accepted that the need for manual skills decreases as mechanization increases. Professional knowledge is degraded. In our opinion this is an erroneous or hasty conclusion. "Skill" is not only, or even primarily, an instrumental act. It also involves propositional knowledge and the knowledge of familiarity. All these three forms of knowledge go to make up a single kind of professional skill. It is a skill that is only in part explicit, and all three forms of knowledge are internally interdependent.

It is taught and understood only within the framework of a given practice, where practical knowledge, propositional knowledge and the knowledge of familiarity are gained together.

If this is the case, then training must also include some form of apprenticeship. This does not mean that a new work organization and production technology can, or should, be linked to the traditional forms of apprenticeship in workshops. We may have to look for a new apprenticeship model. The experiences of the senses and practical intellect are perhaps both an essential complement to and a prerequisite of the successful automation of industry. A model for this kind of apprenticeship, paradoxically enough, may be found in the 1700s, in Rousseau's Emile.

Of all the senses, sight is that which we can least distinguish from the judgments of the mind; so it takes a long time to learn to see. It takes a long time to compare sight and touch, and to train the former sense to give a true report of shape and distance. Without touch, without progressive motion, the sharpest eyes in the world could give us no idea of space. To the oyster the whole world must seem a point, and it would seem nothing more to it even if it had a human mind. It is only by walking, feeling, counting, measuring the dimensions of things, that we learn to judge them rightly; but, on the other hand, if we were always measuring, our senses would trust to the instrument and would never gain confidence. Nor must the child pass abruptly from measurement to judgment; he must continue to compare the parts when he could not compare the whole; he must substitute his estimated aliquot parts for exact aliquot parts, and instead of always applying the measure by hand he must get used to applying it by eye alone. I would, however, have his first estimates tested by measurement, so that he may correct his errors, and if there is a false impression left upon the senses he may correct it by a better judgment. The same natural standards of measurement are in use almost everywhere, the man's foot, the extent of his outstretched arms, his height. When the child wants to measure the height of a room, his tutor may serve as a measuring rod; if he is estimating the height of a steeple let him measure it by the house; if he wants to know how many leagues of road there are, let him count the hours spent in walking along it. Above all, do not do this for him; let him do it himself. (Emile pp. 107 – 108)

References and Further Reading

Abrahamsson K (1982) Vagval i kunskapens land, ur Vad ar den goda erfarenheten vard. Stockholm
Babbage C. (1825) On the economy of machinery and manufactures. (Reprint, New York, 1963)
Gierz E (1986) Det framtida verkstadsarbetet. Uppsala
Kuhn T (1970) The structure of scientific revolution. University of Chicago Press, Chicago, Illinois
Noble DF (1977) America by design. A. A. Knope, New York
Noble DF (1984) The forces of production. A social history of industrial automation. New York
Ostberg G (1982) Om konsten att diskutera nya material.
LO/TCO konferens om nya material och materialforskning.
Rousseau JJ (1762) Emile (J. M. Dent and Son, Edition London 1982)
Taylor FW (1906) On the art of cutting metals. 3rd Edn. ASMA, New York
Uhre A (1830) Philosophy of manufactures
Wiener N (1948) Cybernetics. Avon Books, New York
Wiener N (1961) The human use of human beings. Avon Books, New York

Chapter 5

Computerization and Skill in Local Weather Forecasting

Maja-Lisa Perby

Increased information through computerization does not mean greater reliability in decision making. Consider the case of weather forecasting. Skill here is the ability to select and interpret information. Computer solutions are general and standardized whereas skill is developed through use of concrete, specific examples. Traditionally, meteorologists used solely historical material to build up a "comprehensive idea" of the weather situation in their minds. This "comprehensive" idea is the shaping of an inner weather picture which gradually builds up in the minds of meteorologists and leads to understanding and development of skill. Its creation depends on the reflection and digestion of information. Forecasting is a continuous process. The problem with the new methods and information presented by computerization is that there is less importance placed on reflection and therefore understanding through consideration of a variety of knowledge sources, communication between workers, and practical experiences.

Introduction

"Are our weather forecasts today actually better and more reliable than those of 30 years ago when I started working? Personally, I doubt it." This comment made by an experienced meteorologist working at the weather forecasting service at Sturup airport could be regarded as a starting point for the discussion in this chapter. He had himself experienced a dramatic increase in weather information available, and especially he had experienced a long-reaching development of numerical forecasts made by computers.

The weather forecasting service at Sturup airport is one of four regional weather forecasting centres in Sweden. The main task is to produce forecasts for flight purposes and to give other kinds of weather information which are important for the safety of air traffic (e.g., watching out for weather phenomena which are especially dangerous for flight, briefing of pilots before a flight). Today there is an increasing number of forecasts produced for other customers. The forecasts vary in time span from half-an-hour to 24 hours and vary in area from a local forecast for the airport to regional forecasts.

The opinions about the quality of the forecasts may vary, but the introductory comment indicates that the availability of numerical forecasts which predict large-scale weather for a time over 12 or 24 hours ahead are not necessarily sufficient for making a good *local* forecast. Another meteorologist said in reference to this introductory statement: "At the airport we have not had so much benefit of the kind of computerization which numerical forecasts represent. We work with an emphasis upon 0–9 hours. Whether our forecasts have improved or not during the last 30 years that depends on *other* factors than computer-based forecasts."

Here, I consider the skill of the meteorologists in performing their work, e.g., their skill in selecting, interpreting and using a huge amount of information about various weather elements. Since the notion of skill is not well-developed I have attempted to develop a theoretical framework for considering skill in work. After analysing the job of the meteorologists it is quite evident that the computer applications which they encounter can cause some problems in relationship to a skilled performance of their tasks. Finally, using the perspective upon skill, I discuss some alternatives to a one-sided use of computers and more data about weather. The alternatives are founded in proposals from a group of meteorologists who have discussed their work and their knowledge in work in a trade-union context.

In my study I have tried to highlight some questions which can be of general interest. One such point is that computer solutions tend to be general and are always standardized whereas skill in work is formed by concrete and specific circumstances. Another point is the use of advanced computer models – here numerical forecasts, more generally expert systems – in relationship to the skill of those using the systems in their work.

Method

The framework for this study has been a project between Lund University and the local weather forecasting service at Sturup in a trade-union context. Researchers participated in a group which was formed in 1982. Most participants in this group are meteorologists, a few are meteorological assistants.

The original aim of the project was to discuss the influence of computerization upon working environment. But within a short time the discussion in the group spontaneously centred around meteorological work and the preconditions for doing a job in which the meteorologists themselves are satisfied with the quality of their work. The discussion can be characterized as a discussion about knowledge in work in a trade-union context. According to trade-union-active members of the group, the group has been a support in long-term trade-union work.

In addition to participating in the group I have conducted in-depth interviews with the members of the group to further elucidate questions of skill, outcome of work and computerization.

What is the Weather Like Today?

Weather is dynamic; it is in movement; it is continuously changing: Air masses move, centres of high pressure and of low pressure form, develop and then disappear. Weather is three-dimensional; processes in the upper strata of the atmosphere influence the weather development at ground level. There are weather phenomena of very different geographical extension. There are phenomena of very different time-scale. There are interactions of many kinds between weather phenomena.

As a consequence, to be able to make a local forecast the meteorologist must have an overview of the development of the prevailing weather pattern in a large geographical area and in upper strata of the atmosphere. "Also when one makes a forecast such as the half-an-hour forecast for the airport one must look outside local weather. You can find for example a newly formed low pressure centre, that may end the life cycle of an old one."

The work of the meteorologists includes analysing the weather. Traditionally, meteorologists have used historical material, i.e., observations, in their analysis. Today the numerical forecasts provide additional raw material directly oriented towards the future.

When a meteorologist comes to work, he is briefed by his departing colleague on the current weather development. At the beginning of a work shift the meteorologist also checks the material on the walls. He takes about ten minutes to look at this material: he notices some traits in the development predicted by numerical forecasts; he notices whether the numerical forecasts from various sources are in accordance or not; he may take down a particular numerical map which he finds especially interesting and bring it with him to his desk

The main part of the hour or so it takes to form a rough picture of the weather patterns the meteorologist spends with a pen in his hand analysing the so-called synoptical map where the latest available observations at ground level are plotted individually. (Synoptical means that the observations are made at the same point of time at all places.) Each single observation contains a number of weather parameters, i.e., wind, visibility, air pressure, change of air pressure for the last 3 hours, temperature, dewpoint temperature, amount and type of clouds, the cloud base.

To analyse the map the meteorologist traces patterns in the weather situation. He draws isobars, isallobars (lines of the same air pressure change), areas of precipitation, areas of fog and mist, fronts, rain showers etc.

One important reason why meteorologists defend this traditional work method is, as expressed by one meteorologist: "Analysing the map is the quickest way of assimilating large amounts of weather observation data". In fact, during the analysis the meteorologist uses many other kinds of material in addition to the synoptical map in front of him, e.g., observation maps from upper strata in the atmosphere and satellite pictures. He also looks at a sequence of maps which have been analysed earlier and at analyses and forecasts from other sources.

On the one hand the visible result of the analysis is a map showing the weather situation at ground level at a specific point of time. But, on the other hand, the meteorologist has simultaneously formed a notion of the weather development in all three dimensions of the atmosphere over a period of time which stretches into the future.

The meteorologist's ideas about possible directions of change in the weather come from a number of sources. He is guided on the route by the briefing from his colleague: "It is useful to have an idea about the weather development at the outset of the analysis; you make a better analysis then. The judgement of your colleague gives you a sign-post to follow. During the analysis you have to be critical; you keep asking yourself if his suggestions seem all right to you or if you can see signs of other changes."

The sequence of previously analysed maps is an important source of ideas about the weather development. The meteorologist looks at the position of a front on the maps from 9, 6, 3 and 0 hours ago, and he checks the distance between two isallobars. This is interpreted against the background of a theory which allows for movement (inclusive accelerations) of weather phenomena and also takes the life-cycle into account.

The numerical forecasts are used as comparisons during the course of analysis like "Does this development seem plausible when taking into account the development which one can trace oneself from the synoptical map?"

The first idea about the weather situation which has emerged as a result of the analysis is completed during the course of the work shift. The meteorologist follows and takes in all kinds of information. He talks to pilots on the radio; he checks all kinds of material which arrive; he is also open to casual information.

Weather Forecasting and Computerization

I will consider two kinds of computerization. The first one (dating back to the 1950s) is the use of computers for making numerical forecasts. This is an example of the use of computers for making scientific calculations; an incredibly vast number of calculations have to be carried out in order to make weather forecasts on the basis of a mathematical model.

Briefly, a numerical model works in the following way. The state of the atmosphere is given (or rather calculated through interpolation) in a grid. A computer model in accordance with physical laws (but containing many simplifications) is used to calculate in an enormously vast number of small steps how the state of the atmosphere will change for several days ahead.

The models used in numerical forecasts are developed to show large-scale weather development. In addition, the methods used during the last 25 years are developed with an emphasis upon 24–72 hours. Or to put it in other words: the forecasts are not constructed in order to cover such short intervals as 0–12 hours. Here old methods have proved to be superior, and the traditional methods work well also up to 24 hours.

The continuing technical development of computers as well as of the scientific basis for making numerical forecasts has continuously increased the number of computer-made forecasts. The first model used at the Swedish national forecast centre represented the atmosphere above ground level by one upper stratum; the models of today use perhaps 10 to 15 upper levels. Large centres – like Reading in England where they have at the moment the fastest computer of the world – have been established to give the computer capacity necessary, for example, for making numerical forecasts over 72 hours. Today there are numerical forecasts made up to 10 days ahead.

The situation at Sturup airport today is that forecasts from various sources are available. There are numerical forecasts from, for example, England and Sweden. The numerical forecasts are made upon observation material once or twice every 24 hours. They are presented in the shape of maps showing the predicted weather situation at given fixed points of time in the future, e.g., 00 +12 hours, +18 hours, +24 hours, +36 hours etc. In addition there are large-scale so-called subjective national forecasts from, for example, Germany and Sweden. These forecasts are made by meteorologists and are partially based upon an interpretation of numerical forecasts.

The second type of computerization I will consider is a computerized system for plotting maps, which was introduced in 1983. The idea of automatic plotting was originally put forward in order to replace the chartographer assistants who had done the plotting of observations manually. During the systems development other facilities were introduced into the system. One example is that the kind of meteorological data which have been received by teleprinter now are presented on VDUs. A second example is that a computer program has been developed to make local calculations of the development of fog in the area around the airport.

Working Knowledge and Skill

The various kinds of knowledge needed in order to perform a job have been labelled "working knowledge" (Kusterer 1978). The focus of my interest is the skill people acquire in using their working knowledge, an ability which increases over time. In other words, what I discuss here is *skill as an aspect of every job* (Goodman and Perby 1985; Perby 1985).

The following examples from meteorological work illustrate the kind of knowledge and ability which I include in skill – compare the concept "tacit knowledge" (Polanyi 1962; Göranzon 1983b). "In the beginning I had to say to the pilots, just a minute I'll see – now I know in advance what they will ask for. It took me many years to develop this ability." A meteorologist who had worked for some years observed about a more experienced colleague: "It strikes me repeatedly that he knows more about the prevailing weather than he has really been informed about – and he is right." A third reply: "It is hard to tell why one thinks the weather is in a certain way; you just have a comprehensive idea of the weather in your mind."

The third reply raises the question of whether it is possible to say more about the knowledge and ability inherent in skill. What is the "comprehensive idea" like? In order to discuss skilled work, Goodman and I have introduced two concepts, integrated understanding and sensibility (Goodman and Perby 1985). By *integrated understanding* we stress skill as a fusion of different kinds of knowledge and experience to form a totality in the mind of a skilled person.

In a study of the effects of computerization upon work within the public social insurance system in Sweden there is a statement about the working knowledge of the employees. Their working knowledge is characterized as a combination of their knowledge about the content of rules and laws *and* their practical experience of the many types of situations which they meet in their contact with customers; an experience which tells about *complications* in the use of laws and rules (Johansson and Josefson 1980; Göranzon 1983b). In the terminology used here, this is an example of integrated understanding in work.

The "weather knowledge" can also be characterized as integrated understanding. The background knowledge about weather that a meteorologist uses in work is a fusion of many elements of various kinds, e.g. education, experience of a large number of weather situations, an acquired understanding of the role of local geographical conditions in relationship to large-scale weather, knowledge about and experience of all the various types of information material about weather which arrive at the work place (e.g., experience of the reliability of numerical forecasts from various sources depending on weather situation and mathematical factors in the models), experience of what kinds of questions pilots and other customers are likely to ask etc. (What falls outside "weather knowledge" are a few parts of work like the knowledge directed towards the handling of the computer in the map-plotting system.)

The integrated character of all these elements which constitute "weather knowledge" can be illustrated by the fact that it is not obvious to the meteorologists themselves what the quite-pronounced differences in educational background actually mean in the performance of their tasks.

Just as in the study at the insurance system, the weather knowledge can to a large extent be described as a fusion between some types of *general* knowledge (i.e. knowledge common for meteorologists irrespective of their working centrally or regionally) and experience of *specific* circumstances and preconditions in predicting local weather. Weather knowledge, like all working knowledge, is developed in response to what is needed in order to perform the tasks of the job (Kusterer 1978).

Weather knowledge is formed by the local viewpoint upon weather also in some ways which are not *a priori* evident: "We have a telephone conference every day with the national Swedish forecast service. When we draw attention to some local weather phenomena their attitude is too often to neglect that which does not fit into their general pattern of weather development. Here at the airport we are more open to look out for phenomena which may be a first sign of *changes* in the weather situation."

The concept "integrated understanding" has been used here to characterize the background weather knowledge of a meteorologist. But the concept is also applicable at quite another level, the knowledge about the weather of the day, which I will consider in the next section.

With our second concept, *sensibility*, Goodman and I refer to an aesthetic consciousness that a skilled person has and also to an interplay between different kinds of intellect and our five senses. In connection with this concept I am interested in the role of information received through our senses for skill in work. When interviewing meteorologists I have found a tendency to stress sensual aspects of their work.

The meteorologists use a vast body of abstract knowledge in their work: they use abstract models for explaining weather behaviour, they use abstract terms to characterize aspects of weather etc. But the aim of the job is to give weather information which is so concrete that the receiver can relate it in some way to his sensual experience of weather.

Many of the meteorologists have stressed the importance of looking out of the window when performing their work, although they know that the idea about the weather that they get in this manner may be in some ways misleading. What they see outside the window at the moment colours their opinion about the weather at other places and at other points of time. An interpretation of their attitude is, in accordance with Mike Cooley, that they want to have a "feel for the physical world" (Cooley 1980).

One of the meteorologists referred to a retired colleague who was deeply engaged in the usefulness of the weather information he gave to pilots. "He said that the best part of work was the contact with the pilots and to listen to them describing weather at the height of atmosphere where they fly; then he was able to compare their description with the picture he had himself of what weather is like at ground level." Another meteorologist said: "You learn about weather by talking to pilots; they can tell you what the weather is like at places where you have not been yourself, so you get to know what a storm can be like at the Canary Islands."

The discussion of skill would be incomplete without considering the *social recognition* of skill. The amount of working knowledge that goes into a job can only be judged from inside (Kusterer 1978). In some jobs – like a traditional craftsman or in the case of a medical doctor – there is a general respect for the tacit knowledge required to perform the tasks. In other jobs – e.g., manual jobs without formal training – there is a general lack of recognition of the workers' contribution in terms of knowledge and skill.

At the weather service at the airport there is now a pronounced tendency from management to try to diminish the costs. As a consequence there is a tendency not to respect aspects of the work process which are important for using one's skill in performing the daily work and for maintaining skill in the long run. "They look in our time schedule and find that there is half an hour where we do not have anything to do. We get more and more specific tasks filling our time schedule and less and less time to think and reflect upon weather. Now it is only a question of sending the forecasts on time – the content does not seem to matter."

The Inner Weather Picture

Using the framework for considering skill, and especially with the concept integrated understanding in mind, I will return to the process whereby the meteorologist gains an understanding of the weather situation of the day. Integrated understanding is not to be regarded as a static concept; I use it in order to describe an integration process rather than a finally reached state.

During the work shift the meteorologist assimilates a vast amount of information about various weather elements, using his background weather knowledge to interpret the information and to integrate it into a pattern. In the course of time, as he assimilates more information, the pattern of the weather becomes more complete and clear.

But it is possible to say more about the "comprehensive idea" about weather in the mind of the meteorologist. The emerging pattern takes the shape of an *inner weather picture* showing the prevailing weather situation and the directions of change. At first the picture is quite crude, and gradually it becomes more elaborate and more established in the mind of the meteorologist. The picture represents a more and more comprehensive idea of the weather of the day with its general patterns and specific points of interest, for example, for the meteorologist's further outlook for more information. The understanding which he builds up in the shape of a weather picture for himself includes knowledge useful for making forecasts, to issue warnings and for the briefing of pilots.

One meteorologist described how he builds up an inner picture as follows: "My first picture is quite abstract – I use a theoretical model of the strata of the atmosphere. During the work shift the abstractions disappear more and more. The picture is filled out by the weather as it actually is – there are always aspects which do not fit into your theoretical expectations. I get acquainted with the weather of the day; it is a new acquaintance, unique; we have not met before although there may be similarities to the weather of other days. I get a better and better picture of the atmosphere as it is."

That the inner picture becomes more established during the work shift means that the meteorologist knows more and more by heart, without needing to look at the sources of information which he has used. His ability to answer questions, to make forecasts, etc., improves during work (apart from fatigue).

The meteorologists have repeatedly stressed the importance of reflecting upon information. They have also stressed the need for digestion: "Pieces of information fall into place when you take a cup of coffee and do not think of work for a while or when you move around looking like you were doing nothing."

To make a forecast is not a distinct step in the work of a meteorologist: forecasts are made continuously, as an integrated part of elaborating an inner weather picture. At the very moment when the meteorologist is to make a specific forecast he looks at the latest available data in order to *check* his ideas about the course of development. This step is a very small part of the totality of making a forecast, but helps the meteorologist to establish further his ideas or to choose among alternative courses of development which he bears in mind – or to find out that he should reconsider his ideas.

One meteorologist stressed the importance of having a well-founded inner weather picture when checking the latest available information: "If you do not have a firm picture yourself when you look at the data on the screen, you become a victim of circumstances."

To summarize, in the meteorologists' work there is a complete integration of making an analysis of the weather and of making forecasts and other tasks.

These elements of work are not separated in time. One meteorologist expressed this in the following words: "You do the various parts of the job in optional order or everything at the same time."

Experiences of Numerical Forecasts

Here I will concentrate upon some problematic aspects concerning the integration of numerical forecasts into the inner weather picture.

The numerical forecasts are ready-made products which arrive at the local weather forecasting service. The meteorologists have insight into the principal construction of the numerical models, but they have little insight into the specific preconditions of a model.

A new synoptical map is plotted and analysed every three hours. The distance between the arrival of numerical forecasts is so great (as already mentioned, 12 or 24 hours) that there is no comparable sequence of maps to look back upon. In addition, the information content of numerical forecasts is far from the very precise and detailed level of information of the synoptical maps.

Consequently there are some problems in interpretation. The meteorologist may, for example, be uncertain whether a low pressure centre shown on the map means that an old one will move or whether it represents the forming of a new one, a kind of problem which never occurs in connection with synoptical maps. Another example of a difficulty in interpreting numerical forecasts is that such a forecast shows areas of precipitation but gives no help as to what type or what intensity one could expect. There is a need for a great deal of complementary information to arrive at the level of detail demanded in the forecasts produced at the airport: "The elaborate numerical models are coarse in comparison with the needs we have when making local weather forecasts."

Each numerical model has its advantages and its drawbacks. The construction of a model and mathematical conditions of a model means that any particular model is better suited for some weather situations than for others.

Furthermore, this means that the meteorologists have to acquire experience of each model in relation to different types of weather situations. A central problem here is the difficulty in building up a sufficiently reliable knowledge through experience as was discussed by a meteorologist: "It takes you at least one year to get to know the model during all four seasons – that is experience of how it works in common weather situations. It can take you a couple of years more before you know how to rely upon the model in situations which occur more seldom. The numerical meteorologists keep changing the models; they try to make the models better. But from our point of view this causes new problems. We cannot use our experience of how the models work."

To summarise, there are difficulties for a skilled meteorologist to use the information from numerical forecasts in his elaboration of an inner weather picture. There are problems in interpreting the information from this source and of building up a reliable experience. These limitations are added to the well-known ones from a viewpoint of local forecasting: that numerical forecasts predict large-scale weather for a period of, in the first place, over 24 hours.

Experiences of the Computerized Map-Plotting System

The map-plotting system is physically present at the work place. The meteorologists use VDUs to some extent in their work. The problems of the map-plotting system in relation to the development of the inner weather picture are mainly due to changes in the work process.

In the study of computerization within the public social insurance system in Sweden already mentioned employees have noted that a great deal of their knowledge is directed towards the working of the computer system. The risk they see is that their "insurance knowledge" – the aim and the rules of the insurance system – comes in second place (Försäkringsanställdas förbund 1980).

At the airport the meteorologists have noted a conflict of a similar type. Especially during night shifts, there has been a great deal of computer trouble. More than one meteorologist has noted that the time absorbed in getting the system to work again, in loading lost information into the system, and so on, can come into conflict with keeping the weather picture current. I have heard two similar descriptions where the point is the same: "I concentrated upon getting the system to work again; I thought I had time because the weather situation seemed straight-forward. In the morning I noted suddenly that I had missed a subtle start of a weather change – if I had used my normal time and routines for keeping up with weather development it would not have happened, I am quite sure."

When a weather phenomenon which is dangerous to flight has occurred somewhere, the computer system automatically gives an alarm signal. This interrupts the on-going work process. Here is a potential conflict with the meteorologists' building up of an inner weather picture – which is crucial for his ability to predict dangerous phenomena.

In order to brief a pilot before flight the meteorologist has to get additional information so as to form a picture of the weather along the flight route. After the introduction of the computer system this information is available on a terminal screen. In many ways this makes briefing the pilots easier. But as one meteorologist commented about this relatively new work situation: there are short thoughts and there are long ones. With this he meant that the earlier method of gathering information from different sources naturally gave time for reflection and digestion so as to form a coherent picture.

Finally, the meteorologists mention the calculation program included in this computer application as a good example of tools useful in their work. The program for calculating the development of fog proved to be practically useful. The program runs quickly; the meteorologist can use new in-data and within a short time receive the result. In this way the program is a help in the creation of the inner weather picture.

Skill as a Basis for Alternatives

I have related experiences from Sturup airport concerning the use of new types of information and technology in work. I have focussed upon complications in relation to the meteorologists' forming of a well-founded weather picture.

The alternatives here are based upon a conscious attitude towards the creation of the weather picture of the day as well as contributing to the background weather knowledge. Such a perspective means considering all the factors influencing work, such as technology, organization, and time aspects in carrying through work. It is necessary to have time to assimilate information; an excess of views between colleagues is crucial for the picture etc.

During the discussions in the group of meteorologists many ideas have been put forth which are in accordance with this line of thought. Here I will put some of the ideas together, interpreting them in my framework. Many of the ideas seem to be interesting alternatives to develop further, as they can contribute to making work efficient at a low cost. In contrast to the alternatives emerging from the meteorologists, several proposed ideas to rationalization seem unfruitful as they do not take the inner weather picture into account.

To begin with I present some examples from the past showing that the meteorologists have not accepted some types of changes in work which would lead to a weakening or deterioration of the inner picture. The meteorologists have, for example, resisted a division of labour making and communicating forecasts. Furthermore they have resisted a view of the synoptical map as a product; they maintain that the map is a working material. To describe their motives is to further elucidate some features of the inner picture.

The splitting-up of the work process between making and communicating forecasts – a division of labour which in fact exists at other airports – means that the meteorologist responsible for briefing takes over a ready-made analysis. Their resistance can be easily understood from the reasoning in an earlier section; they have no inner picture of their own to fall back upon. As one meteorologist put it: "There are always questions which fall a little outside the expected ones".

Defending the analysis of the synoptical map does not only mean preserving a traditional work method. The meteorologists defend an *active assimilation* of information about various weather elements instead of *passively receiving* a lot of *information*. Own activity is not only an effective means of assimilating a large quantity of information; it also affects the quality of the work result. When the meteorologist gradually forms his understanding of the weather situation with a pen in his hand some traits in the weather pattern emerge as a natural part of the process. While looking for a high-pressure centre among the observations he can be struck by the fact that the centre has moved farther than one would have expected at first. This type of experience can be important for being alert in selecting from the continuous stream of information. To summarize, an active analysis guarantees a certain depth in the intepretation of information.

This discussion leads on to another issue. The introduction of many new kinds of information and materials – whatever their benefits and advantages – has lead to a *weakening* of the traditional parts of the work process. "There is no possibility of analysing the synoptical map in the way one used to. There is no time to discuss single observations between colleagues."

Before presenting the alternatives I want to consider the inner weather picture from a somewhat different angle, now in terms of *information* and *assimilation* of information. To be able to form an inner picture it is necessary to be well informed about the prevailing weather, i.e., to have sufficient information about those aspects of the weather which are relevant for the meteorologists' tasks. On the other hand, in order to assimilate the weather information, the meteorologist must have a background weather knowledge, and he must have enough time to integrate new elements in the pattern already formed. In other words, assimilation is essential for the usefulness of information.

The first alternative emerging from the group of meteorologists is that they should verify their forecasts. This is not the same as the following up of forecasts, but a systematic approach to looking at the outcome of their efforts. Such an extension of the work process would deepen their basic weather knowledge. This is an interesting proposal as it means more resources in terms of knowledge, which can be contrasted to a general tendency to one-sidedly provide more information.

The second alternative concerns *information through personal contacts with people*, e.g. pilots. This kind of information represents a comparatively small part of the totality of information received today, but it has a number of qualities which makes this kind of information especially useful and important in work. For a variety of reasons such information from person to person has qualities which facilitate assimilation. The sensual aspects have already been stressed; other examples are that a pilot can tell a number of aspects in a nuanced manner in interaction with the meteorologist. In addition, there are pilots who are especially interested in weather and understand themselves when it is important to contact the meteorologists in order to tell them about weather they experience on route.

The reason for presenting this as an alternative is a continuous weakening of the contacts with pilots which has taken place. There is a tendency to regard pilots as receivers of information and to neglect that they contribute by giving information. The contact today with pilots is shorter and more formal than it used to be for a variety of reasons, and there are plans for a further weakening.

The third alternative concerns *information* directly useful *for local weather work*. When talking to the meteorologists it is striking that they say, on the one hand, that they cannot assimilate all the information available and, on the other hand, that they want more information. This seeming contradiction is easily resolved. However massive the stream of information, the meteorologists have expressed a pack of several kinds of observation material about the multi-faceted weather situation suited for the forecasts etc. that they are to produce. Data about observed weather phenomena can be more useful to a meteorologist in the building up of his inner weather picture than the available future-oriented material. This implies a real conflict between the relative abundance of numerical forecasts in comparison with other needs expressed by the meteorologists.

The meteorologists have proposed some technical alternatives as means of supplying them with the type of observation data which they are interested in, e.g. radar and satellite pictures. These wishes have not emerged recently but have been sought after for about 20 years.

Concerning radar, one meteorologist has stressed the contribution to a building up of his own experience: "By returning to the screen every ten minutes during the course of an afternoon you will get a good overview over how the showers move and get a lot of useful experience." This alternative can be summarized in comparison with the line of development which numerical forecasts represent: more historical material and information which supports the building up of own experience in interpretation, i.e., to rely on human sensibility instead of upon standardized ready-made solutions.

This leads on to the fourth alternative, which represents *a new type of future-oriented material*. In short, the idea is to leave the sophistication of numerical forecasts of today and instead use other types of calculation programs (which show similarities with the program for development of fog mentioned earlier). These are programs with limited scope, and they are often consciously crude, i.e., leaving space for the sensibility of the experienced meteorologist. An example from the USA which one meteorologist has referred to can serve as an illustration of this line of thought. The program in question calculates the movement of showers according to airstreams, but does not make any attempt to take the life-cycle of the showers into consideration. The meteorologist receives raw material from the computer and fills in with his knowledge about the formation and disappearance of showers. Forecasts of this type are less complete than numerical forecasts, but they can be easier to integrate into the inner weather picture; hence there is a hope that they can be more useful in work.

Conclusion

In this section I have discussed the seeming contradiction that the meteorologists want more information although there is more information available than they can absorb. The meteorologists have stressed information with sensual qualities, information via people and information about aspects which they themselves find important for carrying through work. Their emphasis upon certain types of information has a correspondence at a work-place of quite another type which I have studied: a department for manufacturing of steel-plates where a group of workers put demands upon a computerized system for controlling the production flow (Perby and Carlsson 1979).

To be useful in work, information has to be assimilated into the conceptual framework (here: the inner weather picture) of those who perform the work. The discussion has shown that more processed information (here: numerical forecasts) which generally is regarded as advantageous can be difficult to assimilate. Paradoxically, information in a more crude form can be preferred from this point of view. Background knowledge (here: weather knowledge) has an important role for the ability to assimilate information. This means that, in a situation with scarce resources, work can benefit more from a development of background knowledge than from providing another source of information.

References and Further Reading

Allard R et al. (1984) Sjukvårdsarbetet och datorn Stockholm: Arbetslivscentrum (In Swedish)

Burroughs W (1985) Favourable outlook for weather forecasts New Scientist 24 January

Cooley, M (1980) Architect or Bee? The human/technology relationship Langley Technical Services, Slough

Försäkringsanstalldas Forbund (1980) ADB inom försäkringskassorna. Handlingsprogram for Försäkringsanstalldas Förbund (In Swedish)

Goodman SE, Perby M (1985) Computerization and the Skill in Women's Work. In Olerup A, Schneider L, Monod E (eds) Women, Work and Computerization Elsevier Science Publishers B V, Amsterdam

Göranzon et al. (1983a) Datorn som verktyg Studentlitteratur, Stockholm

Göranzon, B (1983b) editor Datautvecklinens filosofi

Carlsson & Jönsson bokförlag, Malmö (In Swedish)

Johansson K, Josefson I (1980) Datateknik och abstraktisering av kunskap unpublished paper presented at NAVF's conference Kvinnor, datateknologi och arbete Oslo 1980 (this paper is extensively referred to in Perby (1981)) (In Swedish)

Kusterer K C (1978) Know-How on the job: the important working knowledge of "Unskilled" Workers. Westview Press, Boulder

Perby M, Carlsson J (1979) Att arbeta i valsverket DEMOS rapport nr 11 Arbetslivscentrum, Stockholm (In Swedish)

Perby M (1981) Kvinnor, datateknologi och arbete. Kvinnovetenskaplig tidskrift nr 1-2 Årg 2 (In Swedish)

Perby M (1984) Yrkeskunnande och datorisering. Arbetsliv och Utbildning nr 24 (In Swedish)

Perby M, Svenstam A (1985) Report from the project at the local weather forecasting service at Sturup airport (forthcoming)

Polanyi M (1962) Tacit knowing: its bearing on some problems of philosophy. Rev Mod Phys 34: 601–605

SMHI (1973) Vädret, vattnet och vi, SMHI fyller 100 år (In Swedish) Internal working material from the group at the local weather forecasting service at Sturup Airport

Chapter 6

Tacit Knowledge, Working Life and Scientific Method

A. Janik

What is "Tacit knowledge"? What role does it play in working life? What implications does it hold for understanding, for example, implications of expert systems for working life? What do philosophers of science have to learn from working life studies?

Certain things defy precise description by their very nature: some non-visual sensory experiences and the procedure involved in following a specific rule, hence what is in the strict sense "tacit" cannot be studied scientifically. Knowledge entails understanding which makes for creativity. Creativity is therefore linked to the mastery of conventions, that is, rule-following. One can only achieve an element of this creativity through long, intensive sessions with practitioners to gain experience. Armchair speculation is futile. Understanding and grasping the context is fundamental. Western philosophical tradition has failed to take working life seriously. Working-life studies embody an epistemological revolution which philosophers ignore at their peril.

What is tacit knowledge? What role does it play in working life? What does this imply for our understanding, say, of the implications of new technology such as expert systems for working life? What do philosophers of science have to learn from working-life studies? These have been the principal issues which preoccupied me in the course of my stay at Arbetslivscentrum. In what follows I propose to answer these questions, at least in a preliminary way, with a view to elucidating the perspective of the project Utbildning–Arbete– Teknik with which I have been associated. This amounts to clarifying a number of issues about which there is a good deal of confusion relating to the crucial notion of tacit knowledge, the ways in which theory of knowledge (a term I much dislike but employ for want of a better one) can clarify our understanding of working life, as well as the role working-life studies can play in the development of the theory of knowledge. It is, then, at once a compilation of the ideas which have been most central to my work in the Centre as well as a statement of what I take back to the academic world from my experiences at the Centre. It is hardly intended to be comprehensive; rather it is a sketch of what I, as a philosopher, take to be the most challenging and exciting notions that I have encountered confronting the "real world" of work. My aim, then, is to provide a certain orientation with respect to the role that philosophy can play in helping us better to understand working life but also to suggest how philosophers can learn a great deal about certain vexing problems from working-life studies. It is, therefore, important to emphasize that what is presented here is at once a resumé and a programme rather than an analysis.

With that in mind, we can begin by asking: what is tacit knowledge? In the face of misunderstandings as widespread as they are erroneous, the first thing that has to be said loudly and clearly is that there is nothing whatsoever mysterious or arcane about tacit knowledge. It has nothing whatsoever to do with extrasensory perception (ESP), Rosicrucianism or any such esoteric lore. It is a familiar part of our every-day experience. Indeed, it is that very familiarity which tends to lead us to overlook its importance when we are dealing with such "deep" issues as what thinking or knowing is all about.

What, then, does the term positively cover? There are two senses in which philosophers have come to speak about tacit knowledge. Unfortunately, they have not always been as clearly distinguished as they might have been. It is crucial that they should not be confused with one another. The first refers to things we could say if we wanted to but either do not choose to or just never get around to putting into words. The second refers to those aspects of human experience which are *wholly* knowable self-reflectively – and, therefore, anything but esoteric – but by their very nature are incapable of *precise* articulation. We know things without being able to put what we know into words when, for example, we are able to distinguish the sound of a viola from that of a 'cello in a musical broadcast, or in the way that an experienced cook knows how to vary a recipe when he discovers suddenly that he does not have exactly what the recipe calls for, as opposed to the way in which we know the time, the date or the temperature.

The first sort of tacit knowledge is the sort that could be articulated but happens not to be. It comprises several species which we can distinguish for the purposes of analysis (in situ they are not so neatly distinguishable). First, there is the sort of thing that is kept secret for political (in the loose sense) or economic reasons. Trade secrets typify this sort of tacit knowledge. Guild masters from time immemorial have been acutely aware of the ways in which their status, power and standard of living often depended upon keeping the tricks of the trade from the uninitiated. We find this concern reflected, for example, in Peter Gullers' study of surgical-instrument makers (Gullers 1982). In a similar (but by no means identical) vein medical doctors in the US have resisted efforts to systematize their methods of diagnosis and prognosis on the grounds that the basis for making claims about a patient's development is a knack that has to be acquired over years. Perhaps this is so, but we shall only be certain of that to the extent that we have ventured to systematize their practice. This sort of problem is reflected in Ingela Josefson's work with the medical profession (Chap. 3). Briefly, there are good reasons for thinking that we can say more about this sort of thing than we have till now, but no less good reasons, as we shall see, for insisting that such expert judgment can by its very nature never be fully articulated in such a way that it might be, say, machine reproducible. Be that as it may, one aspect of tacit knowledge has to do with the ways in which elites, such as guildmasters, maintain their power by political manipulation of knowledge.

Another sort of tacit knowledge has to do with the sort of things that people, for whatever reasons, have never got around to articulating. It is typical, for example, that nobody pays much attention to the practice of blacksmiths until those practices are in danger or going out of existence. Crisis is usually the motive for articulating things that people have never found interesting or important enough to try to systematize. Many homely skills such as cooking can be passed from generation to generation without anybody getting around to writing down how they proceed. The evolution of cookery book from lists of ingredients with neither precise measurements nor instructions beyond "take milk, flour and eggs, beat together, cook in oven till done" to the introduction of precise measurements and step-by-step procedures, often profusely illustrated, exemplifies a sort of tacit knowledge that has found articulation. Many skills incorporate tacit knowledge of this sort which has not as yet been articulated but can be.

A third sort of tacit knowledge which may be articulated but in fact has not been, has been described with crystal clarity by R. G. Collingwood (1940) in Chapter 3 of his *Essay on metaphysics* under the rubric of "absolute presuppositions". Collingwood spelled out his reasoning there in relation to the inquiries of natural scientists but they are by no means so restricted. In fact, every practice incorporates absolute presuppositions – which, by the way, are only relatively absolute in that they are absolute relative to a certain enterprise. In fact, Collingwood argues, any effort to answer a question with precision entails making assumptions. The most general and widely held of these are so obvious that it would be silly and tedious to remind ourselves of them continually. It is only when we run into crises, i.e., *wholly unforseen* trouble that it makes sense to consider them.

An example will help here. We all assume without giving the matter the slightest thought that the money we have in our pockets will be worth something similar tomorrow to what it is worth today. We base not a little of what we do on that assumption. But consider the case of Europe in the early 1920s, when sudden enormous inflation hit the continent. All of a sudden one of the rock-bottom pillars of European social life crumbled. Thus what is silly and tedious to question in normal circumstances, i.e., what we absolutely presuppose, can suddenly and shockingly be challenged. Then it becomes urgent that we reconsider what we have tacitly been assuming all along. Much of what we "know" falls into this category. It too is a kind of knowledge that can be articulated when there is a point to doing so. Nevertheless, none of the sorts of tacit knowledge as yet mentioned merits the title in the strict sense, even though we have in fact brushed up against the real thing, because all of the sorts of considerations discussed till now can be articulated if we want, or have, to do so. However, there is another sort of tacit knowledge which cannot. This is, obviously enough, the most important type.

There are two sorts of things that defy precise description by their very nature: certain non-visual sensory experience and the procedure involved in following a specific rule. In both cases our inability to describe what we know by no means indicates that our claim to knowledge is dubious. We do not claim that the objects of tacit knowledge are unknowable, for that would be self-defeating: we would be identifying something as something that could not be known. No, the claim is that what is known in the strict sense of being known tacitly cannot be studied scientifically. We are, therefore, talking about the limits of science.

Those who have problems with the concept of tacit knowledge tend to identify all knowledge with science and to consider that, as a non-scientific mode of knowledge, tacit knowledge must be defective. But this misses the point massively. In fact the sort of knowledge normally designated as scientific is based upon tacit knowledge, as Michael Polanyi (1973) always emphasized.

The first sort of tacit knowledge in the strict sense is sometimes referred to as knowledge by acquaintance or familiarity. It results from sensuous experience. Wittgenstein chose to exemplify this sort of knowledge by contrasting what it is to know and what it is to describe the smell of coffee or the sound of a clarinet. The distinguished English philosopher, Peter Strawson (1972) once posed the question – without being able to say very much that was interesting by way of an answer to it – what would an epistemology be like that was not based upon the comparison between the mind and the eye, but, say, upon that of mind and ear. He is not alone among philosophers in mooting this question. It is Wittgenstein's merit to have illuminated the issue in ways that directly bear upon our theme – though philosophers have for the most part not realized that. We have to direct our reflection to the relationship between sensuous experience and description. If we think of the difference between smelling or hearing and describing what we smell or hear, the smell of coffee or the sound of a clarinet we discover that it is not possible to *begin* to describe any such experiences in such a way that people who had not themselves experienced them could recognize them. The best we could do is supply metaphors, analogies and hints – "well, its sort of like this . . .". In the absence of these comparisons, metaphors, analogies etc. there is no way to describe what it is to "know" these things. Moreover, once the people in question have had the requisite experiences for themselves, they will be satisfied that our inability to describe them belongs to their nature. The sign of this is that once having had these experiences the demand for explanation ceases to press itself upon us. To have had these experiences and to have reflected upon them – which is what most of us normally, and philosophers *never*, do – is to realize that we do not have to be able to describe them to understand them. The kind of knowledge, then, associated with the ability to make subtle discriminations, such as that between the sound of a clarinet and that of an oboe is rightly described as skill. Here it is important to point out that, while everybody is capable of such judgment (assuming they do not have some special auditory problems), not everybody is *equally* capable of making judgments of the same calibre in these matters. We do not all develop identically with respect to sensory discrimination in much the same way that we do not all grow tall enough to play basketball competitively.

The second strong sense in which we can speak of tacit knowledge depends upon the open-textured character of rule-following behaviour. Rule-following activity entails the kind of knowledge that is only acquired through repetition or practice. Learning to play the piano or to compete in the high jump are two cases in point. We must first be drilled in such a way that we come to eliminate obvious mistakes. Only at this stage can we speak of a "right" and "wrong" way to play or to jump. Once we have mastered the technique, once we are "experienced", the idea of a right and wrong way to play ceases to be a significant part of discourse. Indeed, the idea of an algorithm for, say, a piano sonata is as epistemologically absurd as it is aesthetically abhorrent. Mastery of the rules brings with it a freedom to extend them say, in a way that Vladimir Horowitz can bring his expertise to bear upon a Chopin polonaise in such a way that we experience it as wholly new. Clearly, here, inventiveness is dialectically linked to mastery of conventions. This, I submit, is what expertise is all about: the ability to master a set of rules in such a way as to be in a position to extend them when circumstances warrant it. Rule-following activity may originate in rote behaviour but it terminates in creative activity. It is essentially creative.

Yet, there is a problem here. It has to do with a widespread misconception with respect to rules, which is deeply rooted both in the popular imagination and in the liberal philosophical tradition from Mill to Rawls and Habermas. I refer to the notion that rules are independent of practices. On this view, we first learn what the rules stipulate, and then how to apply them. Kjell S. Johannessen (1988) has trenchantly demonstrated just how this puts the cart before the horse. This is not to say that there are no rules which function in this way, for there are: however, these rules have the character of norms with respect to some activity we can already perform. They correspond in our musical analogy to playing with a particular style when there are alternatives to choose from. However, this is not the basic sense of rule-following; for we already have to be able to accomplish something to apply these rules. It is the sort of rule-following activity through which we learn how to perform a specific sort of action in the first place – what Kant called constitutive as opposed to regulative ideas – that has to be primary. Here the rule is scarcely to be distinguished from the behaviour through which it is constituted. Insofar as the rule can be distinguished at all from the actions through which we stabilize our lives, it is an *order or command* to repeat a particular action. We are ordered to follow a pattern. No rule need be explicitly formulated, strange as that may seem. It is in fact not strange; for there is as yet no capacity in the child to understand what a rule is. It is through learning to take orders that we come to understand in the first place. At first we learn to carry on mechanically; we soon learn, to our surprise, that we have to take significant variation into account. Basically, rule-following has a peculiar internal order which is determined by our natural history, i.e., by our being the kind of creature we are. It is important to emphasize that what is being claimed here does not challenge any particular theory of child-rearing because it is what all theories of child-rearing have to take into consideration. The internal order in learning to follow rules, then, begins with a kind of dressage (*Abrichtung* is Wittgenstein's exact phrase) but terminates in creative activity as we learn that we have to guess how to continue to follow the example we have been given and, ultimately, as we learn to invent new ways of carrying on. Because this procedure is open-ended, mastery of the rules, expertise, consists in being adept at dealing with unforseen circumstances. It is largely a matter of seeing analogies between situations or simply seeing where we are. This activity resists being put into words because there is a very real sense in which we do not know what we do till we have done it.

In short, it is an analogical rather than a digital activity. Another way of putting the matter would be to say that there is always and ineliminably the possibility that we can follow the rule in a wholly unforseen way. This could not happen if we had to have an explicit rule to go on from the start. If that were so there would never be the sort of surprises that we normally associate with discovery. Moreover, if constitutive rules were known before their application, we could never learn to apply rules without more rules. But this is a logical impossibility; for we would have to have a rule to understand how to apply our original rule, another to apply the second and so on to infinity.

It is important that we see what is being claimed here clearly and precisely. It is not that nothing relating to expertise can be put into words. The development of cookery books from the Middle Ages to Fanny Farmer and Mrs Beaton down to the venerable Julia Child shows that this can be done magnificently. However, precisely because this is a skill upon which we continue to depend and will apply in yet wholly unforseen situations, it cannot be systematized according to the rules of formal logic. The technical reason for this is that the open-textured character of our rules is such that there is no way of determining in advance whether the Principle of the Excluded Middle is always going to hold in the way it currently does. But we should not find this claim daunting; for its obverse is the claim that human skill is something very real and irreducible to rote activity. It is, then, not incompatible with the notion that skill involves an irreducibly tacit element that we urge the skilled to articulate the basis of their activities. The possibility of radical innovation is, however, the logical limit of description. This is what tacit knowledge is all about. To the extent that work is built upon skill, tacit knowledge is an essential part of the analysis of its internal order.

How is all of this reflected in the case studies of the Centre's "Utbildning–Arbete–Teknik" programme? In answering this question I shall restrict myself to examples drawn from Ingela Josefson's studies of medical skill (Chap. 3), Peter Gullers' study of surgical-instrument making in Sweden and Maja-Lisa Perby's work on local weather forecasting (Chap. 4).

It is not my aim to recapitulate those studies here but to try to put my finger on the ways in which tacit knowledge turns up as a central element in them.

The first and most obvious point to be made here is that the extent to which tacit knowledge is central to an understanding of working life is tied principally to the extent to which we are discussing *skilled* work. It is, therefore, precisely the extent to which quality in products or services demands skill or expertise that tacit knowledge enters intrinsically into any accurate account of work. The most dramatic way of seeing how this is so comes perhaps from Maja-Lisa Perby's work, which takes its point of departure from questions about decline in competence in local weather forecasting. No small part of the importance of this research lies in the fact that the question of decline in quality of local forecasting has arisen from within the community of weather forecasters. Their doubts about the quality of their own work has arisen in the minds of the forecasters from the proliferation of abstract models of the weather with which they have become confronted. Their intuition is that these models force them to work in ways which prevent them from exercising their skills to the fullest extent. In short, there is a clash between abstract models and the concrete practices and procedures in terms of which those models are employed to produce a local weather forecast. Put differently, formalized knowledge comes into conflict with tacit knowledge. Ms Perby has sensitively portrayed the way in which the skills of the local forecaster, like those of the athlete or opera singer, require a "warming up" period before they can be exercised to their full capacity. For the forecasters this means putting themselves into the position where they can synthesize huge amounts of data into an "inner picture of the weather". Tacit knowledge turns up in this process in terms of the role that not only conversations with pilots and colleagues with respect to details about the weather but also the most seemingly casual contacts with them over coffee, say, serve to "fine tune" their sensitivities. Ms Perby suggests that the exercise of this sort of intellectual skill, the process of "concretizing" the inner weather picture, is intimately and inextricably bound to sensual skill such that the most precise way of describing the sort of competence involved is to designate it as a mode of aesthetic sensibility. Now, this is something which can be described, to the extent that the practices of local forecasters generally permit description, but it cannot be "analysed" in the sense of being reduced to a series of effective procedures. Interestingly, the same point concerning the aesthetic character of the skill of surgical-instrument makers has been stressed by Peter Gullers. It is not the least significant implication of this research that it shows graphically and dram-atically that virtually the whole internal structure of such skilled work is lost in a Taylorist analysis.

Ingela Josefson, upon whose research Maja-Lisa Perby to a large extent relies, has emphasized the extent to which medical expertise resists form-ulation in the form of precise description. This has long been recognized in the area of diagnosis. Physicians have often been able to recognize a patient's condition without being able to say exactly how they drew their conclusions. Ms Josefson's work with nurses has provided further documentation of the crucial role that such tacit knowledge plays in medical care. Here the ability of nurses to form sound judgments with regard to medical care, correspond-ing to the doctor's judgment with respect to cure, also turns to a great extent upon factors which tend to resist description. As with Maja-Lisa Perby's work with local weather forecasters, Ingela Josefson emphasizes that there is a great deal about the practices of nurses which does permit description. Nurses, too, can say a great deal about what they know at a factual level. It is the process of forming judgments which are accurate that resists precise formulation.

In view of the sorts of considerations which I have drawn from Wittgen-stein's later philosophy (1960) with respect to tacit knowledge, this is just what we should expect. There is nothing mysterious or implausible about this inability to put what we know into words. Ms Josefson rightly insists that the problem in our inability to see this lies far more with the mystique of formal education and professionalism in our society than it does in the concept of tacit knowledge. It is an essential element in what we normally term experience that experienced persons have a facility for handling a wide variety of unforseen situations. Just as it is not possible to describe an unforseen situation, by definition, it should be reasonable to think that our ability to deal with the situation should not be taken to imply that we *must* be able to articulate the knowledge which enables us to do so. As we have seen, it is Wittgenstein's distinction to have provided an account of why that experience defies precise elucidation. Here, however, the very achievement of these researchers is to show that it is only possible to come to see the problem of describing how expert judgments are formed in the concrete through long and intense discussions in which the researcher comes to understand the perspective of the worker to the point of being able to articulate it. This sort of articulation is best described as a sort of hermeneutic activity; it is a form of interpretation which is dependent upon the researcher's ability to come to grasp the practice of the worker, as a participant in those practices might, and not merely as an "observer". This sort of hermeneutics is by no means based upon the idea that there is nothing to be said about those practices; rather, the very achievements of Maja-Lisa Perby, Ingela Josefson and Peter Gullers consist in having listened sufficiently to workers to be able to describe their activities in such a richly nuanced manner as to lay bare their complexities and, consequently, the competence they require. Thus, we can come to learn why it is that skill rests upon tacit knowledge precisely through a detailed, sympathetic description of agents' practices.

It is not, then, as though one can say "tacit knowledge" like "Open Sesame" and thereby solve a problem instantly; rather, it requires considerable diligence to be in a position to be able to articulate a situation in working life – and this is crucial – to the point where we can grasp why it eludes precise description. In fact, it is the task of articulating that sort of tacit knowledge which can be put into words but normally is not expressed that brings us to the point where we are able to grasp the limits of description. It is the merit of the case-studies mentioned that they do this graphically and excitingly. Moreover, on the basis of the account of tacit knowledge that I began with, it should not be surprising that these studies have been occasioned to a large degree by the efforts of computer scientists to replicate human skill; for the sort of knowledge that these case-studies have yielded, as Wittgenstein and Collingwood were fond of pointing out, is only valuable when the certainties upon which the order in everyday life rest are called into question. So, curiously, we have indirectly to thank those very unrealistic aspirations of computer scientists for motivating researchers to undertake those studies through which we have attained an enriched grasp of the order intrinsic to working life. It remains to look at the significance of Peter Gullers' study of surgical-instrument making in Sweden to see the connection between tacit knowledge and yet other important aspects of working life.

The most skilled surgical-instrument makers are a very appropriate group to study, since, without being craftsmen themselves, their work requires considerable skill; it is not the sort of work that just anybody can undertake. The importance of this difference is such that it accounts for a certain social differentiation between workers on the basis of their "virtues" – in the Greek sense of *arete* or excellence. Here it is best to let Peter Gullers (1982) speak for himself:

What do these various voices then say about work in a workshop making surgical instruments and the changes that have taken place over the years? "The old instrument makers" certainly belonged to what we may call an aristocracy of labour, they were regarded – and regarded themselves – as a cut above others who worked in the same shop. Once, long ago, they wore bowlers and stiff collars, and they were as close as could be to craftsmen. This did not mean that they had any great freedom: what was to be done was closely determined, and their security lay in the fact that they were irreplacable. Pay was never particularly high, and hardly higher than other workers in the same workshop got. It was the work itself that was skilled and that gave them prestige rather than anything measured in money terms.

It is only on the basis of such a state of affairs that we can understand, say, Marx's hope that work should be transformed from a necessary evil to life's prime want. Here the aesthetic sensibility involved in producing a quality product is seen to be intrinsically linked to the self-differentiation of workers, and, if you like, the moral world of work.

But what of the implications of the working-life perspective for the theory of knowledge? They are profound indeed. I should like to begin by identifying two themes near and dear to Karl Marx that these studies in working life call into question. First, these researches imply that skill remains highly *particular*. The modern (post-modern?) worker is, *pace* Marx, far from becoming a universal agent for production. Secondly, and more importantly, these studies show that to the extent that industries produce quality products or provide quality services, the interests of labour and those of management in maintaining the quality level are identical. To this extent, then, a class-struggle model of labour relations is suicidal. The sooner this is recognized the better. Now to the question of the implications of working life as a perspective for scientific method.

Looking at issues raised within theory of science from the point of view of working life injects a healthy pragmatist humanism into the discussion. The fact that the working life perspective imposes a "real time" framework upon discussions such as those concerning the nature and scope of artificial intelligence, for example, demands that the programme's actual performance, its actual achievements and its impact upon living human beings be placed squarely in the forefront of discussion. The working-life perspective rules out the relevance of promises, speculations, thought experiments etc. as irrelevant, by placing the issue of performance squarely at the centre of the discussion. It forces academic ideologues such as structuralists, behaviourists or cognitivists to one side by requiring that researchers take as their point of departure the practices and procedures of living agents. From there it proceeds to inquire into the impact of development upon concrete individuals. This, of course, does not mean that research into these areas becomes easier, only that scientific questions take their sense from human practices, i.e., from knowing as embedded in acting, rather than from theories about what it is to know or act. Whatever problems there are with the working-life perspective, it serves to wrench us away from the kind of pseudo-sophistication of armchair speculation – something not incompatible with what is normally, and dubiously, termed "experimentation" – in an area like psychology, which leads us to ignore the actual circumstances under which real people function. No small part of the significance of the working-life perspective for philosophy of science, then, follows from the contextual character of the "real time" point of view which it requires. My claim is that it is a healthy antidote to the sort of metaphysical speculations which dress themselves in the guise of "experimental" science in areas such as psychology, linguistics or sociology.

This perspective is particularly important for an area such as social philosophy inasmuch as it chastens us to form our expectations for the future in terms of the realities of the present. Thus, from the perspective of a working life researcher like Bjørn Gustavsen the Promethean efforts of Jurgen Habermas to develop a theory of communicative action turn out simply to be irrelevant to labour relations because the stipulations relating to dominance-free dialogue simply do not obtain nor can they be expected to in the forseeable future. Thus, while such a normative theory might conceivably be of some help in judging just what progress we have made, it is too far removed from the actual situation under which communication takes place in working life – from the "essentially contested" character of the concepts involved – to be of much help in facilitating the kind of discussion that must characterize industrial relations in an industrial democracy today. Once more, it is the pressing need to confront the world as it is, rather than as we would like to have it, that is so refreshing with respect to the way the working-life perspective illuminates philosophical issues. This Gustavsen rightly sees as the essential presupposition for effectively introducing change. It does not eschew change by any means but ensures that what changes are brought about are cemented into conditions as they actually are, rather than as we would like them to be, or as they "ought" to be. It is not simply that the working-life perspective on communication proceeds from the actual conditions obtaining in a particular situation, it seeks in those conditions the "logic" or dynamics of change and in that the limits of the possible. Since this is something that philosophers have had great trouble in doing, the suggestion is that they can benefit considerably by looking at traditional questions about social science and social reform from the working-life perspective. This suggestion is more radical than it might seem.

One of the most important points in the development of western thought was the point at which Socrates, as the standard story goes, decided to test the Oracle's assertion that he was the wisest of men by "interviewing", as it were, the other prime candidates for that title: poets, politicians and *craftsmen*. He came away from all of them with the same disappointment. He came away from them convinced that they did know something or other but that whatever they knew could hardly count as wisdom, since they could not verbalize what they knew. It was the service of Ludwig Wittgenstein to challenge Socrates – and the Western philosophical tradition after him – by suggesting that there were in fact good reasons why craftsmen should be taken at once as primary instances of knowledgeable human beings and at the same time unable to express what they know in words. In all this, it is hardly accidental that Wittgenstein was as committed as Tolstoi to the notion that humanly useful work, from which he tended to exclude the activities of academics, was an integral part of any life that was worth living. As for Socrates, legend has it that the main source of his marital problems was his wife's complaints about his refusal to practice his stonemason's trade! Be that as it may, the problem with Socrates, as with so many subsequent philosophers right down to today, is that he sought the wrong sort of answer to his question. In short, he failed to see that the sort of wisdom that attaches to craftsmanship is tied precisely to the sorts of examples and analogies which he found wanting. So it might be said that the main problem with the Western philosophical tradition, starting with Socrates, is its failure to take working life seriously. If this is right, it is not only the concreteness and humane character of the working-life perspective – that point at which the Marxian concept of praxis meets Pope Leo XIII's concern for the dignity of labour – that makes working life studies so philosophically impressive, it is the epistemological revolution that they embody. Philosophers ignore that at their peril.

Acknowledgements. I am grateful to Kjell S. Johannessen for many stimulating and enlightening conversations concerning the philosophical questions discussed here. He is currently preparing an in-depth study of Wittgenstein and Polanyi which will be of great significance for understanding the epistemological issues treated here. I am equally indebted to Bo Göranzon, Peter Gullers, Birger Viklund and the other authors cited here for rewarding discussions of working-life research, industrial democracy etc. I am not sure to what extent they share the opinions herein expressed. They are certainly in no way responsible for the shortcomings of this chapter, which are wholly my own responsibility.

References and Further Reading

Collingwood R G (1940) An essay on metaphysics. Oxford University Press, Oxford
Gullers P (1982) Verktygsmakare och operatörer. Swedish Center for Working Life, Rapport 37.
Gustavsen B (1985) Workplace reform and democratic dialogue. Economic and Industrial Democracy 6: 461–480
Gustavsen B, Engelstad P H (1985) The design of conferences and the evolving role of democratic dialogue in changing working life Human Relations 39: 101–116
Gustavsen B, Hunnius G (1981) New patterns of work reform. The case of Norway. Oslo University Press, Oslo.
Göranzon B (1988) Education-Work-Technology. An overview of a research programme. Swedish Center for Working Life
Göranzon B et al. (1982) Job design and Automation in Sweden, Swedish Center for Working Life
Janik A, Toulmin S (1973): Wittgenstein's Vienna, A Touchstone Book. Touchstone, New York
Johannessen KS (1988) To follow a rule, In Göranzon Bo (ed) Culture Language and Artificial Intelligence. Swedish Center for Working Life
Josefson I (1987) Knowledge and experience. In: Applied Artificial Intelligence 1 Hemisphere Publishing Corporation
Lewis GA (1986) News from somewhere: Connecting health and freedom at the workplace. Greenwood Press, New York.
Polanyi M (1973) Personal knowledge. Routledge and Kegan Paul, London
Strawson P (1972) Einzelding und Logische Subjekt. Stuttgart
Wittgenstein L (1960) On Certainty. Basil Blackwell, Oxford
Yates F (1986) The Rosicrucian Enlightment. Ark paperbacks, London

Skill and Artificial Intelligence

Chapter 7

Can Skills be Transferable?

R. Ennals

When real practical problems need to be solved by people in a particular social and economic context, the technology has no more than an instrumental function. Technology itself is politically, socially, and economically neutral but is political in its use, reflecting and possibly strengthening the value system and the economic and political interests of those who control it. This has implications for concepts entailed in the idea of transferring skills through its use. The preconditions for the transfer of skills are the motivation of the recipient, shared practical context, some common language between those imparting and receiving skills. There are severe limitations as to how far the computer can satisfy these conditions. The issue of the transfer of skills should be of central importance in any political programme. For what future are people to be trained? What skills are to be transferred, and to whom? Who is involved in preparing a solution to perhaps the central problem of our era and who is left to form part of the problem?

Introduction

The account of skills and the transfer of skills which follows is derived from personal practical experience in a number of different settings over many years, during which particular methods and techniques have been developed and explored. Some of this work has been reported in recent and forthcoming books; more should come to fruition in the new Staff Development Unit based at Kingston College of Further Education, where an Information Technology Development Unit has been working with industry and education for two years.

The emphasis of my work is far more on working with groups of people than on working with technology such as Information Technology, though the appropriate use of technology can facilitate new ways of working in general. I have worked in youth clubs based on music and drama, developed team-teaching in history and the social sciences in secondary schools and in an African college, managed the recycling of waste materials for a co-ownership company which employed former hospital patients and ex-prisoners, conducted and managed research in advanced computing for a university department and a national collaborative programme, and consulted for public and private sector training projects using advanced technology. I have been fortunate in being able to study and work in a number of overseas countries, in some of which I have helped establish projects, many of which now form the PROLOG Education Group.

The Politics of Skills Transfer

Skills and their transfer are at the centre of contemporary economic and political debate. Economic development depends critically upon the skills of the workforce, and the change required is a political process in which many potentially conflicting interest groups are involved. The diversion of scarce skills and financial resources into infeasible and ill-advised military projects can further threaten prospects of civil development. Swords are of less practical long-term benefit than ploughshares, but skills may need to be transferred in a radical manner if ploughshares are to predominate.

In the United Kingdom the Alvey Programme for Research and Development in Advanced Information Technology, for which I was coordinator of work in logic programing, was established to build on the nation's undoubted technical skills, and to try to transfer the necessary skills and technology for wider industrial use to the benefit of society. The technology of expert systems, in particular, is intended to assist in capturing the expertise of the specialist, making it available as a marketable commodity.

The Manpower Services Commission in Britain is seeking to take advantage of such technology in enhancing the quality of training through programmes in Artificial Intelligence Applications to Learning and Training Access Points, on which I acted as technical consultant. In pilot projects they are encountering both the potential and the limitations of advanced information technology addressing problems of human skill.

In the London symposium we considered the acquisition of an illustrative new skill: the manipulation of the "microclip". The task was new to all participants, and some approached with trepidation and a lack of confidence. After initial experience confidence grew, and paper clips were successfully dropped into wine glasses from nose height. Exercising this new skill was one thing: offering a full description of how it was done was much harder, indeed impossible.

What are Skills?

Some insight into the conceptual complexity of this field is offered by Wittgenstein in his *Philosophical investigations* (1968, §150). "The grammar of the word 'knows' is evidently closely related to that of 'can', 'is able to". But also related to that of 'understands' ('Mastery' of a technique)".

Skills are demonstrated in the performance of a task; they are observed and described by a third party who sees the actions of the agent as constituting the performance of the particular task.

If we are seeking to develop the skills of a young colleague, at a certain stage we may decide that he knows how to go on; he has learnt the rules of the game; he has become part of this form of life.

The exercise of skills requires the application of knowledge of the subject domain and the development of competences (defined in terms of the task). Sometimes these can be formalized in terms Von Wright described as a "practical inference": a certain conclusion or action follows for an agent if he believes that certain conditions hold. In computational terms this approach is adopted in production rules and expert systems, whereby the system takes or recommends particular actions when given conditions are satisfied.

Skills are clearly enhanced by experience, whether through habit, increasing skill, or improvements derived from feedback. The process of skill acquisition is cyclical and recursive, with the practical use of the skills playing an essential role.

Assessments of skills depend on the belief that a particular task, under a particular description, is being attempted and confidence in both the intentions of the agent and the judgment of the observer.

The Strategic Significance of Skills

A report of the IT86 Committee in the United Kingdom was concerned with the future development, application and use of information technology in industry and commerce. It recognized the central importance of skills, and put forward a naive but superficially attractive technological solution:

We are faced with the anomalous situation in the UK where there are a large number of unemployed, many of whom are young people, with, at the same time, a shortage of skills in many walks of life. One field in which the shortage of skills is evident is IT itself, and the use of technicians to provide a greater pool of IT skills which, in turn, can be used to create wealth in other sectors of the economy seems, to say the least, very worth while. The mechanism is interactive distance learning and the market for such systems is potentially very large in the UK with considerable export opportunities.

On this view skills are seen in technological terms as a marketable commodity: the human element drops out of consideration. In contrast, if one starts by examining the real practical problems to be solved by humans in a particular social and economic context, the computer or other enabling technology in effect drops out of consideration, having no more than an instrumental function.

Transferring Skills

We can see the transfer of skills at three levels.

1. Skills can be transferred by and with an individual between different

tasks, applications or domains. A good education will involve learning skills in one subject area which are then applied in another. The work of the psychologist Piaget (1971) was concerned with exploring the nature, learning and transfer of skills, and with the cognitive development of the individual. The objective of education programmes such as the British Technical and Vocational Education Initiative and the Certificate of Pre-Vocational Education is to develop transferrable problem-solving skills rather than remaining narrowly task-specific or conventionally subject-based.

2. Skills can be transferred between people, as in the processes of education and training. When a senior specialist in a company nears retirement there is concern lest his expertise be lost, and there is often an attempt to transfer his key skills to a younger colleague. When an apprentice joins a firm (though the system of apprenticeship itself has weakened considerably in the United Kingdom in recent years) he is likely to be assigned to work under the direction of an experienced worker, whose skills he is encouraged to acquire. This acquisition will be through practical experience as well as theoretical guidance.

3. At the social or institutional level skills can be transferred between groups, so that skill and influence is concentrated in a particular area. New technology such as computer-controlled machinery can diminish the requirement for specialist skills from the operative. Alternatively word processing can put more executive power into the hands of intelligent secretaries.

Models for the Transfer of Skills

The following suggested models reflect different emphases on the three levels of skill transfer outlined above, and may offer us insights into the nature of the transfer of skills in institutions.

Transmission

The transmission model assumes the existence of an established body of knowledge, held by the expert or teacher, which is transferred to the novice or student. Such knowledge is likely to be propositional, factual and non-negotiable. It may include knowledge of official procedures which must be followed without question, and thus applies particularly in military training, multinational corporations or an uncritical civil service. The transmission model embodies a one-way system of communication, where neither the expert nor the knowledge is open to question: indeed the "expert" may in turn have received the knowledge in the same way, and may be unable to answer questions or explain the knowledge even if he wished to, for it is not "his own". Transmission implies the existence of a system of education, training or control that has its own "meta level" rules concerning who is entitled to know what information, or to ask what questions, and what constitutes an answer or an explanation.

Transfusion

The transfusion model assumes the existence of an organic institution or system, whose working can be affected by the addition of new knowledge to its "bloodstream", so that it can flow to the different parts. The acquisition of a new skill, or the use of a new technology which embodies a skill, can have radical effects if appropriately applied. Keeping the medical metaphor, certain transfusions can provoke the development of antibodies by the receiving system. Caution must be taken as to the purity of materials used, and as to their appropriateness for the type or group of individuals contained in the institution.

Catalysis

The concept of catalysis applied to transfer of skills is that different individuals within a group or institution will each have skills and abilities which others need, but that conventional institutional structures may not enable those skills and abilities to be shared to the maximum overall benefit. The purpose of the catalyst is to bring individuals together in a constructive social interaction, rather than itself being of central lasting significance. Artificial intelligence technology can perform this function by offering a unifying representation of a common problem to which different individuals with varying expertise can relate. Artificial intelligence, on this view, cannot solve human problems, but it can make them amenable to solution, showing the flies, as Wittgenstein put it, the way out of the fly bottle.

Infection

Ideas can be catching; certain environments make it more likely for new ideas to spread; association with another person who holds strong ideas can lead to first a breakdown of resistance, and then acceptance of the ideas. The objective of ideologies is to render the holder immune from infection from outside; however, when a tenet of the ideology appears to conflict with observed reality (cognitive dissonance) resistance may be permeable. Institutions may seek the protection of "conceptual condoms" to inhibit the conception of new ideas and practices, but they can never be fully effective, and the ideas themselves have to be addressed.

Acquisition

Piaget (1971) studied the processes of knowledge acquisition and conceptual accommodation in children and adolescents, and considerable work continues in the field, in particular, of artificial intelligence and expert systems. Piaget wrote of "genetic epistemology" and took a structuralist view of knowledge and social science, thus locating processes of individual action and learning in a broader context. Knowledge cannot be simply, almost passively, acquired in the sense of being taken off the shelf in a pre-packaged form: it requires action by the learner – acquisition without accommodation is worth very little. This view has radical implications for the current explosion in the development of "open", "distance" or "flexible" learning packages, many of which appear to have adopted a consumer marketing approach to skills transfer. We have all seen advertising messages such as:

"Choose any five modules from our attractive range"

"Learn in the privacy of your own car"

"Impress your colleagues with your knowledge"

"A Complete Training Course in 13 weekly episodes"

"Learn from the Experts with an Expert System on your Personal Computer"

Revelation

All will be made clear by the international expert at an expensive one- or two-day seminar in a prestigious hotel, possible targeted at senior management who are too busy to think through a complex problem, but may be persuaded to buy a complete solution from a consultant. Where this revelatory approach succeeds, it tends to result in a contract for the consultant to take on the problem, for a continuing fee. The consultant will not reveal his methods in his answers to questions or his explanations: the element of mystery is maintained as his source of income. Revelation is thus normally partial and phased, with control and profit in the hands of the "prophet" (this is what Mikes has called the "prophet motive").

Preconditions for the Transfer of Skills

Whichever model of the transfer of skills we adopt, there are certain common precautions.

There must be the potential for the application of the skill in question, or it can never be exercised and thus internalized. This precondition may be met by either a real or a simulated situation.

There must be some motivation in the recipient in order for the skill to be taken on and added to his repertoire. The motivation could take various forms, including:

Personal danger (which can help in learning to swim)

Instrumental need (motivating students to learn typing)

Financial gain (where a bonus payment is made for additional skills or qualifications)

Social concern (for those learning first aid skills)

Personal goals (as with athletes or religious believers)

Pressure from employer (employees without certain skills may be made redundant)

There must be some shared practical context, some common language between those imparting and those receiving skills, though this may well be mediated by a number of different educational technologies of individual or mass communication. In order to learn how to play a game there is a need in some sense to know that the objective is to play the game, though the skill may be imparted before it is named, or fully put into practice. Wittgenstein used to teach the principles of basketball without a ball, showing how it was done by running in and out of the trees by the river in Cambridge. His students should know how to go on if they found themselves in a game. Such insights could not be acquired in conventional texts or lectures.

Technology and Skills

If we regard technology as the partial realization of particular defined human skills, as implementations of "the extension of man", then there is clearly a dynamic and controversial relationship between the two. Given some understanding of what is technologically possible, it is a social and political issue as to how the balance should be struck, and by whom. Technology is of itself politically, socially and economically neutral: it is inevitably political in its use; reflecting and possibly strengthening the value system as well as the economic and political interests of those who control it.

Many of the terms which are causing concern in present-day industrial relations demonstrate the interconnectedness of technology and skills. We talk of "de-skilling", when the introduction of new technology means that a task no longer requires the same degree of human skill: instead of carrying out a complex process the operative may just press a button. Where the workforce had been trained using one generation of technology, and face a new generation of technology in the workplace, we talk of "re-skilling". Where the workplace has incorporated so much new technology that the nature of the process and the worker's place in it has changed, we may find discussion of "multi-skilling", where the worker is expected to apply himself to a number of different tasks rather than being a specialist in one.

There is a clear danger in this technological "advance" that the nature of skill becomes defined in terms of technological and industrial processes, as constituting a human response to the needs of the technology, rather than the reverse. When the industrial base collapses, as is happening in the United Kingdom at present, it may take with it the narrowly defined human skills which it embodied. Such a drastic form of alienation of the worker from the products of his labour cannot but have explosive effects.

Technology and skills are also associated in the sense that both require the support of long-term investment. Neither can be treated as a short-term cost to be cut without calamitous consequences, for which the United Kingdom again serves as an example. Research, development, education and training are inseparable essential elements of a society's continuation.

Technology policy had to be determined with regard to the social and economic needs of society. The newest, most advanced and expensive technology may well not be appropriate. A country with a large working population may not give priority to a technology which replaces human labour: that would not be authentic for the interests of the society as a whole, though it might make a few company directors extremely wealthy. There has been concern, based on the work of Schumacher (1973), to identify intermediate, appropriate technologies, which extend the effectiveness of people in meeting their own particular goals. Enabling technology can be liberating; inappropriate technology can provide a form of enslavement. The same physical objects, such as printing presses, steam engines or computers, could in themselves be enabling or enslaving: it is the context of use which is crucial and defines the social meaning of the technology.

Artificial Intelligence and Skills

Artificial intelligence is being applied to the complex process of training and skill transfer. Training clearly happens in particular cases, but the critical elements are not proving easily amenable to automation. There are definite limits to what is possible with Artificial intelligence, and these limits are currently being encountered in both research projects and practical applications.

There were those who thought that the process of Training Needs Analysis could be automated, that from a description of a task to be performed and of the employee who should perform it, an account could be generated of the training required, and that much of the necessary training could then be provided through the computer. Such a view derives from a mechanistic approach to human behaviour, closely related to a Taylorist view of the division of labour in manufacturing processes. If instead we start with an understanding and appreciation of the human, and regard the job description as adaptable, our conclusions and work practices will be different.

When we use artificial intelligence tools or techniques in a practical situation we are constrained by the extent of our knowledge. Our systems can only be as good as the description of the problem to be addressed, and the chosen knowledge representation. Human experts can never make all their expertise explicit, and we have to resort to various knowledge-elicitation methods in order to try to make up the deficit. As our knowledge of a problem can never be complete, our system can never be fully dependable in the real world. We can thus never build a system which cures all illnesses, solves all business problems or destroys all incoming ballistic missiles. There will, furthermore, always be limits to the extent to which the system can offer acceptable explanations of its behaviour and conclusions. In order to give a satisfactory explanation to somebody else we need to know a good deal about that somebody: there will always be severe limitations on what computers can be said to "know" about their users.

Artificial intelligence tools offer the potential of making social complexity more tractable, if we can arrive at an adequate representation of the institutional structures, problems and interest groups concerned. This involves a shift to seeing artificial intelligence as a tool for social, or collaborative, problem-solving, rather than for individual procedural problem-solving of the conventional kind.

The Politics of Skills

Politics is concerned with people and the deployment of human resources. A political philosophy must include some view of the future, in which both the individual and society play parts. Politics includes the pragmatics of the management of change, but in a manner whereby success or failure are not purely calculated in terms of short-term profit and loss, and policies are seen as means to longer-term ends, or goals.

In this context training, and the transfer of skills, must be of central importance in any political programme. For what future are people to be trained? What skills are to be transferred, and to whom? Are we at present mortgaging our future to finance current profligacy? Who is being consulted and involved in preparing a solution to perhaps the central problem of our era, and who is left to form part of the problem?

References and Further Reading

Benson I (ed) (1986) Intelligent machinery: theory and practice. Cambridge University Press, Cambridge

Bide A (chairman) (1986) Report of the IT86 Committee. Department of Trade and Industry, UK.

Cotterell A (ed) (1988) Advanced information technology in new industrial society. Oxford University Press, Oxford

Ennals JR (1983) Beginning micro-PROLOG. Ellis Horwood, Chichester

Ennals JR (1985) Artificial intelligence: applications to logical reasoning and historical research. Ellis Horwood, Chichester

Ennals JR (1986) Star wars: a question of initiative. John Wiley, Chichester

Ennals JR (ed) (1988) Artificial intelligence. Pergamon Infotech State of the Art Report, Maidenhead

Ennals JR, Gwyn R, Zdravchev L (eds) (1986) Information technology and education: The changing school. Ellis Horwood, Chichester

Ennals JR, Cotterell A, Briggs JH (1988) Advanced Information technology in education and training Hodder and Stoughton, London

Gill K (ed.) (1986) Artificial intelligence for society. John Wiley, Chichester

Mikes G (1972) The prophet motive: Israel today and tomorrow. Penguin Books, London

Piaget J (1971) Structuralism Routledge and Kegan Paul, London

Rahtz S (ed) (1987) Information technology and the humanities. Ellis Horwood, Chichester

Schumacher EF (1973) Small is beautiful: a study of economics as if people mattered. Blond and Briggs, London

Wittgenstein L (1953) Philosophical investigations. Basil Blackwell, Oxford

Yazdani M (ed) (1984) New horizons in educational computing. Ellis Horwood, Chichester

Chapter 8

Artificial Intelligence and Social Action: Education and Training

K. S. Gill

One of the central planks of development is the enhancement of people's potential for creative participation in the development process by enhancing the provision of basic human needs such as education, health and welfare. If AI technology has any relevance to these developmental issues (as like any other technology it should), then it must also concern itself with the knowledge of human needs and the nature of expert knowledge which contributes to the design of relevant technologies. In order for people to participate in the development process, they must have knowledge and skills to affect such a process. The machine-centred approach of current AI technology restricts its application to those problem-solving domains which can be formalized in logical rational rules. This approach thus takes account of non-intuitive knowledge and ignores the intuitive component which is embedded in the personal experience and in the social and cultural traditions of the user. The human-centred approach, on the other hand, is based on the human–machine symbiosis and provides for creative participation of users in the design of "developmental" systems.

Introduction

As advanced computing technology continues its transformation from a data-processing to a knowledge-processing technology, there is an increasing tendency to seek technological solutions to many of the decision-making problems. The application of expert-systems technology in social domains such as education, medicine and law raises issues of computerizing professional knowledge which have wider social implications for the nature of human knowledge itself. Current developments in expert systems in social domains deal mainly with propositional knowledge and ignore the practical knowledge and knowledge of familiarity which belong to personal experiences, practices and social traditions.

The central focus of these developments has been the design of an autonomous intelligent knowledge-based machine which aims to automate human knowledge and human decision-making processes. This focus arises from the "rationalistic orientation that not only pervades artificial intelligence and the rest of computer science, but much of the linguistics, management science and cognitive science" (Winograd and Flores 1986). Rationalistic styles of discourse and thinking representing this orientation have determined the theories, methodologies and assumptions that have been adopted by the proponents of the "intelligent machine".

Human knowledge, in this orientation, is assumed to be rational and therefore can be objectified and represented in the form of systematic rules. Michie and Johnston's *Creative computer* (1985) perhaps represents the most significant development in this tradition.

To achieve the demanded objectivity, paraphrasing Cooley (1980, 1987), human knowledge is eliminated of the very human traits such as subjectivity, uncertainty and imprecision, and is stripped of the social and cultural contexts which give meaning to human knowledge itself. Moreover, what this tradition also ignores is that the traits such as uncertainty, imprecision, error and lack of objectivity are a human resource and are crucial to the iterative processes of optimization which humans apply and experience in achieving rational knowledge and objectivity. Errors and uncertainty occur in a context and therefore not only help us in understanding the process of optimization but also in avoiding their consequences in similar contexts. For example by correcting one uncertainty, we may correct other uncertainties, and therefore enhance our understanding of the process of optimization. It seems that by focussing on the means of objectifying human knowledge, the rationalist tradition not only ignores the contexts of knowledge transfer, it also ignores the process by which humans acquire the formal knowledge in the first place.

Underlying the whole enterprise of the "intelligent" machine are the assumptions of the universality of culture and the universality of human needs. These assumptions not only deny the diversity of social and cultural contexts which enrich human knowledge but also reflect the inequalities inherent in the power structures of the dominant culture. Such an enterprise, therefore, tends to equate human knowledge with the knowledge of the dominant culture, the dominant group or a dominant individual (e.g., an expert in expert systems). The transfer of knowledge among people and across cultures and societies is seen in terms of its transfer from a dominant giver to a dominated receiver. Knowledge in this context is thus predominantly seen merely as a marketable commodity rather than as a rich human resource. This view of human knowledge allows its valuation in economic terms and therefore its description and representation in logical forms (e.g., logical rules). Knowledge transfer in this context is therefore seen in terms of the transfer of quantifiable factual knowledge and technical skills from an expert to a learner. Current work on expert systems illustrates this dominant focus of knowledge transfer.

This technical view of knowledge transfer forms a basis for the current machine-centred approaches to processing human knowledge. New technology is thus seen to provide technological solutions to many of the complex human decision-making problems without considering broader social issues arising out of such an approach. There is, however, a growing awareness amongst many concerned artificial intelligence (AI) researchers and practitioners (Ennals 1986; Göranzon 1987; Gullers Chap. 5) of the inadequacy of new technology in dealing with all aspects of professional knowledge, Expert systems may be used for transferring technical skills and technical knowledge from an expert to a learner in "limited but well defined domains"; their role in developing user-centred systems is limited because of the difficulties of formalizing and automating the processing of human knowledge, particularly the personal knowledge and the knowledge of familiarity. On a technical level, the inadequacy of expert systems to represent the background and the contextual environment of the domain limits the construction of explanation systems which are meaningful to both the learner and the teacher.

If new technology is to play a beneficial and effective role in the human domain, then its design must take into account the social and cultural practices and traditions of its users. The contention of this chapter is that human-centred approaches developed by researchers such as Cooley and Göranzon offer a practical alternative to the machine-centred approaches practised by the dominant AI community. Human-centred approaches provide a basis for creative and democratic use of new technology for the benefit of people. The health/welfare project discussed here is an attempt to design a human-centred system for training which deals with some of the issues of knowledge transfer in the human domain and emphasizes the need for designing AI systems appropriate to the needs of people.

Nature of Expert Knowledge and its Transfer

Behind the machine-centred approaches, we find a view of knowledge described by Peter Gullers as "knowledge in which all human thought and action can be logically described in a formalized language, and in which all conceivable activities are predictable". According to this view of knowledge, professional knowledge is often regarded as having a manual skill. Since it is generally accepted that manual skill decreases with the increase in mechanization of production processes, so the professional knowledge gets degraded to a form of factual knowledge or propositional knowledge. This degradation of professional knowledge ignores the knowledge gained through practical experiences and social and cultural interactions, and hence regards the issue of knowledge transfer in terms of transferring only factual knowledge from a technical expert to a learner.

The design of AI systems for social domains such as education, medicine and law cannot choose only one aspect of professional knowledge, propositional knowledge, and ignore other aspects, practical knowledge and knowledge of familiarity, which give meaning to the very propositional knowledge used by expert systems. Bo Göranzon describes these three forms of knowledge and comments that "practical knowledge contains experiences obtained from having been in practice. At the same time there is a great deal of knowledge within this practice that we learn by examining examples we are given by others who have been working within the practice. It is from this aggregate experience that we also build up our competence and learn from first-hand experience. The interaction between people in the same professional group is of decisive importance here. The latter kind of knowledge, knowledge that we acquire from learning a practice by examining examples of tradition, we call the knowledge of familiarity. That part of a professional tradition that has been expressed in general traditions, theories, methods and regulations and that we can assimilate from a theoretical study of activity, we call propositional knowledge."

Gullers discusses the interdependence of these three forms of knowledge and comments that "one kind of knowledge cannot be separated from the other two kinds. Formal expert systems can therefore neither replace nor compensate for shortcomings in propositional knowledge, the knowledge of familiarity or practical knowledge. Professional skills cannot be completely formalized".

Göranzon emphasizes the importance of practice and on-going dialogue in gaining professional skills and competence, and says that "Being a professional implies extending one's perspectives towards a broader view of one's own skills. Being aware of anomalies – failures – is of particular importance in terms of accepting professional responsibility. The historical perspective is a central factor in the knowledge of familiarity." He notes the paradox of this argument and comments that "if we remove all practical knowledge and knowledge of familiarity from an activity we will also empty it of propositional knowledge".

From the above discussion, it should be clear that machine-centred approaches focussing on propositional knowledge only are totally inadequate for designing AI systems for the transfer of professional knowledge.

Fundamental to the consideration of the issues of knowledge transfer is the dynamic nature of human knowledge itself. Issues of knowledge acquisition, representation and retrieval are all intertwined with the generative, creative and interactive nature of human knowledge. These aspects of human knowledge are discussed in the book *AI for Society* (Gill 1986).

The Nature of Knowledge Acquisition

The dynamic nature of human knowledge requires it to be organized in a form which when transmitted allows the user to apply it in new contexts and thereby generate new knowledge.

Knowledge as a Socio-Cultural Resource

If knowledge acquisition is to have in-built dynamic creativity, there must be a strong resonance between the mode of knowledge representation and a user's own social and cultural experiences.

Cultural Hermeneutics

Knowledge transfer between different cultural groups must involve us in the joint activities of interpretation and translation. Cultural hermeneutics is part and parcel of our enterprise and we should not be over-timid in embracing it.

Design Issues

Social Domains: Design Criteria for AI Systems

Knowledge-based systems for knowledge transfer should put human needs at the centre of their developments and should focus on the inextricable intertwinement of benefit and accessibility. Such systems should:

1. Build upon the individual's life experiences and expertise, and aim to provide those skills, expertise and cognitive competence which enhance the individual's life chances and access to institutional structures and resources of society on an equitable basis

2. Take into account the individual's social and cultural contexts and constraints within which the transferred knowledge could be meaningfully interpreted and validated

3. Be concerned not only with the issue of whether the control of technology and knowledge exists but where does the control actually lie. If such a technology is to enhance the participation of users and the democratization of knowledge, then it must allow for equality of autonomy. Implicit in the question of autonomy are the questions of evaluation and responsibility. For example it may not just be a question of designing a technology but who is allowed to evaluate it and under what criteria. The question of responsibility may not just be concerned with the issues of design and maintenance but also with issues such as: the choice of the symbols of presentation and representation; dealing with the failures of the system; and the suitability, accessibility and reliability of AI products.

Human-Centred Approach for Knowledge Transfer

The limitations of the machine-centred approach has much wider implications than the design of technical rules for knowledge transfer. The rule-centred ethos of technology leads to an uncritical acceptance of computerized techniques (Weizenbaum 1976). According to Cooley (1987), perhaps the most alarming aspect of this state of affairs is that the technologists and designers see nothing wrong with the limitations inherent in these techniques. There is an urgent need to view alternative systems, in particular those which may be regarded as human-centred. Such alternatives should reject neither human judgment, tacit knowledge, intuition and imagination, nor the scientific or the rule-based methods (Cooley 1987), The human-centred approach allows a collaboration between the user and the computer in such a way that they complement each other's capabilities. The computer provides storage memory and high speed of processing the data while the human provides rich pattern-recognition skills and creative knowledge for developing interactive human-centred systems. This approach assumes that the user has skills which can be effectively used in the collaborative mode or can be further enhanced.

Participatory Model

The participatory model may be regarded as an extended form of the human-centred model. In this model the user has the freedom to use a computer system as an expert-centred system or a human-centred system or does not use any computer system at all. In such a model users and human experts may interact with each other, and may use a variety of computer and non-computer resources for transferring knowledge and skills. What is of concern here is the type of boundaries and constraints which are needed for designing and implementing such a system. Such a model is also relevant to those who may not possess necessary skills and appropriate knowledge for participating either in human-centred systems or expert-centred systems.

The Human Domain: AI Technology and its Limitations

One of the domains which provides rich socio-cultural contexts for the design of human-centred systems is the domain of health. The rapidly changing nature and composition of users of health services require that these services must be adapted and enhanced to meet the multi-facet need of its users. One of the areas of health which provides a considerable challenge to the AI technologists and health educationists is the application of new technology to meet the education and training needs of health/welfare professionals and carers who are involved in the provision of these services to disadvantaged groups who have disparate social, economic and cultural backgrounds. In the UK, there are large groups of users: people from black and ethnic minority communities, the elderly, single-parent families, women's groups and the disabled people whose health needs may also depend upon factors such as race and culture, social, environment, and gender. Such factors may not only contribute to the disadvantagedness of these groups in gaining access to health services, they may also contribute to the provision of inappropriate services because of the lack of knowledge of these disadvantages among the carers and providers. There is now a growing awareness and understanding among health and social services professionals of the need to take into account these factors for providing effective health services to these groups. In order to provide these services, health and social services professionals must first understand the socio-cultural contexts within which users' health-needs arise and are cared for.

Although health educationists and trainers are aware of the importance of socio-cultural contexts for designing training programmes, many AI techno-logists seem to consider these contexts as a periphery to their interests and developments. As far as I can see, most of the AI work in the area of health is concerned with the issues of diagnosis and administration (e.g. MYCIN-type systems, Alvey Demonstrator Project on Social Security 1985). This work seems to be dominated by the expert-centred approach of many commercial expert systems. Because of this approach, AI work in health services assumes that the health needs of its users are universal irrespective of the social, cultural and environmental factors discussed above. The consequence of such an approach is that not only may the technological systems be inappropriate to the needs of users, they may also restrict the richness of AI development for dealing with the propositional knowledge, practical knowledge and knowledge of familiarity as an integrated whole rather than dealing with the propositional knowledge only.

Effective and appropriate use of new technology for the benefit of all groups in society requires that we must accept the diversity of both the needs of users and the socio-cultural contexts within which these needs arise and technology becomes relevant. This means that technological systems in the human domain must consider issues of knowledge and skill transfer within the contexts of their users and not just those of the experts and technical designers. The domain of health offers an opportunity for developing AI technologies which benefit people and at the same time enrich the development of AI techniques for the acquisition, representation and interpretation of human knowledge.

An AI system for the education of health professionals within broader socio-cultural contexts should aim at both the practitioner and the policy-maker. The design of such a system should be based on the practical experience and expertise of the professionals, educationists, and trainers. It should take into account the multi-disciplinary nature of health services, and should focus on the diverse needs of users of health services. Such criteria for an AI system require that it must deal with not just the rule-based propositional knowledge of the experts, but it should also deal with the tacit and experiential knowledge of professionals and users. This diversity of the health domain makes it unrealistic and inappropriate to develop education and training programmes based on the AI technology of expert systems which are applicable to restricted and well-defined domains of technical knowledge. It is therefore important for the educationists and trainers to be aware of the limitations and inadequacies of the expert systems approach in order to participate in developing knowledge-based systems in their domains. Some of these limitations are discussed below.

Winograd and Flores (1986) note that the area of artificial intelligence arousing the greatest commercial interest is the creation of systems that perform some detailed tasks, such as analysing chemical spectograms (DENDRAL, Lindsay et al. 1980), identifying a particular kind of bacterial infection (MYCIN, Shortcliffe 1976) or checking a proposed configuration of computer equipment (R1, McDermott 1982). Buchanan (1982) lists some characteristics of problems that are suitable for expert-systems applications:

Narrow domain of expertise

Limited language for expressing facts and relations

Limiting assumptions about problem and solution methods

Little knowledge of own scope and limitations

They note these limitations and comment that "these are exactly the characteristics that make it possible to create a program to do "problem solving" within a systematic domain, and there is no reason to believe that any future state of the art will transcend them".

They point out that there is a danger inherent in the label "expert systems": "when we talk of a human 'expert' we connote someone whose depth of understanding serves not only to solve specific well-formulated problems, but also to put them into a larger context". Another problem of creating expert systems, they point out, is the difficulty in conveying and understanding a sense of the limitations of a particular program and of the approach in general. Using medical "expert systems" as an example, they note that: "In order to produce a set of rules for a medical expert system, it is first necessary to pre-select the relevant factors and thereby cut out the role of the background. But . . . this process by its very own nature creates blindness. There is always a limit set by what has been made explicit, and always the potential of breakdowns that call for moving beyond this limit."

Towards Designing Human-Centred Learning Systems: A Research Initiative at the Seake Centre

A research initiative on human-centred learning systems being undertaken at the Seake (Social and Educational Applications of Knowledge Engineering) Centre has two interrelated objectives:

1. To combine AI, interactive video and electronic design technologies for developing human-centred systems which benefit people
2. To develop a multi-disciplinary approach for human-centred systems which regards learning as a social process and focusses on the issues of the transfer of human knowledge and human skills among the participants

The Centre's work includes projects on

A knowledge-based system for language development for adults in continuing education
An interactive learning system for language development for young children with learning difficulties

Interactive video (both tape and disc) work includes projects on:

1. Social and moral skills for youth in special education
2. Cognitive development and communication skills for children in special education
3. Health education for youth in special education

Previous pilot work on interactive video (mainly video tape) has included projects on interviewing techniques, handling anger and aggression among youth, and on safety at home for mentally handicapped adults.

A New Initiative in Health Care Training

Recently the Centre has initiated a research programme on a knowledge-based interactive video system for training health and social services professionals within an equal opportunity context. Its aim is to raise awareness of the health needs of groups in the community who are disadvantaged due to cultural, racial, gender, age and disability factors. Effective health care must cater for the diverse needs of its users which may arise from factors such as race, culture and gender etc. The project aims to assist health and social services workers to respond to and to deal more effectively with health-care needs of these disadvantaged groups. The training system will also be useful for voluntary organizations working with black and ethnic minority communities, women's groups, single-parent families, and those working with elderly and disabled people.

Some of the issues which are being considered for developing a human-centred system for health-care training are:

Human knowledge – both formal and informal

Communication – human–human and human–machine

Background – social, cultural and environmental

Learning needs – recognizing disadvantages and providing appropriate services; adapting and initiating good practices, self-awareness and social relationships, handling uncertainty and hopelessness, involving users in their own care; working together with other interest groups

We believe that the convergence of AI, interactive video, and graphics-design technologies provides an opportunity to develop knowledge-based learning systems for health education and training. Both video tape and video disc can be used to capture and store social and cultural contexts of the domain-knowledge in rich visual and sound forms. Formal and informal knowledge can be represented within defined contexts and backgrounds. Photographic, graphics and computer-graphics forms can be used to represent the contextual and background information which cannot be either formalized or captured through audio-visual forms. These representations of the backgrounds provide contexts within which meaningful explanations and interpretations of the domain-knowledge can be constructed. The randomness of the video disc and the knowledge-centredness of AI can be combined to develop interactive learning systems which can be both proactive and reactive, and enable feedback which can be meaningful and relevant.

The Domain of Health: Some Concerns of Automating Social Knowledge

We have chosen health education/training as a domain for our research and applications work because of our concern with the use of advanced technologies in the human domain. Our concern is that the automation of human knowledge is likely to lead to the development of machine-centred training systems which can only deposit limited technical knowledge onto the learner and fail to build upon and expand human skills and life experiences of the learner.

From the earlier discussion on expert systems, it is clear that rule-based and machine-learning methodologies are too limited to deal with the social nature of human knowledge. Moreover, such machine-centred systems only deal with technical knowledge in limited professional domains, and are therefore limited in their application to only those domains in which the technical knowledge of the expert can be transferred to the learner. However, human domains such as health and education are social domains in which human learning takes place within the complex socio-cultural contexts of the learner and the background knowledge of the domain.

The domain of health provides a rich learning environment in which providers and users of health services share each other's knowledge through a common language whilst bringing to bear their own expertise and life experiences.

Both the providers and users of health care may have, in common, many of the health needs and health experiences, and yet may differ in their perceptions, beliefs and myths about health care. A provider or a user of health care could be both an expert and a learner depending upon the role and the context. In the domain of health, the knowledge of the expert is the product of the technical expertise, practical knowledge gained through professional experience and the background knowledge arising out of social and cultural interactions. The knowledge of the domain consists of formal and informal rules and practices which are applied with varying degrees of flexibility and sensitivity. The interpretation of the user needs and the expert knowledge may itself be dependent upon the background knowledge of the domain. The domain thus cannot be considered either as an expert-centred domain or as a machine-learning domain or as an MMI (man–machine interaction) domain in the Alvey Programme sense. If we are concerned with the use of knowledge-based technologies in the multidisciplinary domain of health, then the most appropriate approach is the human-centred approach. In this approach, the human expert and the learner collaborate with the machine in such a way that the machine deals with the storage and processing of formal knowledge and the human deals with the informal and tacit knowledge.

The design of an AI system for health care must deal with the complexity and diversity of knowledge of professionals such as nurses and doctors. Ingela Josefson (1987) discusses theories of knowledge that are most likely to capture the versatility of the nursing profession. She poses a fundamental question as to why nurses (which could apply equally to other professionals in social domains) are so bad at formulating their knowledge and comments:

If, unlike the physician's profession, the basis of the nursing profession is care, then a different kind of knowledge needs to be developed in the nursing profession than in the doctor's profession. Theoretical training inculcates important medical facts; information that is essential to the nurse. But it does not prepare her for dealing with unexpected events in the care of patients . . . Work in medical care is full of unexpected complications. To deal with this degree of complexity the nurse must have the ability to make a reasonable interpretation of events not covered by the descriptions in the rule book. This requires a multi-faceted practical experience, through which information acquired through formal training can be developed into knowledge. That knowledge is built up from a long series of examples which give different perspectives on an illness. Different kinds of knowledge are acquired, some of which can be described explicitly in generally applicable rules (called propositional knowledge). Another equally important type of knowledge is the knowledge that becomes apparent in encounters with unforseen complications in everyday care. This knowledge of familiarity cannot be described in a meaningful way in general rules because its core is the ability to act with good judgement in unique situations.

Josefson's observation on the complexity of the knowledge of a nurse illustrates the difficulty of expressing her professional knowledge in a form suitable for designing AI systems for health care. The multi-facet nature of the knowledge of a nurse is rooted in the tradition of the nursing profession "a tradition which, to a large extent, is inculcated through role models, such as older, more experienced nurses, who, through their actions, pass on their ethics to younger nurses and student nurses."

The complexity of the nursing profession's knowledge necessitates the development of AI systems which exploit the convergence of audio-visual and communications technologies for expressing various aspects of professional knowledge.

A Knowledge-Based Learning System for a Social Domain: a Case-Study in Adult Literacy Using the Domain of Diet Planning and Health

A project on a knowledge-based system for language development for adult students in continuing education was undertaken in collaboration with a local adult education centre, Friends Centre, Brighton. It was part of the EEC (European Economic Community) Social Fund-sponsored project on basic education in literacy, numeracy and technology. Students involved in the project were mainly women from ethnic and minority communities in Brighton. Their learning needs included the use of English language for enhancing their social communications skills and gaining access to various resources and knowledge sources relevant to their own life skills. In addition to these basic needs, they also wanted to gain confidence in the use of the computer as a word-processing tool. Students not only had different cultural backgrounds, they also had varying levels of proficiency in English language. Teachers involved in the project came from backgrounds of linguistics, sociology, mathematics, and computing. Their concern was to develop a teaching tool which complements their teaching practice especially in the teaching of English, basic numeracy and the use of the computer. AI researchers involved in the development of the project had backgrounds in philosophy and computing and had practical experience in community work.

The central focus of the project was to design a knowledge-based tool which enhances the transfer of knowledge among students themselves and between the students and their teachers. What was needed was a domain which was familiar to the students and teachers, and which provided a knowledge base rich enough for achieving the objectives of the project.

The domain of diet planning and health was chosen because all women students had expertise in cooking, were interested in the issues of diet planning and health, and were concerned with gaining access to health services. Moreover, they could communicate their cooking expertise and knowledge to each other with confidence and also learn from each other about various ways of cooking dishes. Teachers and AI researchers were also interested in the domain of diet planning and health and were also interested in learning how to cook dishes from various cultures. The domain of diet planning and health thus provided a context in which students, teachers and researchers could act both as experts and learners.

Designing the System: Using Learning as a Social Process

As discussed above, the domain of diet planning and health provided a social model for learning. In this model, formal learning was complemented by informal discussions among the teachers, students and AI researchers. Teachers acted as education experts and designers of educational material; students acted as experts in the art of cooking and consultants in their own cultural practices; AI researchers acted as designers and producers of the system.

Throughout the development, the students and the teachers also acted as assessors and evaluators of the project.

Learning Through Designing the Knowledge Base

The knowledge base consists of various dishes, their descriptions, ingredients and their descriptions, methods of preparation, food value, healthy methods of food preparation and explanations. The main activities involved in designing the knowledge base was acquiring knowledge from students about various dishes and making students express their knowledge in simple English. Informal one-to-one sessions and group discussions were used to select appropriate vocabulary, formulate rules and explanations (e.g. for preparing dishes), and designing rules for reasoning (e.g. giving reasons why certain foods may be healthier than others). A simple pilot program in meal planning, COOKING, was developed. It allowed students to input their recipes. The students had already prepared such recipes as part of their homework. The discussion of input formed an important part of the formal lessons. This was particularly true of the questions relating to descriptions of the meals and their various ingredients. This simple program was also used by students to express their knowledge in the form of formal expressions in English and to design formal forms of rules and relevant explanations. The program was also used by the system designer to formulate explanations in a form which was understood by students. Thus the process of designing the knowledge base was considered a part of the learning through practice.

Health visitors and dieticians were consulted to provide knowledge about the nutritional food values of the ingredients and dishes, and on the methods of preparation. Knowledge was represented as a combination of scripts and rules. Teachers helped in the English-like formulation of these representations.

Piloting the System with Students and Lessons Learnt

Jones (1987), a researcher at the SEAKE Centre designed the system DIET which was implemented in MICRO-PROLOG on an Apple II microcomputer.

It was used with groups of students (two or three students at a time) on a weekly basis from January to March 1985. The program was tested with students from a broad section of ages, nationalities, backgrounds and linguistic abilities. The opinions of staff and students were sought in order to find ways in which the program could be improved, and it was modified continuously during piloting. An example of a piloting session with a group of German and Vietnamese ESL students is described below. S stands for the writer of the program, ST for student, and SYS for the system:

ST: What is B vitamins?
     What is vitamin B?
S: No, one has to use the language of the program.
     What are B vitamins?
     (Note that a discussion takes place between the student and the writer, other students are also encouraged to participate in the discussion)
SYS: B vitamins are needed to protect against anaemia. Vegans may also need to take vitamin B tablets
ST: I find that tablets are not good for me. Is there not another way?
SYS: When you boil cabbage, some of the vitamins will be absorbed by the water, but you can use this to make a sauce. Frying the cabbage will mean that there is more fat in the meal. If you like fried food, it is best to use vegetable oil. Do you like fresh cabbage?
ST: No
SYS: Perhaps you should, because it will increase the amount of vitamin C.
     (Students explain to each other the meaning of the words)

Lessons Learnt: Some Examples

1. Topics of personal and social interest are suitable for this type of learning application, as they are motivating to the students and their appeal and relevance is largely unconfined to any particular culture.

2. The concept of using a deductive data base which can respond to queries in a restricted subset of natural language is a viable one for teaching English as a second language to adults.

3. The more commonly used types of expert-systems shells do not appear to be suitable, as they are inflexible and use language which is hard for students to understand. Programming environments such as PROLOG and APES are promising.

4. Such knowledge-based systems should be used as an integral part of an overall learning programme.

5. Knowledge-based interactive video systems are likely to provide more creative and effective learning tools. Background knowledge of the learning domain can be represented through video film and video disc. In addition to providing contexts for meaningful explanations, these representations can also provide a context for student discussion about relevant topics of the domain.

Back to the Health Care Project: Preliminary Work

A pilot interactive-video-tape program has been designed to demonstrate the feasibility of using an interactive video system as an effective training tool in the domain of health. Four video films produced by other organizations have been edited to produce one video film which deals with the issues of health and social-services provision within a multicultural and a multiracial perspective. The original four films were shown to a group of health trainers for their comment on the effectiveness of the original films. They were also asked to discuss how they would deal with health-care situations covered in the films. The discussion of these trainers was filmed, edited and included in the first edited film. We have used video film not only to elicit knowledge from health trainers, we have also used it to elicit new explanations and interpretations which are, in many cases, different from those given by experts in the original films.

Currently, software is being developed to control interactive video systems through PROLOG and the next stage of the pilot is to develop a rule-based interactive video system. Our plan is to develop a video-disc-emulator system for our further work on knowledge-based interactive video systems.

Concluding Remarks

Until recently there has been very little impact of advanced computing technology on education and training. While new technology is being used by the military, by industry and by commerce as an effective tool for automating many processes, its role in social domains has been limited to research projects in medical diagnosis and intelligent computer-assisted learning systems. However, as computing technology enters the area of human knowledge processing, there is bound to be either temptation or considerable pressure to use knowledge-based technologies such as expert systems for mechanizing some education processes on the grounds of cost-effectiveness of advanced computer technology.

As the discussion on expert systems has shown that although it may be possible to use expert systems to transfer technical skills and professional knowledge in limited domains, these rule-based systems are inadequate for designing human learning systems in the education domain. Moreover, expert-centred systems are unsuited to learning systems in which the aim is to enhance human skills and human cognitive competence of the learner. The machine-learning approach is inadequate to deal with issues of self-adaptation and self-modification which are essential for automating any human information-processing systems.

Since education is essentially a social domain, it is crucial that we do not turn education into a technical training domain and then justify the use of expert systems to automate the transfer of technical skills and technical knowledge from the expert to the learner. There is, however, an alternative approach of "human-centred systems" which can use knowledge-based technologies as an integral part of an overall learning resource. Growing convergence of AI, video disc/video tape and communications technologies makes it possible to design human-centred learning systems which can be used to enhance people's opportunities to participate creatively in the acquisition and transfer of human skills.

Fundamental to the design of AI systems for social domains is our understanding of the complex and dynamic nature of human knowledge. Propositional knowledge cannot be separated from the practical knowledge and knowledge of familiarity which are rooted in professional practices and are gained through social and cultural interactions over time. AI technology has now become a significant economic and political resource, and we must, therefore, ensure that it is also used as an effective tool for socially useful purposes.

References

Alvey DHSS Demonstrator Project (1985), Alvey Programme Annual Report, 1985, Alvey Directorate Millbank Tower, Millbank, London SW1P 4QV

Buchanan B (1982) New research on expert systems. In: Hayes JE et al. (eds) Machine intelligence 10. Ellis Horwood, Chichester, pp 269–299

Cooley M (1980) Architect or bee?: the human-technology relationship. Langley Technical Services, Slough, England.

Cooley M (1987) Architect or bee?: the price of technology (revised), Chatto & Windus, London

Ennals R (1986) A way forward for advanced information technology: SHI-a strategic health initiative. In: Gill KS (ed) AI for society. Wiley & Sons, Chichester

Gill, KS (ed) (1986) Artificial intelligence for society. Wiley and Sons, Chichester

Göranzon B (1987) The practice of the use of computers: a paradoxical encounter between different traditions of knowledge. AI & Society: Hum Machine Intell 1: No 1

Gullers P (1987) Automation, skill, apprenticeship. Proceedings of the London Symposium on AI Based Systems And The Future Of Language, Knowledge And Responsibility In Professions, The Swedish Centre For Working Life, Box 5606 S-114, Stockholm, Sweden.

Jones SG (1987) A knowledge-based system for language development for students in continuing education, learning English as a second language. MPhil thesis, SEAKE Centre, Brighton Polytechnic

Josefson Ingela (1987) The nurse as an engineer – the theory of knowledge in research in the care sector. AI & Society: Hum Machine Intell 1: No 2

Lindsey R et al. (1980) Applications of artificial intelligence for organic chemistry: the DENDRAL project. McGraw-Hill, New York

McDermott J (1982) RI: a rule-based configurer of computer systems. Art Intell 19: 39–88

Michie D, Johnston R (1985) The creative computer. Penguin Books, London

Shortcliffe EH (1976) Computer-based medical consultations: M Elsevier, New York

Weizenbaum J (1976) Computer power and human reason: from judgement to calculation. Freeman Press, San Francisco.

Winograd T, Flores F (1986) Understanding computers and cognition. Ablex Publishing Corporation, Norwood, New Jersey

Skill, Education and Social Value: Some Thoughts on the Metonymy of Skill and Skill Transfer

J. Hilton

Skills are necessarily representative of value systems of which they are a part. Hence the transfer of skill has to be considered as the transfer of a skill and part of a value system without which the intrinsic skill is meaningless. Knowledge transfer is better termed knowledge exchange. At present, training (intrinsic skill acquisition) is being divorced from education as a whole (location of skills in a value system) leading to the danger that skilled groups will lose touch with the social value system within which its skills are located, and probable erosion of skill. The intelligent system can be another powerful tool of the expert or it can be designed to be transparent to the non-professional. To ensure the democratization of knowledge the system must be transparent i.e., the learner is at the centre of this process such that acquisition and personalization of a skill is achieved by transforming what one observes another doing into something of value to oneself.

Introduction: Skills and Social Interaction

When I go to London, I often stay with my sister. She has two children. The younger, just two years old, likes my visits. After his breakfast he comes to me with a book, wakes me up and asks for a story. I read to him, concentrating on the pictures. He does not listen to the story for long before he goes and gets a second book, asking me again to read a story. He evidently likes the power he has to make me do things even more than he likes the story. This behaviour made me ask myself what the real skill is in his behaviour. Is it choosing the book or making me do things with him, or both together?

It is surely both. Our story-telling together functions on two levels, which we may distinguish as *practical* and *social*. On the one hand, my nephew has the practical skills intrinsic to choosing a book, bringing it to me and asking me to read. He can walk and see. He can recognize shapes and colours sufficiently clearly to find his favourite stories. He has sufficient linguistic control to ask me to read and to direct my reading. On the other hand, he has the social skill to make me enjoy reading to him, based on his, perhaps intuitive, recognition that of all the many things he could do with me, reading is the one I most value. So when he exercises power over me, he chooses to do it through asking for a story. It is the social context which legitimates and informs with meaning the practical skill.

This social context has certain types of rules, specific to our relationship and our situation. First, *preconditional*: he must eat his breakfast before he can have a story, and I must have a cup of tea before I can read. Secondly, *behavioural*: he relies on his knowledge of the fact that I like reading to him and that I will tolerate frequent changes of book, neither of which conditions are given in his expectation of a reading situation. Thirdly, *psychological*: as a younger brother he likes the fact that I am interested in him so the special nature of the event depends on the fact that his sister is seldom awake at this time, which means that he has my undivided attention. If we consider the reading process itself in the context of such rules, how may we define its parameters?

1. *History*. The fact that we read together often gives the event its own history, from which certain rules (traditions) have emerged. When, therefore, he asks for a story, we both know that what he means is that he wants an elaborate social interaction with me lasting up to about thirty minutes.

2. *Will*. On a specific occasion, he must want to have a story and I must want to read to him. Further, he must choose a story that I am prepared to read.

3. *Enactment*. I must actually read to him and follow the rituals we have developed: we turn the pages at specific intervals, we identify animals and the sounds they make, I deliberately falsify the answers and he corrects me, he then jokes about this process. Reading is itself, therefore, a multi-layered process.

4. *Social Legitimation*. We must both regard the event as part of a special bonding process which gives the reading a social legitimation. The special nature of our relationship is expressed symbolically through the joint act of story-telling, in which a listener is just as important as a narrator.

In the light of these conditions, which in themselves are relatively blunt categorizations of skills of great complexity, we may describe the story-telling event as *metonymic*, the skill of story-telling which is invoked by the request "Tell me a story" being part of a much wider interaction of social skills.

If there is another common thread running through these observed conditions, it is that it may be inappropriate to talk of skill or knowledge transfer at all, for in each condition I have outlined there is complete *interdependence* of my skills and his. This principle is inherent in story-telling, the teller being perhaps more dependent on the listener than *vice versa*. In other words, even in reading to my nephew I may be engaged less in knowledge transfer than in knowledge exchange, in which I trade my knowledge of reading for his knowledge of how to be taught to read. These principles of interdependence suggest that only knowledge and skill transfer predicated on the partnership of both sides in the transfer has any real chance of functioning as a communication system. It further suggests that the concept of *knowledge transfer* itself may be inappropriate and that it should be replaced by *knowledge exchange*.

At the same time, the interdependence principle highlights another aspect to our story-telling, the fact that it has such a central role in our particular relationship. In the way I presented the relationship between practical and social skill, there is an implicit sense in which practical skill is to be understood in the broader context of social skill. Yet in practice, the social skill has narrowed the real meaning of the practical skill to something unique to my relationship with my nephew. While he is unwittingly learning to read he is also learning about the specific social problem of how to get on with me. There is nothing new in this observation: we all know that our ability to be taught depends very heavily on our personal feelings towards our teacher. Yet to what extent is the knowledge exchange between us itself specific to our relationship? Can our knowledge be made accessible to a third party? Is my nephew learning a general life skill in his particular dealings with me?

The Metonymy of Skill

Thinking about this issue in terms of the theme of this volume, *Knowledge, Skill and New Technology*, I began to observe my nephew in his dealings with others. His mother is studying at university, so has a seventeen-year-old girl to look after him. This girl is strict on forms of behaviour. One day when my nephew was in the room with me, but playing on his own, she came in. My nephew started to pick his nose in the presence of his nanny, which I had not consciously seen him do before. Immediately the girl told him to stop. He would not. She told him again. Eventually the battle of wills resolved this way: she offered to read him a story if he would stop picking his nose. He stopped and she read a story. Once again, it seemed clear to me that the skill my nephew had acquired in picking his nose was only secondary to the recognition that he had come to that by picking his nose he could cause stories to be read. In my nephew's relationship with me, his nose-picking had no value, but in his relationship with his nanny it was central. Paradoxically, it was the nanny's insistence that he should not pick his nose which gave that skill to him special significance. When then he could associate nose-picking with story-telling the skill became of great value to him.

The problem this sets us is subtle and complex. We are probably agreed that public nose-picking is not a form of behaviour we wish to encourage, for whatever reason. So we would not criticize the nanny for wishing to control my nephew. But we will need to teach her how to exercise her control without creating false or unacceptable value systems by doing so. If we do not, we may discover that she is remarkably efficient at achieving the precise opposite of what she and we would wish.

If we express the practical and social values of nose-picking in semiotic terms we can see how the ambiguity of all skill works. The nose-picking itself is iconic: the skill signifies itself. But the skill is also symbolic: nose-picking is a symbol of social power. Practical skills enable me to do or make things, to achieve concrete results. I may have the skill of carpentry and be able to make a table. The finished table iconically signifies my skill. But if my table enables me to entertain people to dinner and gain influence over them both because they admire my carpentry and because they like my company when eating, then the table signifies my social worth. We may resolve the iconic and symbolic functions into a single expression, that of an index. The table is an index of all my skills. To transfer knowledge, therefore, of how to make an equivalent table I must also transfer the knowledge to which the table itself is only an index. This is the basis of the metonymy of all practical skill.

In the example I have given of my nephew and his nanny, knowledge transfer undergoes distortion, a process which turns the metonymic value of nose-picking into the skill of securing a story-telling session. Such distortions can occur to much more devastating effect, when a skilled group loses touch with the social value system within which its skills are located. Such a professional distortion occurred in Chernobyl amongst the research scientists, such an ideological distortion in Nazi Germany. Such a distortion appears to have begun in western industrial society where the economic benefit of automation and machine intelligence has been allowed to precede and predetermine the management of its social impact.

The practical consequences of this impact are unemployment and de-skilling. The social consequence, which may be even more profound, is the dislocation of work (applied skills) from social value systems, which threatens the concept of commonality on which the welfare state is based. This consequence only fuels the de-skilling process. If culturally we enjoin people to acquire skills but then give those skills little or no value, by making it clear that our real political and economic interest is to replace these people with machines, we cannot expect the skills to be learned and retained over any length of time. De-skilling is being accelerated by cultural attitude.

Power and Knowledge Transfer

The transfer of knowledge is the transfer of power. This metarule is in itself a very powerful piece of knowledge, which has substantially determined the politics of knowledge and skill transfer. If the thesis is accepted that skill is metonymic, then any act of skill transfer is simultaneously the transfer of power. Historically, the growth of democratic power from the sixteenth century onwards has been paralleled by the democratization of knowledge through mass education. The growth of trades unions has been enabled by the solidarity of those with common knowledge and skills banding together for common purposes. In such purposes it is the skill-base that, *ipso facto*, determines the membership of the union, the skills themselves, when located in a social context, acting as indices of political power. For example, the heavy dependence of the British energy system on coal in the early 1970s gave those with the skill of mining an enormously powerful social position. Now that the social value of mining has been weakened by the broadening base of energy-generation skills, the power-base of the miners has largely been broken.

Despite the historical trends towards democratization, there has been, particularly in recent years, an equally powerful refusal to transfer real power from a minority to a majority in society based on a resurgence in the belief of the power of elites. This refusal is embedded in a political attitude to knowledge which sees knowledge, and power, as pyramidic. The higher the knowledge the fewer can obtain it. Powerful knowledge (i.e. knowledge with high social value) is stored in complex symbolic systems (special professional languages and numerical codes) which only those who invent them and a deliberately restricted number of others may interpret.

In the light of one of the most significant finds of artificial intelligence (AI) research so far, it is possible that we may have to reassess this pyramidic structure. For AI has shown that it is the domain of common sense which is in fact hardest to embed in any artificially intelligent system. Yet common sense, by definition, is that which is common to all, or nearly all. The possible implication of this re-evaluation of the significance of common sense is that the capacity of people to access and understand high and powerful forms of knowledge may be radically different from our current experience. It may be that the real reason why only a small number of people enjoy, for example, the highest levels of education has more to do with long-term social conditioning of the majority who "fail" to expect "failure" than with any innate cognitive weakness. If a child can master the enormous complexity of speech why are the principles of electronics regarded as so difficult? If now, therefore, it is beginning to leak out that a new democracy of knowledge is possible, predicated on an application of the rules of "common sense" to a far wider variety of knowledge domains than ever before, a profound social revolution becomes a distinct possibility.

Two factors are contributing to the development of such a revolution. The first is that human intelligence, benefitting perhaps from the results of a mass education process, is beginning to question the manner in which professions conduct themselves. This very act of questioning is tantamount to an assault on the power-base of professions, traditionally self-regulating and hitherto protected by the traditional devices all professions use to render their knowledge arcane. The second is that machine intelligence promises to make the non-professional as able a decision-maker as the professional.

In professions such as medicine, there is a tradition of self-regulation, the arcane language of the doctors, their white coats and emblems of office (stethoscopes, prescription pads amd ECG machines) all being used to protect themselves from incursions into their power-base even by nurses, and, still worse, by their patients. Yet nurses are obviously aware that the imbalance in their pay as compared with doctors vastly overvalues the skill differential between them, to the great economic disadvantage of the nurses. Likewise, the public, irritated by the distance of most doctors and their reluctance to treat patients as intelligent beings, question whether the price of medicine is worth the cost. When into these perceptions we add the potential of machine intelligence, which will eventually give the nurse and even the patient access to the doctor's diagnostic knowledge in a manner uncontrolled by current conventions of decision making (the patient goes to the doctor, feels politically his inferior, is unable to understand information he is given), then the grounds for preserving special powers for doctors start to become even more unstable.

The generic issue this challenge to the doctor's power raises is that of the relationship between knowledge transfer and knowledge exchange. In the current power situation, the knowledge held by the doctor is transferred to the patient, in the expectation of cure. The tendency is to ignore the patient's own knowledge of himself in the process. Yet might it not be that better medicine would result from knowledge exchange: the patient exchanges his knowledge of his own symptoms with the doctor's knowledge of a possible cure? If this were the case, the principal skill the doctor would need is interpersonal – the ability to ask questions, the ability to elicit knowledge from someone else.

Another aspect to this issue is highlighted by the debate within the Swedish Social Security Service as to whether or not to allow local offices the power to make decisions hitherto reserved for the central administration. In such a case, the problem of power is geo-political than professional, but the concept of democratization is nevertheless common. With the new technology the local officer will have the means to make decisions hitherto reserved for the central power. But will the executive authority to make such decisions be granted? And if not, will it be stolen?

Two Models of Knowledge Transfer: Colonial and Independent

The current pre-occupation with the role of machine intelligence in the professions has thrown up two potentially contradictory ways in which such intelligence can be deployed. Either the intelligent system becomes another, powerful, tool of the expert, no more comprehensible to the average person than other forms of intelligent aid; or the system is designed to be transparent to the non-professional. It is hardly surprising that early experiences of such systems tend to reflect the anxieties of professionals at the possibility of being displaced or even replaced by machines, with the result that they have been resisted. Yet even when this resistance is overcome, the underlying issue of who the systems are for remains.

If machine intelligence is to contribute to the democratization of knowledge to which I have referred then we must ensure that the systems we design are transparent. Yet how difficult this may be can perhaps be illustrated by comparing two models of skill transfer, one which I shall describe as *colonial*, the other as *independent*, terms chosen to reflect the metonymic relationship between knowledge and power.

Colonial Model of Skill Transfer

The premise of a colonial nation is that its culture is so good it deserves export to those needing "civilization". These colonial attitudes we may schematize as follows:

1. The learner is assumed to be unwilling to learn
2. The learner expects to be taught by an expert
3. The expert has professional status

4. The learner expects that learning will be unpleasant and that there is a high risk of failure or only partial success.

5. The learner is not expected to challenge the method of knowledge transfer

6. Once expert himself, the learner will be expected to maintain the traditions and attitudes of the teacher, especially in regard to the restrictions imposed on knowledge transfer

In terms of a knowledge transfer system we may describe this as *expert-centred transfer*, functioning as follows:

Learner expecting to be taught goes to

Expert with

Skill (by definition) who

Demonstrates skill to

Learner who

Assimilates skill by

Imitation and

Problem-solves using skill and becomes

New Expert dedicated to the

Interests of the expert group.

The colonial model is reinforced in crucial social ways. Experts are accorded titles, such as Dr or Professor, by which their special status is confirmed. They wear special clothing, such as white coats, which not only iconographically suggest disinterested exercise of knowledge (and hence power) over the non-expert, but visually identify who they are – a kind of priesthood. The moment of knowledge transfer itself, in the social sense at least, is frequently associated with special ceremonies, the taking of oaths, or enactment of special forms of behaviour (rites of passage).

Yet it is an open social secret that the non-expert feel a range of emotions towards the expert ranging from awe and respect to fear and hostility. In either event, there is a barrier created between the expert and the non-expert which any communication theorist would assume automatically is likely to hinder rather than enable good communication of knowledge. The obvious reason why experts do not find this barrier irksome is that it is the barrier which keeps the non-experts out. The barrier protects the power and the privileges of the expert. If such experts accept expert systems into their domains, then we may assume it will be only in the context of absolute assurances that they will be enabled by them to become more expert. It will not be part of the policy to enable the non-expert to gain access to expert skills without resort to the human expert and without going through the mumbo-jumbo first.

Independent Model of Skill Transfer

Yet there is another way. If we accept the premise that there is, analogous to common sense, something like common skill, or common expertise, then the unskilled learner, who is capable of acquiring and mastering rules systems of the complexity of language may be able to encompass a knowledge base far greater than hitherto assumed, on condition that the social context in which he learns affirms to him the value of knowledge and the possibility of attaining it. This premise assumes that the knowledge-transfer problem is essentially an attitudinal one. Knowledge transfer is made problematic because of a deeply-held conviction, coinciding with ideological expediency, that powerful knowledge is necessarily hard to acquire. By challenging this conviction, and this ideology, knowledge transfer may be made much simpler.

There is, however, a further means of changing the terms of the problem: we may argue that by treating machine intelligence itself as a transparent tool, learners may be taught how to manipulate successfully knowledge which they themselves do not understand. In other words, we may teach the skill of knowledge manipulation as distinct from the skill of knowledge acquisition, leaving knowledge acquisition to machine intelligence, knowledge manipulation to ourselves. The analogy here might be driving a car. We can learn to drive without knowing how the engine works.

Taking the analogy further, we might argue that machine intelligence will do to knowledge what the family car has done to individual mobility, making learners vastly more flexible and powerful knowledge-users than hitherto. In such a scenario the new information technology could provoke a revolution as profound as that sparked by the discovery of moveable type. Such a "reformation" of knowledge may nevertheless be unwanted, precisely because of the radical political effects it would have. Yet in the Reformation we underwent a cultural quantum leap of such magnitude that its contemporary equivalent cannot be ruled out. The precondition for such a quantum leap is that we have the courage of our own intelligence before we seek to render machines intelligent.

The independent learning model which would foster such a view of intelligence, we may characterize as *learner–teacher exchange* which functions as follows:

1. The learner initiates the learning process
2. The teacher assumes the learner to be willing to learn
3. The learner expects to learn from an expert learner, expert in a domain but still learning about it
4. The expert has professional status, but only circumstantially
5. Both expect that learning will be pleasant if demanding
6. The learner is expected to challenge the method of knowledge transfer
7. Once expert himself, the learner will be expected maintain traditions and attitudes of the teacher, especially in regard to the open nature of knowledge exchange

We may schematize this model as follows:

Learner
Willing to learn has
Need which is manifest (not necessarily consciously) as
Problem (How do I satisfy my need?)

Experiments lead to *Solution or frustration*
   If frustration persists
   Try again
   Exchange problem for knowledge
Or *If no solution*
   Go to expert
   Get help and
   Exchange problem for knowledge
   If solution
   Memorise as
   Skill and
   Exchange problem for knowledge

The models I have sketched are clearly analogous to the concepts of *assimilation* and *accommodation*, which Jean Piaget (1932) describes as the basis of children's learning. By assimilation he means the mere imitation of the skills of another, which become the basis of the colonial method. A given procedure is held to be correct and learning becomes a mechanical process of repetition and imitation. By accommodation, he means the acquisition but also the personalization of a skill, transforming what one observes another doing into something of value to oneself. This is the basis of the independent model, in which the learner is at the centre of the learning process and in which, ultimately, all learning is accommodatory.

What might this suggest about machine intelligence? Perhaps something very simple. The challenge of machine intelligence is to replicate in a machine the accommodatory capacity of the human intelligence. The principle of this capacity is that it is transparent and universal. We all have the facility and we use it – for it is the foundation of our individuality. If we construct machine intelligence on a merely assimilatory model then we will replicate colonial learning methods on our machines and so surrender not just the boring and onerous aspects of our working lives to machines but, equally, make over our intellectual and political freedoms to the few people responsible for the machine intelligence systems.

References and Further Reading

Ault R (1977) Children's cognitive development. Oxford University Press, New York
Elam K (1980) The semiotics of theatre and drama. Methuen, London
Goffman E (1967) Interaction ritual. Doubleday, New York
Hall E (1959) The silent language. Doubleday, New York
Hilton J (1987) Performance. Macmillan, London
Levi-Strauss, C (1963) Structural Anthropology. Basic Books, New York
Piaget J (1932) The moral judgement of the child. Routledge, London
Turner V (1969) The ritual process. Chicago University Press, Chicago
Van Gennep A (1908) The rites of passage. Routledge, London (1960)

Chapter 10

Knowledge Acquisition for Expert Systems
Anna Hart

Important issues need raising before detailed knowledge acquisition can take place for designing expert systems. It is futile to try acquiring knowledge and constructing systems unless it is known what it is for.

You need knowledge which is useful for users, where useful means being adequately accurate (as checked by the experts), easily accessible, understandable, relevant. Much of this "useful" knowledge is probable, implicit, tacit, and previously unspoken. There are a variety of methodologies one could use to try and access it but its detailed acquisition will only work if the development team understand why the system is being built and how it should perform.

Introduction

I shall work from the premise that human beings are intelligent, clever and versatile. Although we now have clever machines, which are far more sophisticated than those of a decade or two ago, people are far more versatile than computers, and simple tasks which we perform easily can defeat computers. Expert systems are programs with knowledge in them. This knowledge needs to be acquired before it can be modelled on a computer. However, before detailed knowledge acquisition can take place some very important fundamental issues need to be addressed. This paper outlines some of these issues and describes a realistic role for ensuing expert systems.

Human Experts

Intelligence is difficult to define with any precision. We all recognize, and take for granted, intelligent behaviour. In fact there are many facets of intelligence and a person or artefact can display some while lacking others.

Intelligence is complex and cannot be measured sensibly on a single linear scale. An appreciation of this is important when considering definitions of "intelligent" machines. Authorities vary on descriptions of intelligence. I shall take Hofstadter's (1979) as adequate for this discussion. Intelligent behaviour is characterized by the ability to:

Make flexible responses

Take advantage of fortuitous circumstances

Make sense from ambiguity and contradiction

Assess relative importance

Find similarities

Draw distinctions

Form new concepts from old ones

Formulate new ideas.

These qualities enable human beings to solve problems ranging from everyday activities to highly specialized jobs, and also to learn from experience and example.

Certain people are described as "experts". An expert is an expert *at something*, certainly not everything. Similarly knowledge is knowledge for some purpose. Experts have used their intelligence to develop a high level of expertise in a particular area, by training, education and learning from experience. In general, experts can solve problems with more versatility, efficiency, reliability and confidence than non-experts. Dreyfus (1985) describes the progression from beginner to expert in the following way:

A beginner applies rules to context-free features, and then learns from experience to recognize aspects and select strategies

A proficient performer applies the relevant knowledge intuitively without effort

An expert associates a problem with a prototype and produces a solution without recourse to strategies

I see no reason to question this description, there being evidence from analysis of people playing chess, people solving physics problems, and the rich supply of everyday observation and experience.

One important consequence of this analysis is that it is not easy to get an expert to explain in verbal terms what he is doing and why he is doing it. This involves a retrograde step, and means that he cannot actually tell the full truth. The explanations will often be rationalizations and descriptions of rules and strategies for which he no longer has use. These rules and strategies are of use to other learners, but are not the natural way in which the expert thinks. This is demonstrated when experts reply with comments like:

You get a feel for it

I know that's right

You can sense it's different

Furthermore emotion, motive, fear and sensory perception are likely to play a part in problem-solving and learning, and these are almost impossible to verbalize.

Computer Knowledge

The terms artificial intelligence, expert system and knowledge-based system are commonly used in computer science. They denote an attempt to make computer programs behave intelligently, or to process knowledge. Many of the words are used of both people and machines. It is important that we are not beguiled into thinking that the same word means exactly the same thing in different contexts. If machines can be described as *thinking* then they certainly do not do it in the same way as human beings do. Knowledge, as stored and processed by computers, is a high level of information.

DATA: examples are digits 1,0; numbers 68; character strings AMMA

INFORMATION has more meaning than raw data, e.g., PAY = 42

KNOWLEDGE employs symbols and relationships, e.g. DOG IS A MAMMAL; MAMMALS SUCKLE THEIR YOUNG

In fact, machine knowledge can be more sophisticated than this example. But note one important point. The symbols DOG and YOUNG mean something to human beings. Furthermore, a person would immediately deduce from this pair of statements that dogs suckle their young. Computers do not have this common knowledge, nor do they make such deductions *unless* told to do so. They lack common sense, and any knowledge must be put into them. A knowledge-based system (and this is a much more meaningful term than expert system) therefore:

Stores and manipulates symbols

Uses relationships between symbols

Uses reasoning to draw inference

I summarize this situation by saying that intelligent people are *smart* people and intelligent programs are *smart* programs.

Programs may display some facets of intelligence and even outperform human beings in some respects, but this does not mean that they use the same processes. For example Bayesian models of probability are sometimes useful for handling reasoning in expert systems, but the fact that people find probability theory counter-intuitive means that it is extremely unlikely that they use Bayesian probabilities themselves. Knowledge-based systems provide *models* of knowledge and reasoning techniques; some are good and some are poor. A model is never equivalent to the real entity; it is sometimes good enough for its purpose.

Dreyfus argues that expert systems are certainly not *experts* according to his definition: this should now be evident. I shall therefore propose the following useable definition for an expert system:

A program to help people with tasks involving uncertainty and imprecision, and requiring intelligence and judgment.

A few comments are appropriate:

1. These systems enjoy the advantages and disadvantages of being programs e.g. they need programming and testing, they are indefatigable, objective and repeatable.

2. The systems help rather than replace people. This pre-supposes some understanding of who the users are and their problem-solving capabilities.

3. While the tasks demand judgment it is not immediately obvious that the program should perform that judgment, e.g., the system could prompt, remind, outline pros and cons leaving the user to make a judgment, or the system itself could actually make the decision. These situations are *quite* different and heavily influence the role of the system and its ultimate usefulness.

Uncertainty

The problems which we are talking about are subject to uncertainty and ill-definition. This is a sharp contrast with more conventional information systems where the processes or algorithms can be defined (almost unambiguously) and tested fairly thoroughly, so that correct input should produce correct output.

It is useful to classify the areas of uncertainty in the following way:

Expert. As we have described, the expert will almost surely be unclear about what he does even though he can perform well.

Data/problem statement. There may often be missing or contradictory information. The task may be unclear, some data may not be available or uncertain or imprecise. Typically, the classification of pain as "severe" or not is subject to a multitude of ambiguities and misunderstandings.

Domain. Some uncertainty is inherent in the domain. This is exemplified in medical diagnosis where the same disease may manifest itself differently in different patients. The patient knows whether or not he has been sick or has a rash; the question may be how important that symptom is for a particular diagnosis.

(Solution. For some problem domains there are no acknowledged solutions or experts to evaluate them. This category is in parentheses because it seems ludicrous to construct systems to tackle such problems.)

It therefore follows that expert systems cannot be defined unambiguously or correctly, and the knowledge for them cannot be bounded or complete. Some knowledge may be obviously relevant, other knowledge possibly relevant, and there is always a pool of knowledge which people may use for a hard or new problem without dreaming that they would need it. Consider, for example, the dress of a patient. Clothes are not usually taken into consideration when diagnosing illness. However, if the doctor knows the patient and observes that this usually well-dressed person is untidy then this can influence the resulting judgment.

Systems will be:

Open – they interact with people who receive new problems

Not finished – they never contain all the knowledge

Not correct – they are adequate for use rather than correct. They cannot be proven or even fully tested

These conclusions raise the issues of responsibility, authority, and the role of the system. The questions are obvious:

Why should anyone use the system?

Who tells them to use the system?

Who takes the responsibility in case of error?

If a user is told to obey a system then he cannot be blamed if there is a mistake. Note also that the presence of the system changes the job of the user by making extra knowledge available. The questions of integrity, professional responsibility, legal, moral and social issues are not easily answered. In certain domains it is essential that they are considered from the start.

In summary, a useful system addresses a problem and helps to solve it.

System Development

The stages of system development are shown in Fig. 10.1. As it is impossible to pre-define rigorously what the system will do it needs to be built by incremental development, using prototyping.

After building the initial prototype the team gets comments from the experts and users (who may or may not be the same people). These are comments on the actual system (rather than a paper description of it). The knowledge elicitation and acquisition process is therefore central to the whole process, taking place from very early stages right through the system's life. It can be the major bottle-neck in system development.

At some stage in this cyclic process the system is deemed to be adequate for use according to the relevant assessment criteria. This requirement demands that such criteria have been established. Thereafter users may encounter new problems or unsatisfactory system advice and request modifications to the system. John McDermott who wrote one of the most famous

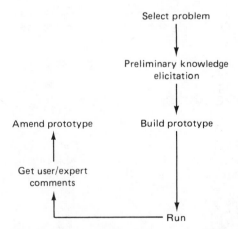

Fig. 10.1. The stages of system development. As it is impossible to write a rigorous specification for expert systems, they are developed by prototyping and successively refined on the basis of comments after use.

systems – XCON – calls this the knowledge maintenance problem. This modification process is not always easy, but may be essential if the system is to retain its usefulness.

Understanding the Problem

This lengthy discussion has been important in order to set the knowledge acquisition process in context. It is futile to set about acquiring knowledge and constructing a system without a realistic idea of what the system is for. Neglecting this will probably lead to the construction of a prototype which never gets used. You cannot evaluate something unless you know what it should do. Evaluation involves checking the adequacy of the knowledge, and its usefulness to the users. It is essential that the early stages of knowledge acquisition tackle the following questions about the problem situation and intended users:

Users
Who are they?
What do they do?
What should they do?
What do they find hard?
What do they find easy?
What do they find interesting?

Experts
What is the nature of their knowledge and how is it used?

Answers to these questions help to determine what is possible, desirable and justifiable. It may take some time, but is essential. At this point it is also appropriate to assess the consequences of the proposed change.

The Knowledge Acquisition Process

This ongoing process involves eliciting the knowledge from the various sources and representing it in the developing system. You need to create an environment in which a model of the knowledge can be built which is useful to the users. Here, useful means:

Adequately accurate (as checked by experts)
Easily accessible
Understandable?
Relevant

This needs to be kept in mind throughout.

Much of the useful knowledge is probable, implicit, tacit and previously unspoken. Other knowledge will be more commonly known. The elicitation process is not at all easy, requiring commitment, interest and enthusiasm from technical specialists, experts and users. It can be embarrassing for the experts to describe heuristics (rules of thumb) and methods. It may sound silly or trivial, and early models may need extensive change. This can be achieved by a team of people or a knowledge engineer (analogous to a systems analyst). The mix of personalities is important as the knowledge is teased out, and people look for patterns, structure, inconsistencies and new ideas. The knowledge engineer prompts, suggests, listens, encourages, argues and acts as a catalyst between experts and users. Intelligence, empathy and communication skills are important as well as knowledge about the domain and computer systems.

Problems can occur if the experts are:

Inaccessible: cannot be freed for periods of time because they are busy, abroad, or unavailable at the same time as other team members

Not really an expert: it is not always easy to identify true experts, who must have knowledge relevant to the problem. Sometimes a team of experts is needed

Inarticulate: completely unable to express and discuss the model of the knowledge

Bored: less enthusiastic about the project or results to date, tired of answering questions and without general commitment

Lie: either deliberately in order to sabotage the project and preserve their status, or subconsciously by inventing plausible reasoning

Experiment: use the project to experiment with the knowledge by "what if" tests.

Methods

In general it is stupid to force experts to use some method which they dislike. The skill lies in finding a method which works in that particular project with those people. Methods have been described elsewhere (Hart 1986; Kidd 1987) and are outlined here.

Background Reading

A lot of information can be obtained from existing documentation which describes methods, problems and terminology. This can help to determine the general framework and background and to establish a working vocabulary for the domain.

Observation

Watching people at work enables you to see what they do rather than what they say they do. They can talk aloud as they work. Video-recording can be useful if the people do not object. Observing experts and users enables you to compare them and get an understanding of the types of problems encountered.

Case Histories

These are often documented case histories (e.g., patient case notes) describing problem descriptions and conclusions. These can be studied away from the expert in a search for general patterns and discussed with the expert to elicit details and explanations.

Simulation/Experiments

If people are willing to co-operate then you can set up a simulation of an expert system consultation by making novices solve problems with access to expert knowledge by dialogue only. This is achieved by telephone or by putting the experts behind a screen so that experts and novices cannot see each other or use body language, but communicate solely by words. (For example, see Shpilberg et al. 1986)

Interviews

The process will normally require extensive interviews which are tape- or video-recorded. Questioning techniques from psychology or social sciences are useful, as are charting methods.

Protocol Analysis

If experts speak aloud while solving problems the recorded comments can be typed up and analysed. This takes hours, but can be fruitful.

Automatic Aids

There are some software tools available that allow the expert to converse with a program which elicits knowledge and builds a model of it. This is good if the knowledge representations are adequate and the expert finds the program easy to use (see Kidd 1987). People are sometimes happier "confessing" to a program but this is countermanded by the fact that a program may be less versatile than a human being.

As general principles it is important to look for structure, and always to bear in mind the explanation facilities and user interface.

Conclusion

This account has set the knowledge acquisition process in context by describing the limitations and possible role of expert systems, and the fundamental issues which must be kept in mind throughout project development. Detailed knowledge acquisition can only work if the development team understand why the system is being built and how it should perform. *Note.* Some of these issues are described in Hart, 1987.

References and Further Reading

Dreyfus SE (1985) Expert systems: how far can they go. The nature of Expertise. In IJCAI 85 Vol.2 p.1306

Hart A (1986) Knowledge acquisition for expert systems. Kogan Page, London

Hart A (1987) Expert systems – a practical introduction for managers. Kogan Page, London

Hofstadter D (1979) Godel, Escher, Bach, an eternal gold braid. Harvester Press, London

Kidd A (ed) (1987) Knowledge elicitation: A practical casebook. Plenum Press, New York

Shpilberg D, Graham LE, Schatz H (1986) EXPERTAX; An expert system for corporate tax planning. Proceedings 2nd International Conference on expert systems, London Sept. 1986. Learned Information, Oxford, UK, pp 99–123

Chapter 11

Knowledge-Based Computer Decision-Aids for General Practice

P. Pritchard

At present there is a huge growth of medical knowledge with increasing specialization in specific fields. This poses a great problem for the general medical practitioner (GP), the sole generalist in medicine, who is unlikely to be able to handle this growth in ten years' time if it continues at this rate. Public expectations and criticism of doctors have increased as people become better informed through the various types of media. Hence there is pressure for the use of computers in the medical profession to assist the doctor, thereby increasing his/her competence.

Most of the communication between GPs and their patients is informal whereas medical records and computers depend mostly on written text. The challenge is to build computer systems that have this informal know-how in a consistent and generally acceptable form. The application of expert systems will only work if the doctor relies on intuition and loosely structured knowledge and ignores overall consistency of the knowledge base to ensure the retention of expertise. The pitfalls will be many if the systems are unreliable, seem remote, and do not take account of the real needs of doctors and patients.

Information Overload in General Practice

Medicine as a whole is pushing out its frontiers at an alarming rate. Knowledge is becoming more plentiful and complex so that hospital specialties and sub-specialties multiply. Each occupies a narrower domain which is now shared with many more non-medical scientists.

General practice occupies the centre ground and tries to exert an integrating and coordinating influence while specialist colleagues race after new knowledge and technology – out of sight over the horizon in some cases. This fragmentation of specialities is inevitable, but as a result, general practitioners (GPs) are now the only generalists in medicine and the quantity and range of information which they need to handle continues to grow. If they can only just cope now it is unlikely that they will be able to do so in 5 or 10 years' time.

Public expectations and criticism of doctors have increased, and people are now better informed, having access to a large number of books, audiotapes and television programmes about health and medicine. In addition, computer literacy is increasing and crude "home doctor" computer programs are already on the market.

Publishers have responded to the GPs' need for more information by producing many more books for them, some written jointly with specialists. Give-away and subscription magazine editors have become more skilled in presenting information in a lucid way. But can GPs read it all, store it away in their brains, and recall just the bit that is needed when faced with a patient who has a problem or an awkward question? For my own part the answer is a clear no (Pritchard 1985a).

When faced with an information overload on this scale, the tendency for the UK GP is to work from a small and familiar knowledge base, and rarely to refer to textbooks when they are most needed – in the consultation. Many doctors think that this would be an admission of ignorance, so they feel obliged to reinforce the image of omniscience, which they do not themselves believe. Shortage of time is also an obstacle. To look up details in textbooks might take several minutes, and if the desired information could not be found, the doctor would feel embarrassed.

A paper-based information system using index cards linked to filed information sheets could suffice, given obsessional zeal and plenty of secretarial help and filing space. Few have achieved it. Is this not just the sort of job that computers are good at? Large data-base-management systems are now in common use, though general practice would probably need a very large data base indeed containing several million medical "facts". That is one facet of the problem, which resembles the "computerized textbook", whereby a large body of information could be instantly accessible to a visual display unit. With optical storage, this has become a reality. But the much more difficult problem remains of helping the doctor to make decisions. There are many reasons why this is an intractable problem.

How Do General Practitioners Make Decisions?

Much has been written about medical decision-making, and some about decision-making in general practice (Sheldon, Brooke and Rector 1985). There is no clear consensus about how decisions are made. Diagnosis is a particularly difficult field of study and Gale and Marsden (1985) considered that the cognitive processes by which general practitioners made diagnoses or defined problems were not well understood. These authors conclude that formal diagnosis does not necessarily precede management action, but rather that they are both a part of the same process.

The use of algorithms (decision trees) and probabilistic methods can be shown to improve clinical inference and, for example hospital referral (Knill-Jones 1977). But "in no way do these methods describe what a clinician, faced with a real patient, actually does" (Gale and Marsden 1985). Algorithms and probabilistic (Bayesian) reasoning is easily handled by computers, whereas the diffuse and poorly understood ways that clinicians reach decisions are less easy to convert into logical form. This chapter aims to discuss ways of bridging this very difficult gap, and to describe the *Oxford System of Medicine* – an ambitious project aimed at helping GPs improve their clinical decision-making and problem-solving ability.

General Practitioners as Experts?

Individual GPs mostly have little idea of how they make decisions, and much of their reasoning seems intuitive. When questioned on how they reached a decision, their knowledge and expertise often could not be articulated (Rector and Dobson 1985). This problem is common to all experts and all expert systems. Experts have a lot of useful knowledge, but ask them how they came to a conclusion, and they may be unable to give a reason, or give an inconsistent one. Experts can use large amounts of knowledge – often in "chunks" – without being aware of the process. When questioned they may give a textbook answer rather than the real one.

As mentioned earlier, medical specialists become expert in an ever-narrowing domain, as specialties split into super-specialties. Yet GPs have to maintain an adequate level of knowledge over a very large field. They have been termed "broad experts" by Rector and his colleagues (Rector et al. 1985). In any specialist field the GP is a non-expert, yet needs a very large amount of accessible knowledge for everyday decisions. There are, in addition, "novices" (e.g. students) and "experts in training" (residents or GP trainees) who have different levels of knowledge, and ways of using it, and their particular needs must not be overlooked.

In every area of medicine in which there are specialists, inevitably their knowledge will be greater than the GPs'. Yet general practice is not just the sum of bits of hospital specialist knowledge. In the areas in which GPs have unique knowledge, they are the experts. This area is increasing, as more knowledge of the social and behavioural sciences becomes an integral part of general practice. So let us take a closer look at knowledge in the context of general practice.

What Do We Mean by Knowledge?

Information includes data – facts on which a decision is to be based; and knowledge – the sum of what is known about a subject. When data is given meaning it becomes knowledge. This knowledge can be formal – as in textbooks, or informal as in the wisdom of a knowledgeable person. Much professional "know-how" is informal and poorly articulated. If the knowledge is subjected to a logical process of inference, it is then part of an expert or knowledge communication system. For such a system to work effectively it must include informal as well as formal knowledge, and this is one of the great challenges of developing knowledge-based systems – how to articulate and include informal "know-how" which is consistent, and generally acceptable. A system which only suited one expert would not be acceptable in general practice.

Techniques have been devised to pry the "know-how" out of experts, and a whole new profession of knowledge engineers has arisen, who know about informal knowledge, but know little about the context. Eventually, one hopes, everyone using knowledge-based systems will become better at articulating their own informal knowledge. These categories and relationships are illustrated in Fig. 11.1.

In spite of the power of modern computer systems, a knowledge-based system can only operate in a narrow domain and represent a very biased model of the world. Human intelligence is still needed to relate a given system to the real world, and to domains of knowledge not covered by the system. Thus a medical knowledge-based decision-aid would have more difficulty in handling the social determinants of illness. To equate machine "intelligence" to human intelligence is liable to mislead, and to raise false expectations of what are at present very primitive knowledge-based decision-aids. Gaines and Shaw (1986) have extended our thinking of levels of knowledge of the world. Their hierarchy is shown in Fig. 11.2.

Events dealt with at Gaines' level 1 would result in reflex, or unthinking action. At level 2, rule-based experience would lead to the development of action rules. At level 3, the development of a model would result in optimal

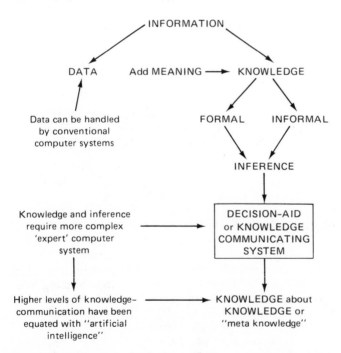

Fig. 11.1. Information, data and knowledge.

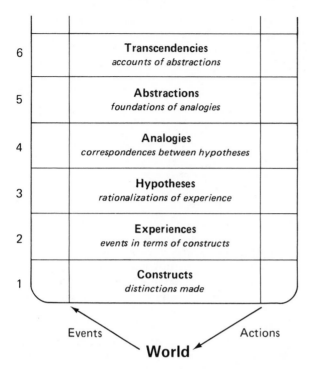

6	**Transcendencies** *accounts of abstractions*
5	**Abstractions** *foundations of analogies*
4	**Analogies** *correspondences between hypotheses*
3	**Hypotheses** *rationalizations of experience*
2	**Experiences** *events in terms of constructs*
1	**Constructs** *distinctions made*

Events   Actions
World

Fig. 11.2. Construction hierarchy of a person modelling a world. (From Gaines and Shaw 1986)

action being computed. At level 4 alternative models would be compared and the optimal model selected. Level 5 would see the development of abstract models which would be refined in the direction of specificity. The highest trancendental level would be even more abstract with distinctions being drawn between abstract models. Conventional computers can be seen to operate at level 1. "Expert systems" would operate at level 2, and possibly 3. The higher levels remain to be colonized by computers. The work of Gaines and Shaw helps to put current "advanced" computer systems into context, and would confirm that they should not be expected to mimic the human brain. Computers should be used for what they do well and not be given human attributes like "intelligence".

General practitioners and patients do most of their communicating by word of mouth and gesture, whereas medical records and computers depend mostly on written text. There is a great divide between spoken and written communication – "orality" and "literacy". Computers have produced a new literacy based on digital signals, whereas the brain developed its analogue thinking processes millions of years before there was any hint of writing. We are now constrained to some extent by having to communicate in print, yet the impact of printing produced a surge in the spread of knowledge, now being overtaken by the tidal wave or avalanche of information technology, with its printed, oral and visual outputs (Hodgkin 1986). Scientific study of the use of gestures and body language in the consultation (Heath 1986) have emphasized how important they are in the doctor–patient interaction, but we are a long way from capturing this information on computer.

Just as early authors had to overcome the difficulties of getting their ideas on paper, so now we face this new hurdle of getting informal "know-how" into a logical setting governed by much stricter rules than those of writing. It is salutary to remember that of the 4000 languages spoken today, only 78 have a "literature" (Ong 1986). How many of those 78 have a "computer literature"?

What Kinds of Knowledge?

For development of medical knowledge-based systems, four kinds and levels of knowledge need to be considered. First, there is knowledge derived from data analysis, which is often statistical or probabilistic. Secondly there is the whole body of formal scientific and clinical knowledge relevant to the domain. Thirdly, there is judgmental or subjective knowledge based on experience and rules of thumb, often difficult to verify yet important in an empirical field like general practice. The fourth kind is higher level strategic or self-knowledge, or knowledge about knowledge. In this category are the professional values which motivate us and guide our decisions, but they are poorly formulated, and vary widely between individuals. The conventional computer is highly appropriate for the first kind of knowledge, but increasing complexity and uncertainty is introduced as we go through the list. So let us look at uncertainty in more detail.

Certainty and Risk in Data and Knowledge

Hard factual data is located at the certain end of the spectrum, and use of this data where appropriate carries a lower risk of error. Formal and rationalized textbook knowledge is less certain, particularly in regard to new untested knowledge and protocols for treating diseases. These varieties are shown in Fig. 11.3.

At the uncertain, high-risk end of the spectrum of knowledge lies much of the everyday work of the GP using subjective data, unverified experience and intuitive clinical impressions. Different methods of drawing inferences from the data and knowledge have been developed, and each has its protagonists. At the low-risk end are algorithms, which are valuable when the topic is appropriate to this approach and the data are available. A computer is only needed to speed their use.

Entirely different methods of reasoning are needed for the different kinds of knowledge. Certain knowledge can often be expressed in algorithms, which hardly need a computer at all, or only a conventional one. In the middle is the probabilistic method of "weighing the odds" – preferably backed by statistics. At the right end lies the informal "know-how" and

CERTAINLY HIGH ←——————→ RISK HIGH		
DATA KNOWLEDGE CONTENT	Hard factual data Certain knowledge	Formal, rationalized knowledge Probability-based knowledge New untested information Agreed treatment protocols	Informal intuitive knowledge Untested experience "Rules of thumb" Unverified data "Clinical impressions" "Wisdom"
INFERENCE METHOD	Algorithms Decision trees Reductionist	Bayesian theory Weighing the odds	Heuristic reasoning Lateral thinking

Fig. 11.3.   Certainty and risk in data and knowledge.

clinical wisdom which we are trying to capture on disc, that need to use rule-based systems or "heuristic reasoning" (rules of thumb). They are often expressed in the "if-and-then" form. The words can be recognized by the computer as "pseudo-English".

If patient has fever
and neck flexion is limited
then meningeal irritation is a strong possibility.

As long as doctors rely on their intuitive knowledge and on loosely structured formal knowledge, as in textbooks, they can get by without bothering too much about the overall consistency of the knowledge base. Even when constructing an algorithm, we realize how much knowledge is missing. But in a very large medical data-base, the logical structure and consistency of the knowledge has to be of an entirely different order. Much work will have to be done on medical knowledge before it can be relied upon in a computer system. But we can start small, and gradually build up a system which can point out inconsistencies and ensure that mistakes are corrected.

Putting Knowledge to Practical Use

Several small knowledge-based systems have been developed in the UK. Few are in general use. Some larger systems have been developed in the USA, but few are functioning outside the research field. Some examples from the UK are listed in Table 11.1 under the headings of problem-centred, patient-centred and policy-centred.

Table 11.1. Knowledge bases and GP program applications in the UK (From Fox and Frost 1985)

Knowledge base	Examples of application
Problem-centred	Terminal care Headache Dyspepsia Diabetes Abdominal pain
Patient-centred	Personal details History Problem list
Policy-centred	Risk assessment Drug selection Investigation Referral

But stitching together a variety of systems will not help GPs who want just one comprehensive system which will cover most of their requirements. A multi-purpose system would need to have most or all of the features shown listed in Table 11.2.

Table 11.2. Features needed in a multi-purpose knowledge-based system for general practitioners (Fox et al. 1987)

Information	Medical library Automated patient record Services available
Assistance	Classification Guide to investigation, treatment and prescribing decisions
Synopsis	Summarize findings Review case. Give opinion on options
Explanation	Ability to question the methods and reasoning involved at every stage

The system would have to be quick and simple to operate. The concepts employed would have to be easily grasped by the GPs operating it. The system should be able to respond to changing requirements as judged by the GP who would be firmly in control of the system, not vice versa. The GP should be able to use the system flexibly, according to the need for information, assistance, review or explanation at any given moment. This framework is the basis for the prototype *Oxford System of Medicine*, an experimental knowledge-based system designed to satisfy the requirements of information processing and decision support in general practice.

The Oxford System of Medicine (OSM)

In 1985 Oxford University Press commissioned a feasibility study of a computerized data and knowledge base providing support for decisions on patient management in general practice (Pritchard 1985b). Early in 1986 a project was set up jointly with the Biomedical Computing Unit of the Imperial Cancer Research Fund to develop a demonstration prototype. Dr John Fox directed the project.

The prototype was successfully demonstrated in September 1985 (Fox et al. 1987), and subsequent development is continuing at the Imperial Cancer Research Fund and Oxford University Press, with the aim of marketing by the mid-1990s a practical system for GPs to use in their consulting rooms. A microcomputer, with enhanced (probably optical) storage would be sited on or near the desk, and could be linked to other systems within the practice. The data would include patients' records, medical (including prescribing) knowledge and information about services.

In order to promote a consistent structure of the medical knowledge base, rather than a collection of separate specialist modules, a unified approach was adopted using the model shown in Fig. 11.3

The outer layer contains information about specific patients, drugs, symptoms and diseases. The next layer has more generic information about diseases and classes of diseases, observations, treatments and investigations. Next comes information about medical methods as listed. Nearer the core is stored information about methods that are independent of medical knowledge and relate to the system design. At the core is PROPS 2 (a knowledge engineering package) written mainly in PROLOG 2.

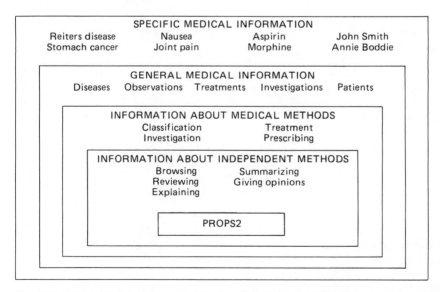

Fig. 11.4. A model of the structure of the first Oxford System of Medicine prototype. Modules are arranged into increasingly specific layers of knowledge with increasing distance from the core (Fox et al. 1987).

The main bulk of medical knowledge in the system (perhaps a million facts or more) is held as a database, not a program. This would facilitate updating. The programs to support the more generic structures are small in comparison, containing perhaps 200–300 rules and would probably need less updating, once the principles of medical knowledge and decision support were established. The process of articulating these principles should advance the logical structure of medical knowledge, but in doing so many inconsistencies could be revealed in the way knowledge is structured. The obstacles to development of a coherent structure of general practice knowledge are formidable, but the *Oxford System of Medicine* offers a clear development path that could advance our understanding of medicine as a whole, as well as benefitting patients involved in everyday decisions.

The User Interface

The user of the *Oxford System of Medicine* would be the individual GP. It would mostly be used in the presence of the patient, which would radically affect the design of the interface. The data and knowledge could well be shared with the patient, but the decision processes might (at least initially) be better hidden from the patient. The GP would tend to follow a "worst case" scenario, such as "could this be cancer?", "what are the possible complications?" or "what drug interactions are possible?". These scenarios might all be rejected, but if shared would leave the patient severely shaken. Though secrecy tends to be counter-productive, there might be a case for the patient having a separate screen which would omit certain processes or diagnoses.

The more the patient can be involved in the decision process the better, once the GP is familiar with the system. The alternative is to have the doctor peering at the screen throughout the consultation, rather than relating to the patient. New technology might allow a horizontal screen on the desk rather than a vertical screen obstructing eye contact.

Though the *Oxford System of Medicine* would be under the control of the GP, there is certain to be parallel development of patient-operated systems, so that in time patients will not accept exclusion from the system. In consequence a "patient-friendly" approach will be an essential design criterion. Experience of general practice computing to date suggests that if the doctor likes the system, the patient will accept it, but the passively accepting patient cannot be taken for granted in the future.

Will General Practitioners Accept a Computerized Decision-Aid?

Evidence of how GPs will react to such a system is difficult to obtain when the system does not exist, and many GPs would find it hard to imagine themselves using one. Yet information technology has shown an inexorable march into banks and other financial institutions, airline booking, retail sales, as well as into many homes and all schools. So the preferred question is not "will it happen?", but "when will it happen?".

Many pitfalls lie ahead if systems are unreliable, or seem remote, or do not take into account the real needs of doctors and patients for information and better-quality decisions. The climate for innovation is changing too. Patients will have access to their own computerized decision-support systems and will expect their doctor to accept and benefit from new technology, rather than be complacent in ignorance. Public expectations of GPs are rising, and litigation is on the increase. These and other factors may produce an irresistible tide for change. The concern of professionals should be to ensure that these changes do indeed benefit patients. Let us hope that doctors will lead the way, rather than be dragged reluctantly into the new era of computers. Francis Bacon (1561–1626) expressed it clearly in his essay *Of Innovation.*

He that will not apply new remedies must expect new evils, for time is the greatest innovator.

Acknowledgements. This paper is based on a presentation to a conference on Computers in General Practice at Bergby Gård on 19 May 1987 organized by Dr Britt-Gerd Malmberg and Dr Ingela Josefson to whom I am deeply indebted. I also wish to thank Dr John Fox and colleagues at the Biomedical Computing Unit, Imperial Cancer Research Fund, and Adam Hodgkin and colleagues at Oxford University Press for their support and help. Mrs Susan Flanders processed the text.

References and Further Reading

Fox J, Frost D (1985) Artificial intelligence in primary care. In: De Lotto I, Stefanelli M (Eds) Artificial Intelligence in Medicine. North Holland, Amsterdam.

Fox J, Glowinski A, O'Neill M (1987) The Oxford System of Medicine. A prototype information system for primary care. (in the press)

Gaines BR, Shaw MLG (1986) A learning model for forecasting the future of information technology. Future computing systems. I: 31–69.

Gale J, Marsden P (1985) Diagnosis: process not product. In: Sheldon M, Brooke J, Rector A (eds) Decision making in general practice. MacMillan, London

Gale J, Marsden P (1987) Medical Diagnosis. From student to clinician. Oxford University Press, Oxford

Heath C (1986) Body movement and speech in medical interaction. Cambridge University Press, Cambridge

Hodgkin A (1986) New technologies in printing and publishing: the present of the written word. In: Baumann G (ed) The written word: literacy in transition. Oxford University Press, Oxford. (Wolfson College lectures 1985)

Knill-Jones RP (1977) Clinical decision making (2). Diagnostic and prognostic inference. Health Bulletin 35A: 213–222

Ong W (1986) Writing is a technology that restructures thought. In: Baumann G (ed) The written word: literacy in transition. Oxford University Press, Oxford. (Wolfson College lectures 1985)

Pritchard P (1985a) The information avalanche: can the general practitioner survive? Practitioner 229: 877–881

Pritchard P (1985b) The Oxford System of Medicine: report on a feasibility study. Oxford University Press (privately circulated document).

Rector A et al. (1985) What kind of system does an expert need? Paper given at Human-Computer-Interface Symposium. HCI 1985 Proceedings. Cambridge University Press, Cambridge.

Rector A, Dobson D (1985) Implications of research on clinical decison-making for the design of decision support systems. In: Sheldon M, Brooke T, Rector A (eds) Decision making in general practice. MacMillan, London.

Sheldon M, Brooke J, Rector A (Eds) (1985) Decision making in general practice. MacMillan, London

Artificial Intelligence and the Flexible Craftsman

Chapter 12

Creativity, Skill and Human-Centred Systems

M. Cooley

We are now at a unique historical turning point. Decisions we make in respect of the new technologies will have a profound effect upon the way we relate to each other, to our work, and to nature itself. Vast computer systems, expert systems, and artificial intelligence systems should not be seen as a technological bolt from the blue. They are in fact part of the historical continuum which is discernible in Europe certainly over the last five hundred years. Scientific and technological change, viewed historically, does seem to embody three predominant historical tendencies. Firstly, there is a change in the organic composition of capital. We tend to render processes capital-intensive rather than labour-intensive. Secondly, it constitutes a shift from the analogical to the digital. The manner in which we perceive our world, analyse it and relate to it is dramatically changed. Thirdly, it is a process in which human beings are rendered passive and the machines become more active. We recall "the more you give to the machines the less there is left of yourself". It is against this historical background that there is an urgent need to view alternative systems, in particular those which may be regarded as human-centred. This paper will describe such human-centred systems.

Introduction

In light of what I shall have to say subsequently, I wish to declare at the onset that I am not opposed to technological change, but stand, I hope, for the best and most appropriate use of it. In saying that, I immediately distance myself from the growing numbers of critics of science and technology, many of whom do seem to take a romantic view and believe that before the Industrial Revolution the populace spent its time dancing around maypoles in unspoilt meadows and writing sonnets in its spare time. It never was like that. There was the squalor, the disease and filth, and science and technology has done much to overcome it. But there were also those elements of our past which should be treasured and linked creatively to modern technology in such a manner as to create a human–machine symbiosis. I do believe, however, that we are now at a unique historical turning point. Decisions we make in respect of the new technologies will have a profound effect upon the way we relate to each other, to our work, and even to nature itself. I share the concerns of the founder of modern cybernetics, Norbert Wiener (1960), when he said that "although machines are theoretically subject to human criticism, that criticism may be delayed until long after it is relevant". By failing to criticize and analyse the systems now being introduced, we may fail to perceive the opportunities for alternative systems which are of a more human-centred variety. Failure to do so may mean that we begin to repeat in the field of intellectual work many of those mistakes made at earlier historical stages when manual work was subjected to the introduction of high-capital equipment.

In the field of manual work, a significant turning point took place in Europe around the fourteenth to the sixteenth century. At that stage there was a growing and discernible separation "between hand and brain" and for the first time most of the European languages introduced the word "design" or its equivalent. It was not that this designing was new but rather that it represented a stage when the conceptual part of work, the design part, was to be separated from the labour process (Cooley 1987). Up to that stage a master-builder would "build" a church. In fact he was not merely building it, he would also design it. Around the time in question, there began to evolve the concept of "designing the church", an activity undertaken by architects, and "building the church", an activity undertaken by builders. In no way did this represent a sudden historical discontinuity, but it was rather the beginning of a certain historical tendency which has still not worked its way through many of the craft skills. The significant feature of this stage is that separating manual and intellectual work provided the basis for further divisions in the field of intellectual work or, as Braverman (1974) put it, "mental labour is first separated from manual labour and then itself is sub-divided rigorously according to the same rules" (Cooley 1987). Dreyfus (1979) locates the root of the problem in the Greek use of logic and geometry and the notion that all reasoning can be reduced to some kind of calculation. He suggests that artificial intelligence probably started around the year 450 BC with Socrates and his concern to establish a moral standard. He says that Plato tries to generalize this demand into an epistemological demand for one might hold that all knowledge could be stated in explicit definitions which anybody could apply. If one could not state one's know-how in explicit instructions then that know-how was not know-how at all but mere belief. He suggests a Platonic tradition in which, for example, cooks who proceed by taste and intuition and people who work from inspiration, like poets, have no knowledge. What they do does not involve understanding and cannot be understood more generally or cannot be stated explicitly in precise instructions. That is, all areas of human thought that require skill, intuition or a sense of tradition are relegated to some kind of arbitrary fumbling. The separation of hand and brain was by no means accepted without controversy. Durer, who was not only a master of the arts but also a brilliant mathematician who reached the highest academic levels in Nuremberg, sought to use his ability to develop mathematical forms which would succeed in preserving the unity of hand and brain. He suggested that it would be possible to develop instruments of labour through the use of which the conceptual part of work could continue to be integrated with the manual part. He had in mind the further development of those instruments of labour which allowed master-builders to define parabolic arches and sine bars which allowed the construction of complex angles, "forms of mathematics which would be as amenable to the human spirit as natural language".

Sadly Durer and those who supported a human-centred solution which linked hand and brain were unable to keep at bay those who sought to separate the intellectual part of work and reify it into abstract and so-called objective functions. Those who had studied these functions and were located in an academic tradition, who could write and talk about design and construction but frequently not in practice undertake it, were gradually held to be more important than those who were capable of doing. Just as today, such people were bitterly resented by those who were capable of embodying hand and brain but found themselves "in an inferior position". Thus we find Leonardo da Vinci saying "they would say that not having learning, I will not properly speak of that which I wish to elucidate. But do they not know that my subjects are to be better illustrated from experience by yet more words?. Experience has been the mistress of all those who wrote well and thus as mistress I will cite her in all cases" (in Kemp 1981). I hold that we are now at a similar historical turning point in respect of intellectual work and the introduction of new technologies and expert systems. Options are still open to us but we are only likely to implement these if we are aware of the consequences of the existing technologies.

Vast computer networks, expert systems, and artificial intelligence systems should not be seen as a technological bolt out of the blue. They are in fact part of the historical continuum which has been discernible in Europe, certainly over the last five hundred years. I hold that in general we have been asking the wrong questions of science and technology and it is not surprising that we have come up with the wrong solutions. Scientific and technological change, viewed historically, does seem to embody three predominant historical tendencies. Firstly, there is a change in the organic composition of capital. We tend to render processes capital-intensive rather than labour-intensive. Secondly, it constitutes a shift from the analogical to the digital. The manner in which we perceive our world, analyse it and relate to it is dramatically changed. Thirdly, it is a process in which human beings are rendered passive and the systems become more active. We recall "the more you give to machines the less there is left of yourself". It is against this historical background that there is an urgent need to view alternative systems, in particular those which may be regarded as human-centred.

In recent years, there has been a growing tendency to assume that there is only one form of technology – that which we may now think of as "American technology". This view constitutes a form of Taylorism at the macro level, a belief in the notion of the "one best way". A richer and more sensitive way to view new technology would be to perceive it as a culture product, and since culture has produced different languages, different music and different literature, why should it not produce different forms of technology, forms which reflect the cultural, historical, economic and ideological aspirations of the society which will use them? Should there not be a form of European technology reflecting European aspirations (if more in the rhetoric than in the reality) of motivation, self-activism, dignity of the individual, concern for quality etc., and reflecting also the reality of the European manufacturing base which is composed predominantly of medium-sized and small-scale units?

To understand these issues, we shall examine the relationships between knowledge and technology which are embedded in the socio-cultural traditions of society. In the context of work culture, the issues of common sense and tacit knowledge are of central importance for AI developments.

Common Sense and Tacit Knowledge

The use of the word "common sense" in some respects is a serious misnomer. Indeed, it may be held to be particularly uncommon. What I mean is a sense of what is to be done and how it is to be done, held in common by those who will have had some form of apprenticeship and practical experience in the area.

This craftsman's common sense is a vital form of common knowledge which is acquired in that complex "learning by doing" situation which we normally think of as an apprenticeship in the case of manual workers, or perhaps practice in law or medicine.

Tacit knowledge is likewise acquired through doing, or "attending to things".

These considerations are of great importance when we decide which forms of computerized systems we should regard as acceptable. It is said that we are now approaching, or are actually in, an information society. This is held to be so because we are said to have around us "information systems". Most of such systems I encounter could better be described as data systems. It is true that data suitably organized and acted upon may become information. Information absorbed, understood and applied by people may become knowledge. Knowledge frequently applied in a domain may become wisdom, and wisdom the basis for positive action. All this may be conceptualized as in Fig. 12.2 in the form of a noise-to-signal ratio. There is much noise in society, but the signal is frequently dimmed.

Another way of viewing it would be the objective as compared with the subjective. At the data end, we may be said to have calculation; at the wisdom end, we may be said to have judgment. Throughout, I shall be

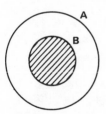

Fig. 12.1. Interaction between subjective and objective. *A* represents the total area of knowledge required to be an expert and *B* the core of knowledge which can be referred to as the facts of the domain (see text for further discussion).

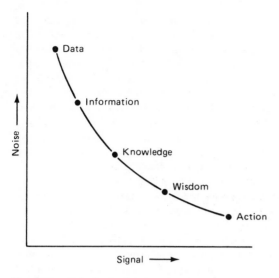

Fig. 12.2.   Cybernetics loop.

questioning the desirability of basing our design philosophy on the data/ information part rather than on the knowledge/wisdom part. It is at the knowledge/wisdom part of the cybernetic loop that we encounter this tacit knowledge to which I shall frequently refer.

The interaction between the subjective and the objective, as indicated in Fig. 12.1 is of particular importance when we consider the design of expert systems. In this context, I hold skilled craftworkers to be experts just as much as I hold medical practitioners or lawyers to be experts in their areas.

If we regard the total area of knowledge required to be an expert as that represented by A, we will find that within it there is a core of knowledge (B) which we may refer to as the facts of the domain, the form of detailed information to be found in a textbook. The area covered by B can readily be reduced to a rule-based system. The annulus AB may be said to represent heuristics, fuzzy reasoning, tacit knowledge and imagination. I hold that well-designed systems admit to the significance of that tacit knowledge and facilitate and enhance it. I reject the notion that the ultimate objective of an expert system should be so to expand B that it totally subsumes A. It is precisely that interaction between the objective and subjective that is so important, and it is the concentration upon the so-called objective at the expense of the subjective that is the basis of the concern expressed in respect of existing systems design.

The Acquisition of Skill

In the processes and systems described below, my concern is not merely with the production but also with the reproduction of knowledge. I frequently refer to the learning by doing, for as a result of this, human beings acquire "intuition" and "know-how" in the sense in which Dreyfus uses these. This is not in contradiction with Polanyi's concept of tacit knowledge; it is rather a description of a dynamic situation in which through skill acquisition people are capable of integrating analysis and intuition. Dreyfus and Dreyfus (1986) distinguish five stages of skill acquisition: i) novice; ii) advanced beginner; iii) competent; iv) proficient; v) expert. I think learning-development situations are absolutely vital, and when someone has reached the knowledge/wisdom end of the cybernetic transformation (see Fig. 12.2) and has become an "expert" in the Dreyfus sense, he is able to recognize whole scenes without decomposing them into their narrow features. Thus I do not counterpose tacit knowledge, intuition or know-how against analytical thinking, but rather believe that a holistic work situation is one which provides the correct balance between analytical thinking and intuition.

Dreyfus and Dreyfus's essential point is to assert that analytical thinking and intuition are not two mutually conflicting ways of understanding or of making judgments. Rather they are seen to be complementary factors which work together but with growing importance centred on intuition when the skilled performer becomes more experienced. Highly experienced people seem to be able to recognize whole scenarios without decomposing them into elements or separate features.

My criticism of the prevailing systems-design methodology and philosophy and "training" stem from the fact that they deny us that "deep situational involvement". Our development tends to be constrained within the novice end of the skill-acquisition spectrum.

Many designers fear to discuss these concerns because they may be accused of being "unscientific". There is no suggestion in this line of argument that one should abandon the "scientific method"; rather we should understand that this method is merely complementary to experience and should not override it, and that experience includes "experience of self as a specifically and differentially existing part of the universe of reality" (Bodington 1978). Such a view would help us to escape from the dangers of scientism which, as was once suggested, may be nothing more than a Euro-American disease (Needham 1976).

This scientism poses a paradox for creativity in science which does not arise from Western scientific methodology which has central to it the notion of predictability, repeatability and quantifiability. Creativity is a subtle process. If you look historically at creative people, they have always had an open-ended, child-like curiosity They have been highly motivated and had a sense of excitement in the work they were doing. Above all, they have possessed the ability to bring an original approach to problems. They have had, in other words, very fertile imaginations. It is usually accepted that imagination is required in music, literature and art. It is less well-recognized that this is equally important in the field of science, and even in the so-called harder sciences like mathematics and physics. Those who were creative recognized this themselves. Isaac Newton said "I seem to have been only like a boy playing on the sea shore and diverting myself in now and then finding a smoother pebble or a prettier shell than ordinary, while the great ocean of truth lay undiscovered before me". Einstein said, "Imagination is far more important than knowledge". He went on to say, "The mere formulation of a problem is far more important than its solution which may be merely a matter of mathematical or experimental skills. To raise new questions, new possibilities and to regard old problems from a new angle requires creative imagination and marks real advances in science." On one occasion, when being pressed to say how he had arrived at the idea of relativity, he is supposed to have said "When I was a child of fourteen I asked myself what the world would look like if I rode on a beam of light". A beautiful conceptual basis for all his subsequent mathematical work (Architect or Bee?). The problem with the notion of the "scientific" entailing predictability, repeatability and mathematical quantifiability is the preclusion of human judgment, intuition, subjective knowledge, sense of feel and imagination in systems design.

Problems of Human–Machine Interaction

The introduction of computers, their enabling technology and accompanying organizational form has given rise to expressions of fundamental concern as to where these forms of technology are taking us (Weizenbaum 1976, 1977). Fears are expressed that by failing to examine the range of technological choices open to us, we are permanently closing off technological options and alternative forms of human organizations which reflect in "a loss of nerve" on the part of engineers and designers (Rosenbrock 1979). Integral to these expressions of concern is the notion that we may be about to repeat, in the field of intellectual work, many of the mistakes we made at such enormous cost at earlier historical stages when skilled manual work was subjected to the introduction of high-capital equipment. Seventy years of scientific management have seen the fragmentation of skills grind through the spectrum of workshop activity, engulfing even the most creative and satisfying manual tasks such as that of tool-making. Throughout that period, most industrial laboratories, design offices and administrative centres were the sanctuary of the conceptual, planning and administrative aspects of work. In those areas, one spur to output was a dedication to the task in hand, an interest in it and the satisfaction of dealing with a job from start to finish.

The notion of scientific management and the basic concepts of the division of labour are so intertwined with Western philosophy and scientific methodology that they are identifiable as far back as Plato, when he argued for political institutions of the Republic on the basis of the virtues of specialization in the economic sphere. If we are unable to quantify something, we like to pretend that it does not exist. To pretend this, we have to rarefy it away from reality and this leads to a dangerous level of abstraction, rather like a microscopic Heisenberg principle, such techniques maybe acceptable in narrow, rarefied mathematical problems but where much more complex considerations are involved, as in the field of design, they may give rise to very real problems and, indeed, to questionable results. "The risk that such results may occur is inherent in the scientific methods which must abstract common features away from concrete reality in order to achieve clarity and systematization of thought. However, within the domain of science itself, no adverse results arise because the concepts, ideas and principles are all interrelated in a carefully structured matrix of mutually supporting definitions and interpretations of experimental observation. The trouble starts when the same method is applied to situations where the numbers and complexity of factors is so great that you cannot abstract without doing some damage and without getting an erroneous result (Silver 1975). Within the design process there is a contradiction at the level of the human–machine interaction itself. The human being may be viewed as the dialectical opposite of the machine in that he or she is slow, inconsistent, unreliable but highly creative. The machine, on the other hand, may be regarded as fast, consistent, reliable but totally non-creative (Cooley 1987). Initially these opposite characteristics were perceived as complementary and regarded as providing the basis for a human–machine symbiosis (Archer 1973). Such a symbiosis would however imply dividing the design activity into its creative and non-creative elements. The notion then is that the non-creative elements may be allocated to the machine and the creative elements left to the human beings. This is a Tayloristic notion and implies at the level of design the equivalent of separating hand and brain within the field of skilled manual work.

The design activity cannot be separated in this arbitrary way into two disconnected elements, which can then be added and combined like some kind of chemical compound. The process by which these two opposites are united by the designer to produce a new whole is a complex and, as yet, ill-defined and ill-researched area. The sequential basis on which the elements interact is of extreme importance. The nature of that interaction and indeed the ratio of the quantitative to the qualitative depends upon the commodity under design consideration. Even where an attempt is made to define the portion that is non-creative, what cannot readily be stated is the stage at which the creative element has to be introduced when a certain part of the non-creative work has been completed. The very subtle process by which designers review the quantitative information they have assembled and then make the qualitative judgment is extremley complex, and much freedom must be left to the designer in doing it.

But there are further problems. The computer can produce quantitative data at an incredible rate. As the designer seeks to keep abreast of this and cope with the qualitative elements, the stress upon him or her can be truly enormous. In certain types of mechanical engineering design examined by the trade union, The Associated Union of Engineering Workers (AUEW) instances were found where the decision-making rate is forced up by approximately 1900. Clearly human beings cannot stand this pace of interaction for long. Experiments have shown that the design efficiency of an engineer working at a visual display unit decreases by 30%–40% in the first hour and 70%–80% in the second hour.

J. Weizenbaum, a professor of computer science at the Massachusetts Institute of Technology, (Computer Power and Human Reason, 1976), highlights the dangers which will surround an uncritical acceptance of computerized techniques. Given the scale and nature of these problems and the exponential rate of technological change within which they are located, it behoves all of us to seek to demonstrate, as Durer did, that alternatives exist which reject neither human judgment, tacit knowledge, intuition and imagination nor the scientific or rule-based method. We should rather unite them in a symbiotic totality.

Unfortunately, there are few examples of such "symbiotic" systems, that is, systems where the pattern recognition abilities of the human mind, its assessment of complicated situations and intuitive leaps to new solutions are combined with the numerical computation power of the computer. They do exist in narrow specific areas, as Professor Howard Rosenbrock of the Control Systems Group at the University of Manchester Institute of Science and Technology (UMIST) has demonstrated with the computer-aided design of complex control systems where the performance is displayed as an inverse Nyquist array on the screen. I have myself described the potential for human-centred systems both in skilled manual work and in design. Furthermore, in the technology division of the Greater London Enterprise Board, we have been working on the development of a expert medical systems through our technology networks. These provide an interaction between the "facts of the domain" and the fuzzy reasoning, tacit knowledge, imagination and heuristics of the expert, and no attempt is made to reduce all these aspects to a rule-based system – the system is seen as something that aids rather than replaces the expert.

The human-centred system will be more efficient than conventional fully-automated systems because the operator can use his skills and experience, with the aid of powerful software tools, to optimize the machine programs and the job scheduling in the cell. It will be more flexible because any job that the machines can cope with can be machined in batch sizes of one upwards. It will be more robust because there is much less dedicated automation and electromechanical complexity, so that when a failure occurs the cell may be instantly reconfiguired to allow for greater human intervention, and the fault will take less time to fix because there are fewer dedicated subsystems. It will be more economical because it is designed to be more efficient, more flexible, have a higher up-time, lower running cost, cost less to buy and take less time to commission.

Human-Centred CIM (Computer Integrated Manufacturing)

An important break through for these human-centred systems has been the recent decision by the EEC's ESPRIT Programme to fund jointly a project to build the world's first human-centred computer-integrated manufacturing system. The project involves nine partners in three EEC countries. Danish teams will research and ultimately design a CAD (Computer Aided Design) system. Partners in Germany will produce the CAP (Computer Aided Production and Scheduling) and the British partners, the CAM (Computer Aided Manufacturing) (with the Greater London Enterprise Board (GLEB) acting as prime contractor and coordinator of the project). It was accepted from the outset that science and technology are not neutral but rather that they embody assumptions of the society which has given rise to them. The project has now been supported by the EEC to a level of £5 million over three years. One of the objectives throughout will be to ensure that the qualitative or subjective judgments of the worker will be treated as valid scientific knowledge and the worker will dominate the machine rather than the other way round. The systems design will be such as to wield upon and enhance the skill, ingenuity and tacit knowledge of the worker. It will reflect the European reality of highly skilled workers and small- to medium-sized companies.

It is held that such a "human-centred" approach could be applied more widely to system design work undertaken by the GLEB in a number of projects that are likewise based on a human-centred approach. Work is proceeding on an expert medical system in which the object is to diffuse knowledge outwards into general practice and the community. The data base will be so structured as to render visible the assumptions to the general practitioner rather than to concentrate knowledge in the hands of a small elite of consultants. Thus it is hoped it will be possible to democratize decision-making, sharing it between the general practitioner and the consultant. More particularly the presentation of the data in the surgery is such as to provide both the patient and the medical practitioner with a range of different treatment options. This, firstly, avoids the major defect in Western scientific methodology; "The notion of the one best way". Also it enforces a dialogue between the medical practitioner and the patient, thus providing a framework in which this relationship can be more democratized. Likewise, an interactive video disc project at GLEB seeks to build upon the knowledge and culture of ethnic minorities, rather than providing them with a series of "commands". It is hoped that such work on expert systems will be ultimately integrated into manufacturing systems since, of course in the best sense, a skilled worker on the shop floor is as much an expert as is a medical practitioner or a lawyer. In designing such systems no attempt is made to reduce the knowledge of the practitioner to a totally rule-based system. It is accepted that there are facts of the domain and that these provide the basis for a rule-based "core" (see Fig. 12.1) but that surrounding this there is tacit knowledge, heuristics, fuzzy reasoning, intuition, imagination and that these cannot or should not be reduced to a rule base. Thus the systems are designed to create a dialectical interaction between the rule-based core and the rest. In designing such systems an attempt is made to concentrate on that part of the cybernetic loop which is knowledge and wisdom-based rather than on the data and information end (Fig. 12.2). Thus we are concerned with minimizing noise in the system and enhancing signal. This model of knowledge should provide a basis and a focus for designing computer systems which build upon the skill of the worker.

References and Further Reading

Archer L B (1973) Computer Design Theory and Handling the Qualitative. Royal College of Art, London

Braverman H (1974) Labour and monopoly capital. The degradation of work in the twentieth century. Monthly Review Press, New York.

Bodington S (1978) Science and social action. Alison and Busby, London

Cooley MJE (1987) Architect or bee: the human price of technology. Hogarth Press, Chatto & Windus Ltd (edition), London

Dreyfus HL (1979) The Limits of Artificial Intelligence. Harper & Row, New York

Dreyfus HL, Dreyfus SE (1986), Mind over machine: the power of human intuition and expertise in the era of computers. New York Free Press, New York

Kemp M (1981) Marvellous works of nature and man. Dent & Sons, London

Licklider JCR (1960) Man – computer symbiosis. IRE Trans Electron 2: 4–11

Needham J (1976) History and human values In: Rose H, Rose S (eds.) The radicalisation of science. Macmillan, London

Rosenbrock H (1979) The Redirection of Technology. Proceedings, IFAC Conference.

Silver RS (1975) The misuse of science. New Scientist 166: 956

Weizenbaum J (1976) Computer power and human reasoning. WH Freeman, San Francisco

Weizenbaum J (1977) The Future of Control. Proceedings 6th IFAC Congress, Boston 1976. Automatic 13: 389–392

Wiener N (1960) Science 131: 1355.

Chapter 13

Professional Knowledge and the Limits of Automation in Administrations

T. K. Karlsen and Maria Oppen

The aim of this chapter is to consider the limits to rationalization and, therefore, the barriers to further devaluation of professional skills. If these limits are not recognized, an erosion in special qualifications acquired through professional training may emerge, thereby adversely affecting the quality of services. It is important to look at how far-reaching are the consquences of using information technologies as a means to distribute tasks and functions of administrative work and to substitute human labour for the devaluation of skills. Examination of two case-studies leaves little doubt that increased rationalization through automation of various parts of the decision-making process causes erosion of skill and professional knowledge, increased division of labour destroying that element of skill gained from the organizational culture, and hence limits the scope for action (inflexibility as technology does not accept the contradictions of social reality) and the ability to act with competence in a context. Only through "careful" strategies of rationalization can flexibility and effectiveness of administrative action be maintained or improved in an increasingly complex environment.

The Problem

For quite some time, strategies of rationalization in administrations have been predominantly concerned with executive assistant functions such as collecting, reproducing, arranging and controlling data or information resulting from both the division of labour and the subdivision of work. With the development of computer technology in the areas of software, ergonomy and artificial intelligence more user options will be available and introduced, which will affect the nature of administrative work: not only the collection and analysis of information, but also decision-making. The use of information and communication technology in the workplace, e.g., the paperless office with electronic data-processing in conversational mode, is leading to an increase in the automation of professional work. The quantitatively and qualitatively most important part of administrative work is no longer considered to be difficult to automate and to rationalize. An ever-larger part of central professional activities will be computer-aided or fully computer-controlled.

The automation of qualified-professional activities will require a large organizational restructuring of the work processes of administrative activities. With automation, office tasks will increasingly be integrated using computer systems. Technically determined universalized access to previously separately stored and processed information enables a new range of forms of work, organization, cooperation and control.

Maintaining or even intensifying the traditional division of labour following from Taylorism will mean a further division of routine work and office tasks, an increasing emphasis on efficiency, low subject-specificity requirements and poor training opportunities. A reintegration of the processes of work can be achieved if human potentials, such as a willingness to learn, creativity, flexibility and personal responsibility are exploited (Gottschall et al. 1985).

Case-studies into the various forms of rationalization in various sections of administrative work do not indicate any uniform trends of development. Rather, distinctive levels of automation and various concepts of rationalization exists side-by-side, according to societal configurations and a company's strategies, and opportunities for office staff involvement. Hypotheses about predominant trends in professional qualifications in the service sector, particularly in the area of public administration, also reflect such developments.

There is a strong argument that computerization causes de-skilling: the domain of skill will be taken over by computer systems to an increasingly larger extent. On the other hand, there is the argument that the technology raises professional status, increases skills and leads to the greater efficiency needed to deal with the increasingly complex demands on administrative action. Another argument of "polarization" points out the adverse effects of developments on professional qualifications, especially concerning societal and internal company functions and areas of responsibility. It is suggested that recent developments would mean that professional skills will increasingly be replaced by more general and unspecific job requirements as a result of the use of electronic data-processing.

In this chapter, our aim is to consider the limits of rationalization and hence barriers to further devaluation of professional skills, by the use of case-studies. These limits will be discussed with respect to maintaining or raising the quality of services, often one of the stated reasons for reorganization in administrations. If these limits are not noticed and acknowledged there will be so great an "erosion" in the skills acquired through professional training that the administrations may be incapable of being flexible, adaptable and having a client-oriented modernization. As a result, the quality of services will be markedly lowered.

We are particularly concerned with the interrelationship between the quality of administrative services and the structures of tasks and qualifications of administrative employees. That relationship has a crucial role which has been underestimated until now in the debate surrounding the use of new technology. It is especially important in the area of communicative administrative services, where the process of the provision of services takes place through interaction with the client or customer. In general there is a high degree of division of labour among office staff as well as between personnel, and computers tend to limit the scope of independent thought and action, hence causing de-skilling.

This does not only result in increasing demands on clients, whose administrative requests are dealt with inadequately within a highly divided process of work. To them, the result of administrative action becomes less "transparent" and controllable because of standardization and formalization of the process. Hence, a comprehensive consideration and processing of clients' claims and rights can be hindered. This hindrance can be caused either by employees who are no longer able to give comprehensive and thorough information and advice because of deteriorating skills, or by clients because of increased barriers to communication and access to their entitlement to benefits. If, as a natural side-effect of rationalization, the quality of services is reduced, there may develop contradictions between demands on the function of services to guarantee the social process of reproduction and the real effectiveness of services. This is particularly true if a potential loss in effectiveness coincides with increasing demands in certain parts of society.

Based on the results of case-studies in two countries (Federal Republic of Germany and Sweden) we shall elaborate further on the destructive effects of the application of information technology on the development of professional skills in public administrations. There is no intention to consider all the consequences of technological applications on the development of professional qualifications or to claim that no other factors affect professional skills. Rather, the intention is to point out how, under certain conditions, the application of information technologies as a means to distribute tasks and function of administrative work and to substitute for human labour, can have far-reaching consequences for the devaluation of professional skills in public administration. Therefore, the initial hypothesis is that expert knowledge or professional skills can only be preserved or developed if they are continuously used in the actual work situation.

Learning from Experience and the Computerization of Administrative Work

Professional skills in public administrations can be divided into two kinds of knowledge. Firstly, knowledge of administrative tasks fixed by statute law, instructions and guide-lines and secondly, knowledge of that section of the social environment to which the particular functions of the administration concerned is assigned. Administrative activities of skilled employees consist in essence of the application of politically established normative rules upon concrete "cases".

Expert knowledge or professional skills in administration can be classified analytically into three types:

1. Theoretical knowledge: reproducible knowledge of fundamental functions and their role in the area of reponsibility. In public administration, this would be knowledge of the legislation which regulates the activities of the administration concerned and also knowledge of the societal context.

2. Practical knowledge: knowledge of the application of administrative tools and material for work (including computers) and how to carry out administrative functions (e.g. setting up records or files, conducting interviews and giving advice, doing calculations, writing memos etc.).

3. Experience-based and "tacit" knowledge: knowledge that is not fully explicit, and emerges from the application of both the theoretical and practical knowledge to individual cases in everyday work and can be applied more-or-less unconsciously in similar situations.

For the formation and acquisition of this "knowledge" from experience certain processes of feedback are necessary; these will vary according to the employee's position within the organization concerned. This knowledge and its quality can, in principle, only be acquired through carrying out professional activities. It is therefore determined by tasks, tools, work conditions, and the like. Theoretical and practical knowledge are thereby transformed into manageable instruments for everyday professional activity and work routines become natural habits. Experience-based knowledge is a necessary component of skill in order to support, facilitate, master, or even to carry out professional activities.

Furthermore, this element of skill is closely connected with individual attitudes and ordinary behaviour. Consequently, it is not formally expressed when describing positions and occupational tasks. It can only be acquired to a certain extent through formal vocational or professional training. This means that the formation and use of this type of knowledge depends more or less strongly on the "atmosphere at work", i.e. on the work culture. If this knowledge is to be used positively for achieving internal company objectives, not only is the ability to socialize in the workplace required, but work conditions that promote the use of this knowledge are also necessary.

Thus, experience-based knowledge is always related to experience gained through the application of vocational qualifications, whether they are of a theoretical or of a practical nature. Those elements that cannot be formalized will be labelled as tacit or implicit knowledge according to Polanyi (1985).

In complex relations involving a great deal of communication, as in that between administrators and clients, very subtle indications (visual and acoustic) are necessary for the effective performance of office tasks and advice services. They are implicit and are assumed for other areas of work (Jazbinsek 1986). The professional employee does not have to decide consciously what particular information he or she is going to select to complete his or her tasks. Therefore, this notion has the problem that it entails indefinable learning processes and therefore knowledge which cannot be described in relative terms. Thus, it always characterizes just the subjective remainder of expert knowledge, which cannot be formalized.

The formation and use of experience-based knowledge in applying administrative rules to individual cases is the prior condition for an efficient mediation between administrative regulations and "cases at issue". Furthermore, experience-based knowledge, coupled with discretionary power in administration, constitutes the basis for effective and continuous adaptation of the application of rules to a continuously changing environment. Hence, the performance of public administrations gains in flexibility and quality. One organizational condition for this is that the bearers of professional skills are settled in positions as mediators or "gatekeepers" at interfaces between the administration and their social environment. With appropriate allocation of time for extensive communication they can then use the legally established discretion (Karlsen 1985).

One prerequisite for integral client-orientated administrative action is that the practical areas of responsibility for public officials be designed in such a way that at least a large part of the knowledge they acquire through vocational training is demanded within their professional practice. A further division of labour and increased specialization means that, in practice, learning from experience can only be developed in the domain of a narrow sector. In the course of time, skilled labour will lose track of the overall processes of administrative work. As this occurs, uncertainties can arise, which can only be compensated for by the individual skilled employee following rules strictly. This, on the other hand, leads to a loss in flexibility and thus in the potential for progress in the entire administration.

The realization of such an organizational principle is neither practically nor logically dependent on the use of technology. In practice, however, the use of visual display units, operating in conversational mode, at the individual workplace, does make for an extreme and precisely controlled division of labour, which can empirically be observed as one of several possible lines of development (Diehl and van Treek 1982; Schafer 1983; Schreyogg, Steinmann and Zauner 1978). In principle, the application of such technology may have negative effects on the development of skills of administrative staff. These effects will be referred to as "distributive effects" because they arise through the utilization of technology to distribute work.

Furthermore, from the definition of experience-based knowledge and its implicit unconscious elements, it follows that such knowledge cannot be formalized and hence cannot be automated. Through informal communication processes, problems can be handled in relation to persons and situations. While the human method of integrating operational sequences is a social, context-orientated process, the essential rules can be distinguished from the irrelevant, mechanically processed information and formulated into algorithmic standardized models (Buck 1985).

Technology does not accept the contradictions of social reality, since it is incompatible with such ambivalent logic. In this respect, efforts to automate aspects of specialist knowledge cannot achieve the same results. If the decision-making processes are taken over by computers, parts of the tasks will be separated from the functions of professional officials with the consequence of a considerable loss in their competence. We shall describe this as the "substitutive effects" of the use of technology.

Distributive Effects of the Use of New Technology

We shall now discuss some findings of a research project on "information technology and the quality of social services' currently being undertaken at the Science Centre, Berlin. They illustrate how the use of technology as a method of reinforcing the division of labour can have an effect on the development of professional skills and on the quality of services within a particular type of public administration. In the field studied, that of public health insurance, the use of computers shows the effects on the distribution of work (distributive effect). Here the decision-making of officials in charge has not been programmed. The files of members and services, which previously served as the basis of administrative case-work, to control entitlements of insured persons and to register benefits claimed, have been stored. In the course of office automation, the files have been put at the officials' disposal in the form of on-line real-time retrieval systems.

Previously, since each file-card had only existed as one physical copy a definite form of organization had been predetermined, mainly based on the cost of labour: the responsibility of each official for one portion of an alphabetical listing of insurants. Whilst a vertical division of work existed within single teams (record keeping, registration of new cases, decision-making), horizontal specialization into special areas or types of services was thus quite effectively halted. With the use of visual display units, temporal and spatial barriers for horizontal specialization were abolished. Data on insured persons became increasingly accessible and an arbitrary specialization or reintegration of professional tasks was made possible.

Within the health insurance organizations examined, various options for reorganizing the service have been used in different directions, with accordingly specific effects on the development of skills. One empirically – established type of organization of work stands out, due to its extreme division of labour. Within each subdivision (section) not only did a vertical division of work exist between assistant activities and actual administrative case-work, but there was also a far-reaching horizontal division of work into particular specialist areas. Besides this, there was a hierarchical division between dispositive and executive activities. In addition, a functional division of work was introduced, where only assistant officers (semi-skilled labour or employees with the lowest standard of vocational training) had been assigned to conduct face-to-face advice and telephone information services for insurants.

Here, the work situation of highly remunerated employees, who had completed professional training at the most advanced levels, showed two characteristics; firstly, competence in decision-making in a narrow specialized field (hospital treatments, sickness benefits, maternity grants, dentures etc.) and, secondly, an isolation from direct contacts with clients. Thus, in practice, the organization of work prevented the use of special practical and theoretical knowledge which professionals had acquired through vocational training when confronted with clients' needs and, thus, the opportunity to develop them further. In this manner, the formation of knowledge was not just restricted to closely defined areas of work, but also within those areas, which had been directed to formal and definite application of rules (completeness and proper filling-in of files, correct calculation of benefits in cash and contributions, obedience to prescribed severence of operations in case processing).

Among these professionals, the feeling of operative competence in the area of their responsibility (the view that work assigned can be mastered) was high. When questioned as to whether they could imagine themselves taking over tasks of other professionals, the answer, however, was a resounding "no". This indicates that those parts of expert knowledge acquired through professional training, but not made use of for some time – one year in this case – ceased to be a productive asset for the organization. Opinions of highly qualified administrative experts differed also over the question of whether they themselves could take over advice services for clients. If positive answers were given, the explanations referred to aspects of job enrichment: "It would be an interesting change from paper-work".

The underlying opinion of positive as well as negative answers was that case decisions, which constituted the tasks of the professionally-trained officers at the time of the questioning, involved much greater responsibility than advice services. They believed that there was little to advise about, anyway, because legal regulations and guide-lines seemed to be clear to everyone. Among the semi-skilled advisers, who also had to give advice within the area of responsibility of the professional officials, a willingness to take over other areas of work was expressed by all persons interviewed (even if they had not been trained in those areas). In their opinions, advisory service had its most important justification in the ignorance of the clients.

These findings indicate that, over a number of years, a high degree of division of labour with corresponding administrative specialization leads to a loss of knowledge among professional officials since the specialist knowledge they acquire through professional training is not demanded in the work environment. The period of time in which this development takes place probably varies from administration to administration depending on the complexity of the specific theoretical knowledge. Moreover, qualified administrative work is only possible if the expertise needed for dealing with complex regulations and formalized language is built up in conjunction with the transformation of such regulations and language into client-related information and advice.

The separation of the recording of information gained through interaction with the client from the decision-making process can lead to a situation where relevant case information is not given its true weight, by ignoring the social context. Formalistic and unrealistic attitudes to work can be the consequence as suggested by the description of clients as "cases" and in the undervaluation of needs for advice services. This totally contradicts the explicitly-stated goal of public health insurance to utilize computers for improving client-orientated and advice centres.

On the contrary, the assignment of tasks requiring more extensive knowledge than that gained through vocational training appears not only to preserve the knowledge already acquired, but also seems to produce incentives to learn, as can be shown in the case of the semi-skilled advisers. However, these developments have set limits, which can only be overcome through an extended training concept of a different strategy for the use of human labour. Interrelations like those shown above can be described as indirect effects of the use of technology: effects due to concepts for the application of technology which are not determined by technological constraints but are outcomes of the relative strength of interests and negotiation processes as well as of available experience and levels of competence.

Substitutive Effects of the Use of New Technology

In this section the substitutive effects of the use of computers, which are in principle mediated through concepts, will be examined. Our concern is about the direct substitution of professional qualifications by computer programs, whereby normative rules of administrations (that is, the theoretical knowledge of administrative employees) become operationalized and translated into computer programs. In this way, expert tasks will be reduced to data input and control of output, while the central activity of adminstrative work, the application of norms, will be taken over by computers. With these so-called "deontic" systems (Bing and Schartum 1985) a conflict can emerge between the framework of norms in administrations and the constraints of computer algorithms. This can lead to changes in the application of rules, which can be considered as the direct effects of computerization.

From the following case-study in Swedish forestry offices (Göranzon et al. 1982; Göranzon 1985) substitutive effects on professional qualifications due to the use of computers can be highlighted. Forestry officers have the task of calculating the value of woodlands and lumber before purchasing and selling and the calculations serve as the foundations for price negotiations between seller and buyer. An exact calculation of the values is of great importance as losses must be avoided when selling wood to sawmills or papermills, which in turn calculate the value of the wood on finely graded criteria.

The multitude of complex processes of calculations, previously carried out by officials, have now been automated. The computer programs were based on a standardization of the principles and rules for fixing the values of plots of woodland and lumber, varying them according to the object of the calculation. They were inflexible and did not allow modifications of calculations that forestry officers, from their specialist knowledge, regarded as relevant and necessary for a realistic fixing of prices. This was partly due to problems of algorithms and partly due to lack of participation by the systems designers and so valuations which did not correspond to reality could be reached. Mainly for this reason, the older forestry officials avoided working with computers. They left it to office assistants to feed the computer with results of investigations they had made by hand: they gave up, therefore, continuous control of program variables and had no influence on individual cases from valuation to decision-making: they had no control over the final result of their work.

Over the years, this lack of control over parts of the process and the outcome of evaluations has led to a gradual loss of the knowledge necessary for other activities. Since the calculations of forestry officials served as foundations for negotiations of prices for purchasing and selling wood, it was also part of the officials' task to explain and justify the methods and results of evaluations when dealing with their customers. In the course of time, they could no longer understand how computerized calculations had been made and to what extent their own calculations had been taken into account, so advice or negotiations with customers became increasingly difficult. The process of the destruction of professional skills through the use of computers, resulting in the deviations from reality in forestry officials' calculations and consequently in the output of forestry offices, can be characterized in three stages:

First stage: Discrepancies between the evaluations forestry officials would carry out on the basis of their professional training and the evaluations computer programs would allow for, lead to demotivation and a retreat from contacts with computers. This leads to a breakdown in the feedback loop. This loop is vital for maintenance of the knowledge concerned as well as for realistic evaluations of results, namely the feedback from an empirical individual case to general rules of evaluation. Since the users of the computers have no professional training, their activities cannot contribute to the modification of rules through empirical control using individual cases.

Second stage: Losing track of parts of the process of evaluation gradually leads to a loss of ability to explain the results of calculations, which is one of the prescribed tasks of forestry officials. This undermines their capability to negotiate with customers and can lead to poor results in administrative action. Apart from this effect, the situation of negotiation also becomes more difficult, due to increased complexity of explanations resulting from the use of computers.

Third stage: Recently appointed forestry officials learn about the evaluation of woodland and wood in relation to existing computer programs and no longer through a method orientated around the actual objects of evaluation. Their efforts will be concentrated on bringing their empirical investigations into line with existing computer programs. If one takes into consideration that user instructions quite frequently do not give any information about principles of design and modes of operation of a computer system, it becomes obvious that altered usage and opportunities for adaptation are hindered. With the loss of understanding by these officials, effects and consequences of the use of computers are no longer possible to evaluate critically.

In this example, there was computerization of the objects of evaluation and the criterion of profit was the yardstick for the quality of estimates carried out. Thus erroneous evaluations on the part of the forestry offices through the use of electronic data-processing can be relatively easily discovered. However, these systems will also be increasingly used within social security organizations for decision-making processes and application of norms, which limit the development and maintenance of flexible and adaptable professional knowledge. Thereby, a loss of reality in the perception of the environment and in dealing with social problems becomes considerably more difficult to overcome. Reasons for this are that the clients are in a position of control whereas they are normally dependent on services from these monopolistic organizations and that generally social realities are concerned and not material quantities.

Conclusions

The results of two case-studies show a marked tendency for the destruction of professional knowledge in the area of qualified administrative work. This can be regarded as a consequence of certain technological and organizational management decisions and "production concepts", for administrative services. The restrictive division of labour and hierarchization to manage computer-aided administrative work, as well as the application of computer systems to automatize professional decisions, involves an "erosion" of specialist knowledge. While the working conditions offer fewer options for the application of theoretical and practical knowledge acquired through professional training, this knowledge will gradually deteriorate. Experience-based knowledge, which depends on the active and comprehensive use of knowledge acquired through training, can therefore be developed only to a limited degree. When required, practical and theoretical expert knowledge can be improved or acquired through measures of further education and training, but such measures cannot revitalize experience-based knowledge. Thus, certain competences and capabilities can be lost forever.

In the longer term, such trends in development can result in various problems for administrative work. These can be described as internal and external consequences of the devaluation of professional skills. Internally, a lack of expert knowledge can prove to be a restriction on processes of restructuring to adapt administrative action to changing demands from the environment. A high degree of specialization and a corresponding limitation of experience-based knowledge among professional administrators can restrict the flexibility of the organization in the use of human labour and in the reorganization of tasks and profiles of job demands.

Equally undermined are the preconditions for officials to occupy positions and to carry out functions which involve fewer tasks open to standardization and rationalization. In the area of activities like discretionary decisions, negotiations with major customers and special cases, or managing disruptions in work routine it can be assumed that expert knowledge and professional experience still constitute the central basis of work activities. Furthermore, with future systems design, devalued parts of professional knowledge will no longer be available as a source of corrective control and productivity, as was described in the Swedish case-study regarding young officials.

External consequences of "erosion" in professional knowledge are the possible unplanned declines in the quality of services for clients or customers. Through losses in knowledge and competence on the part of specialist officials, parts of service work will be passed over to the clients, resulting in their increased responsibility for and dependence on administrative work. At the same time, opportunities for control and influence on the process of service production and on the outcomes will be made more difficult. Because of the extent of division in the work of administrative routine, as well as the use of complex systems for decision-making, there is a risk that comprehensive context-oriented dealing with clients' demands by administrations cannot be guaranteed.

If one therefore wants to avoid a scenario where administrations operate like closed circuits, it seems reasonable to suggest doing without the use of computers as described above. Computers should not be used for any further automation of professional activities and any further specialization of administrative work as long as long-term social effects on the development of knowledge of employees as well as on the quality of services are insufficiently known. At present, one has to start from this premise, particularly if the thesis from the Swedish case-study holds true that professional skills and experience-based knowledge remain intact for 4–5 years after technological and organizational restructuring and then suddenly disappear. Thus the damaging effects of the above-treated modes of computerization to professional knowledge only become noticeable with a corresponding temporal delay, which calls for a high degree of caution to avoid irreparable destruction of knowledge. Only through "careful" strategies of rationalization can flexibility and effectiveness of administrative action be maintained or improved in an increasingly complex environment.

References and Further Reading

Berger U, Offe C (1984) Das Rationalisierungsdilemma der Angestelltenarbeit. In: Offe C.: Arbeitsgesellschaft-Strukturprobleme und Zukunftsperspektiven. Frankfurt/New York
Bing J Schartum DW (1985) Datenverarbeitung und Durchsetzung von Ansprüchen in Organisationen der sozialen Sicherung. In: Karlsen Th, Kühn H, Oppen M (eds) Informationstechnologie im Dienstleistungsbereich – Arbeits-bedingungen und Leistungsqualität. Ed. Sigma Bohn, Berlin
Buck B (1985) Berufe und neue Technologien – über den Bedeutungsverlust berufsförmig organisierter Arbeit und Konsequenzen für die Berufsbildung. Soziale Welt 1
Diehl RO Van Treek W (1982) Sachbearbeiter und Computer im Leistungswesen der Ortskrankenkasse. Kassel: Arbeitspapiere der Forschungsgruppe Verwaltungsautomation Heft 20
Göranzon B (1985) Datoranvändning för skogsvärdering – en fallstudie. In: Göranzon B (ed) Datautveclingens filosofi. Stockholm
Göranzon B et al. (1982) Job Design and Automation in Sweden – Skills and Computerization Swedish Center for Working Life, Stockholm
Gottschall K, Mickler O, Neubert J (1985) Computer-unterstützte Verwaltung – Auswirkungen der Reorganisation von Routinearbeiten. Frankfurt/New York
Jazbinsek D (1986) Vom blauen zum weißen Kragen – die Informatisierung der Fabrik und ihre Folgen für die Industriearbeit. Bielefeld: Universität (mimeo)
Karlsen TH (1985) Die Beziehung zwischen ärbeit und Leistungsqualität in sozialpolitischen Institutionen. In: Karlsen TH, Kühn H Oppen, M (eds): Informations-technologie im Dienstleistungsbereich – Arbeitsbedingungen und Leistungsqualitat. Ed. Sigma Bohn, Berlin.
Polanyi M (1985) Implizites Wissen. Frankfurt am Main.
Schäfer W (1983) Organisationsstruktur und Qualität der Arbeit in Massenverwaltungen. Kassel: Arbeitspapiere der Forschungsgruppe Verwaltungsautomation Heft 33
Schreyögg G, Steinmann, H, Zauner B (1978) Arbeits-humanisierung fur Angestellte. Job Enrichment im Verwaltungs- und Dienstleistungsbereich. Stuttgart/Berlin/Köln/Mainz

The Changing Nature of the Engineering Craft Apprenticeship System in the United Kingdom

M. Cross

This chapter discusses the changing nature of apprenticeship training and describes some of the principles and weaknesses of the system of supplying engineering craftsmen in the UK. The "new" approach to craft training in the UK focusses on aspects such as duration, contents, standards, assessment, relevance, and openness. For example, training needs are increasingly seen in terms of mending and mental rather than making and manual skills and knowledge. This development requires that job structures should transcend existing rigid job boundaries and take into account such features as versatility, adaptability, and diagnostic ability. While there is a move to create a high degree of common skilling amongst engineering craftsmen there is also the recognition of a need to produce both "skill" and "process system" specialists. New apprenticeship in the UK is being developed with three recognizable streams: specialist craftsmen; operator craftsmen; and, process systems craftsmen.

Introduction

To be an engineering craftsman is to be more than an ordinary job holder. It denotes achievement, skill and status. It represents membership of a powerful trade union with a culture and tradition rooted in times pre-dating the Industrial Revolution. Attempts to tamper with the time-honoured method of craft training (craft education has only more recently become a major concern) is no easy matter. Yet if the period from the mid-1960s to the present time is considered, relatively rapid progress has been made in producing a programme of nationally recognized training and education for engineering craftsmen when compared to the previous decades.

The 1960s to the present day

One of the most significant developments has been the reduction in the period of many engineering craft apprenticeships from seven to four years.

In terms of the context, organization and delivery of the apprenticeship as a continuous period of training and education, the changes which have been introduced can be demonstrated by comparing the characteristics of engineering craft apprenticeships up to the early 1960s to those reforms introduced by the Industrial Training Board system (Cross 1985).

The changes in the principles of the engineering craft apprenticeships between the early 1960s and today can be summarized (Table 14.1). The apprenticeship programmes run on the 237 manufacturing sites considered in the study drawn upon by this paper[1] have all been based either directly, or indirectly, upon the Engineering Industry Training Board's modular system with suitable modifications to meet local needs. The rigour with which these training principles are adhered to, and the prescribed tasks within each module undertaken varies. The result of this situation is that the existing stock of engineering craftsmen have been trained under widely differing conditions, and may as a result require a training input to bring them up to today's standard.

Table 14.1 Principles of the engineering craft apprenticeship: the 1960s to the present day (from Cross (1985) and Wellens (1963))

Principle	Pre-1960s	Post-1960s
Duration	Time-based 4–7 years	Standards-based 4 years
Certification	None	National scheme
Age of entry	Rigidly fixed: 16 years old	Still fixed: 16 and 17 years old
Education	Minimum, not mandatory	Integral component
National control	CGLI	EITB, BTEC, CGLI
Craft breadth	Uni-craft	Still mainly uni-craft
Craft status	Low	High
Instuction	Ad hoc	Systematized
Future development and growth	Self-contained	Self-contained: base upon which to build

The aspects of the "new" approach to craft apprentice training which have attracted most attention in the UK over the last five years or so are as follows: duration, content, standards, assessment, relevance, and openness. Each of these aspects represents a further development of the principles established in the 1960s.

Duration

It is claimed that the current four-year apprenticeship is inefficient and costly as a period of programmed education and training. The current duration of

1. Database for the study contains information on the development and diffusion of changes in working practices (and associated changes in pay, hours of work, training, factory budget structures, etc.) on 237 manufacturing sites currently employing 236 900 full-time employee equivalents (including 42 000 craftsmen). Further details are available from the author on request.

the apprenticeship tends to imbalance the training and education received by craftsmen by placing the emphasis on a single, relatively intensive period of training. It might be more effective, for example, to devote only two years to the initial period of training, and then phase all subsequent training over the following years (Annett 1982). Under the existing modular system most craft apprentices take two modules which cover a range of specific tasks which he (or she) must be able to attain. These modules have now been broken down into segments (three segments = one module) which would allow differing training needs to be met of both the apprentice and adult craftsman, and may also offer a means of reducing the overall initial training period. This mini-modular approach also offers a way of accommodating changes in work and technology.

Content and Relevance

There have been questions asked as to the relevance of the apprenticeship system as a means for meeting skilled manpower requirements in many industries because the discrete parcelling-up of skills and knowledge in the hands of a limited group of individuals is inappropriate for the needs of manufacturing industry. What is needed, it is claimed, is the sharing of the craft skills amongst a wide range of operatives. A related aspect to "relevance" concerns the content of current apprenticeships and its relationship to the skill and knowledge required to manage and maintain modern process plant. Here the issue is one of the current job requirements of craftsmen not being related to a single group of skills. The complaint one hears is that training material should recognize the repair and diagnostic nature of maintenance work, and should not be unduly concerned with the manufacturing (machining) aspects. The quick summary statement often used to describe this changing need is that mending and mental, not making and manual, skills and knowledge are required. Some immediate implications of the mismatch of skills and knowledge acquired and those needed to do a job are: to inflate the numbers required to do a repair or overhaul; to create an over-identification with a specific craft trade rather than a particular application of skills and knowledge to do a job; and, to promote the (apparent) transferability of skills and knowledge at the expense of their utility at a specific workplace.

Standards and Assessment

The concern over the duration of apprenticeships is very much related to both assessment and standards. If agreed methods of assessment and likewise a set of standards could be applied to the apprenticeship system it would reduce its duration by allowing individuals to progress at their own rate. Adoption and application of both assessment and standards would reduce many apprenticeships to around three years. Experience in the UK to date indicates that apprenticeships (building on the YTS system) would range in length from two years and nine months to three years and three months. This would reduce apprentice training costs by between 20% and 30% (approximately) which would make training apprentices a more financially attractive proposition to employers. Another significant aspect of developing training to a standard means that the training must be closely specified, monitored and assessed. It calls for a statement of the objectives and standards of training and a means of testing that both the objectives and standards have been acheived. At present progress is being made towards the widespread adoption of a standards-based approach to apprentice training though there is quite some way to go before it becomes as much a part of modern apprenticeships as the modular system.

Openness

The numbers of engineering craftsmen were controlled in part by enforcing a specific age of entry into an apprenticeship. Today that age stands at 16 or 17 years (the Youth Training Scheme might increase the most common age of entry to 17), and the move to a standards-based apprenticeship introduces the acceptance of merit (competence) as the only judge as to whether an individual is, or is not, a craftsman. This means in reality that a thirty-year-old production worker could become a craftsman if he (or she) underwent a recognized programme of training, and achieved the necessary standards. What has not been fully considered is the minimum number of modules of training a trainee must undertake before achieving craft status. Would it be possible, for example, for a production worker to acquire craft skills and knowledge over a seven-year-period and then be designated a craftsman? Or, will it be agreed that a degree of control will still be exercised by the craft unions (amongst others) to stipulate that to become craftsmen, trainees must undertake the bulk of their initial training on a continuous basis, and so bias entry (as at present) to those just leaving full-time education. It is unlikely that a truly open entry system will emerge in the training of engineering craftsmen for a number of years to come.

The points raised above describe the principles of the system supplying engineering craftsmen in the UK, and some of the weaknesses in that system despite major efforts to reform it since 1964. What has thrown these weaknesses into sharp relief has been the introduction of new plant and equipment into many workplaces, and the pressure to reduce operating costs. A situation exists where the engineering craft apprenticeship system is being challenged at the same time as the work undertaken by engineering craftsmen is being redefined. We are witnessing in the UK a period of intense occupational modification and redefinition. The issue for the remainder of this chapter to consider briefly is the utility of the engineering-craft apprenticeship system of initial training given the changing nature of craft work in manufacturing industry. There are two sections. First, the "new" jobs of the engineering craftsman are outlined. Second, the main basis of these changes is considered in terms of the future of the UK engineering-craft apprenticeship training system.

The Emerging Engineering Craft Job Structure

The changes in the work of engineering maintenance craftsmen are giving rise to a number of "new" engineering craft jobs. One of the immediate calls is for engineering craftsmen to work beyond many of their existing, relatively rigid job boundaries. In short, this development requires job structures which go beyond focussing on accuracy, precision and speed within a single trade, but which also take into account such features as versatility, adaptability, and a diagnostic ability. This wide range of demands being placed upon engineering craftsmen as a result of changes in technology, work organization, management style, manufacturing cost structures, and competitive position is giving rise to a number of different types of engineering craft jobs. It is the purpose of this section to describe these new craft jobs in broad outline terms.

In all there are five identifiable types of engineering craft job, each of which is currently being developed from the same basic building block – the traditional engineering craftsman. This situation is changing and the developments in craft apprentice training and education will lead to direct entry routes in the "new" engineering craft jobs. For the bulk of existing engineering craftsmen the five craft jobs (Table 14.2) are probably more appropriately seen as a career structure (Cross 1985; Chapter 15).

It is these five engineering craft jobs which have come to form the main types of role undertaken predominantly by existing (adult) craftsmen. Currently new apprenticeships are being operated to develop cross- or dual-traded craftsmen, or in some instances a combination of the craft and process operator (production worker) role. Whilst these hybrid apprenticeships do develop the skills and knowledge for the running of "optimized" plants, are they a sound basis for the development for future skills and knowledge? Do the new apprenticeships recognize sufficiently the need for practice and learning through exploration? (see Elster 1983, pp. 131–157). The next section touches on these issues based upon new empirical evidence.

Training for Engineering Craft Skills

At the present time in the UK there is a general move to reduce the length of the apprenticeship period via the removal of the learning of infrequently used skills. Thus there is a focussing upon the training of people who can maintain, and in some cases run today's plants. The basis of this shift is the concentration of training effort upon frequently done, "lower" skill tasks. Tasks can be classified in a number of ways e.g., complexity of tasks, working environment, duration and frequency with which tasks are undertaken, etc. (Cross 1986). Taking just one of these factors, complexity, it is possible to consider it in terms of the time it takes to become competent to perform that task. Then taking the frequency and duration of the tasks it is further

Table 14.2. Emerging Engineering Craft Jobs (from Cross (1985) pp. 93–123)

1. Traditional engineering craftsmen
These craftsmen have undertaken a recognized engineering apprenticeship (at least the equivalent of two Engineering ITB modules) in a single trade discipline and work in one of the following trades, amongst others: bench-fitter, welder, coppersmith, tinsmith, pipefitter, instrument fitter/mechanic, electrician, boilermaker, sheet metal worker, plumber, turner, or some combination (at least during their apprentice training) of these trades. These craftsmen at present cover a wide range of tasks from frontline maintenance work to off-line repairs and on-line installation and fabrication work. It is the last three types of task which will tend to form the bulk of their work in the future.

2. Cross-traded engineering craftsmen
Have undertaken a similar type and period of initial training as the *traditional engineering craftsman* but have by virtue of perhaps both experience and a period of further training acquired skills and knowledge in related craft trades. For example, an electrical fitter would undertake work in one or more of the following areas of electronics, microprocessors, programming, and instrumentation. The emphasis here is upon increasing the breadth and depth of (additional) skills and knowledge within the broad categories of either an electrical/ electronic/instrument, or a mechanical trade.

3. Dual-traded engineering craftsmen
Have undertaken a recognized period of apprentice training in common with both the *cross-traded* and *traditional engineering craftsmen*, but have also undertaken a second period of training and education to acquire skills and knowledge in one of the other major trade disciplines. For example, a mechanical craftsman would undertake training and education in electrical and electronics work. Depending on what is required, the range and depth of such training (and more rarely education) can vary from a few days to extensive courses following a recognized syllabus of either the Engineering ITB, or the Business and Technician Education Council. Such craftsmen are "truly flexible" and are not examples of skill-swop, demarcation-relaxation agreements.

4. Machine specialist engineering craftsmen
Have undertaken periods of apprentice and adult craft training which together have provided a range of skills and knowledge across the main craft trade disciplines. In specific training terms these craftsmen might lie between the *cross* and *(full) dual-traded engineering craftsmen*. However, these craftsmen have acquired, through specific training and experience, the application of a series of skills and knowledge relevant to either a single piece or range of inter-related machines ("a line or 'a unit"). Such craftsmen would be the lead-ins for any breakdown work on "their" machines, be able to diagnose and repair most of the units, know which specialist to call upon for assistance (possibly after consultation with a *system specialist engineering craftsman*) and be able to liaise with them, and undertake many of the supervisory and technician-type duties as regards their machines or line. In some cases these craftsmen may either report direct to production, or hold a group leader/supervisory role within production. Within this one type of engineering craftsman these are two main types which range from the "service" engineering craftsman doing all engineering, and virtually no production work to a "process" engineering craftsman spending 40%–50% of their time undertaking production tasks.

5. System (or area) specialist engineering craftsmen
Have undertaken training probably to the level of the *dual-traded engineering craftsman* and will also have held the post of *machine specialist engineering craftsman*. This category of craftsman has specialized in the understanding of the process and the related engineering requirements of a particular plant or section of a plant. This craftsman is more of the plant technician mould and would understand the electronic control and communications aspects on a plant. A significant part of his time would be devoted to project work. The skills and knowledge involved with this job are concerned with the diagnosis of faults in plant hardware and in the control systems, their correction, and the tuning of plant to give optimum control of the process. The job also involves responsibility for ensuring optimum plant performance and they largely need to act on their own initiative.

possible to group (weight) the tasks in terms of importance to a particular job. In the course of this study this type of analysis has been undertaken for sixteen craft jobs on twenty-five manufacturing sites. The combined results of this analysis are summarized in Fig. 14.1.

It is the broad band of tasks falling into the general and multi-semi skill bands which are forming the core of the new apprenticeships. Hence, there is a trading down of the depth of skill and knowledge for breadth allied to a particular manufacturing process in question. In skill terms this means a move from plant to system and process skills (Cross 1985, pp. 198–199). This move in the nature of the skill base does not in fact reduce the absolute number of skills (as defined by the training objectives used by the Engineering ITB) as this has remained around 40–45 (from a possible total number of engineering skills of 210–220 offered under the modular scheme of the Engineering ITB).

While there is a move to create a high degree of common skilling amongst engineering craftsmen there is also the recognition that from this common base there must also be a system to produce both "skill" and "process

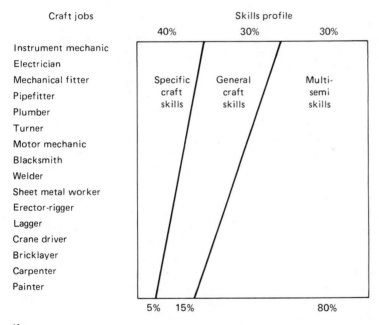

Fig. 14.1. Complexity profiles of sixteen engineering craft jobs. (Source: current research on 25 sites.)

system" specialists. We are therefore seeing an apprenticeship system develop with three recognizable streams: specialist craftsman; operator craftsman; and process systems craftsman. The evolution of this type of system recognizes both the need for the staged development of an individual's skills over a consolidated period of time and also the changed nature of the work done by craftsmen. It is important to note, however, that some of the specialist craft skills are not being trained for on many manufacturing sites but are being supplied by contractors e.g., welding.

It is evident from this very brief discussion that while there has been a change in the system, method and content of the craft apprentice training programmes in the UK, the concept of the apprenticeship remains intact. The most important developments are the opening-up of the access to craft skills to "non-craftsmen", the restatement of the status of craftsmen concentrating their efforts more on craft/technician work, and finally the emergence of more "complex" craft jobs.

Conclusions

Since the launch of the Youth Training Scheme (YTS) and the Technical and Vocational Educational Initiative (TVEI) in the UK there has been an increasing questioning of the value of the apprenticeship system. In some quarters the YTS was seen as a way of reducing apprentice wage rates and a backdoor method for producing "part" craftsmen. Much of this debate was fuelled by defensive trades unions, and education and training bodies resisting change. What in fact appears to be happening is the training of increased numbers of people in technical skills and knowledge as a part of another job. While this development reduces the number of traditional apprenticeship places in the short term this may not be so harmful in the long term as YTS trainees are further trained to full craft status.

In addition the experience of the major employers of craftsmen in the UK clearly demonstrates their continued need for the apprenticeship system. In a number of cases they have experienced the problems (and costs) of trying to dilute, and failing to maintain, an adequate craft-skill base on their sites. As a result these events have spurred them to consider in great detail their skilled manpower requirements and the initial and subsequent training of all their employees. As a consequence therefore the reforms of the apprenticeship system envisaged in the 1960s by the Engineering Industry Training Board are likely to come to a more full realization in the 1990s.

References and Further Reading

Annett J (1982) Distributed Training In: Groupings of Skills: What have we learnt? Proceedings of a symposium held at Warwick University. Manpower Services Commission, Sheffield.
Cross M (1985) Towards the Flexible Craftsman. TCC/Policy Studies Institue, London
Cross M (1986) Multi-Skilling: Costs and Benefits, Work Study, 35: 23–27
Elster J (1983) Explaining Technical Change. Cambridge University Press, Cambridge
Wellens J (1963) The Training Revolution. Evans Brothers, London

Delegation and Decentralization – Computer Systems as Tools for Instruction and Improved Service to Clients

D. Schartum

This chapter deals with issues such as those of delegation of decison making, quality of service and competence, arising from the application of information technology in the domain of the Norwegian National Insurance Administration system. For example, within the context of "national conformity" of practice, the quality of service will demand uniformity in interpretation regardless of the individual insured person's particular circumstances. The emphasis on efficiency and time, and a degree of "tailor-made" information may lead to reduced access and communication between the people who want to use the system and the service itself. Rationalization in complex domains (cases) of decision making may cause the case-handler either simply to ignore the problematic aspects of a case, or to make an intuitive choice instead of conferring with the relevant legal sources. There is empirical evidence from the Norwegian case that in a large number of cases the use of data systems may have a positive effect as they can weed out elementary errors and omissions in calculations, but at a more complex level where legal expertise and judgment is required, such systems may give no insight and support. It is important, therefore, to develop criteria for evaluating the non-time-related aspects of the quality of service, and thereby define aims for, and evaluate, public-oriented activities.

Introduction

Delegation and decentralization are two expressions which to many people have a positive content. In this discussion I will take a closer look at how on-line computer systems in the Norwegian National Insurance Service can be said to affect the realization of these two aims. I will focus in part especially on the use of information technology for information and instruction purposes. In addition I will discuss the effect of computer systems on certain organizational questions in the service. The various effects of information technology will then be evaluated in the light of aims of improved quality of service.

The article is based on the Norwegian part of the joint German/English/ Norwegian project. Naturally, I do not have the opportunity of going further into the details of the background materials this discussion is based on. For those who are interested, I would refer to Parts III and IV of the Norwegian report. Neither do I have the opportunity here of presenting an entire approximation of the question of quality of service, but an introductory effort to develop a method of defining aims and evaluation of the quality of the services offered by the National Insurance Service is found in Part V of the Norwegian report of the project.

It has been discussed in Norwegian legal theory to what degree an administrative organ, which by law or directive has been assigned tasks, can delegate these tasks to subordinate administrative levels. The most important arguments against such delegation is that it can break with Parliament's and the government's intentions if establishments other than those laid down by regulation carry out the work. It has been said that when the legislative powers assign tasks to a superior administrative organ, it is often due to regard for legal protection, because the quality of the work in a superior establishment normally must be regarded as being higher than in subordinate establishments. A second and related argument has been that it would be easier to manage and control the practices in a central establishment instead of several local offices. Important arguments against delegation of administrative authority is, in other words, attached to the regard for the quality of service in the case-handling work.

Development in post-war years has been steadily in the direction of a more liberal attitude to delegation of administrative authority. These changes have been brought about by a strong practical need which has been created in particular by the continuous growth within public administration. Particularly since the 1970s, therefore, attempts have been made to transfer case-work to the local administrative apparatus,while the central organs first and foremost are responsible for planning, steering and control of the work of subordinate units. This division of work has been regarded, inter alia, as being a pre-requisite for sufficiently expeditious case processing. In addition to the regard for efficiency, independent emphasis has been laid on the importance of closeness to the public, both because knowledge of local conditions is regarded as being important to correct case-handling, and because geographic closeness has been regarded as important to people's use of, and attitudes to, the administration. In other words, in addition to efficiency, regard for the quality of service has also been cited in favour of transfer of authority to local organs. On the other hand, delegation has not been justified by demands for greater local freedom in relation to questions of interpretation and practising of the rules.

I mentioned that traditional scepticism towards delegation of official authority has its background in the assumption that subordinate administrative levels do a less efficient job of case-handling than the superior organ. If one is to judge such possible differences in the quality of case-handling, it is in my opinion particularly important to direct attention to the superior organ's right to *issue instructions* to the organ to which it has delegated authority. Surbordinate administrative units (e.g., a local national insurance office), in some connections can be said to be independent. At the same time, however, they are for a large part subject to the authority of the central administration, and must therefore follow the general instructions laid down concerning organization, method of work, legal questions, etc. The effect of delegation must therefore be evaluated in relation to the degree of independence the decision-maker has with regard to the ramifications set by instructions and other conditions.

Delegation and Central Control in the Norwegian National Insurance Service

During the 1970s and 1980s, a large part of the decision-making authority which previously lay with the central National Insurance Administration was delegated to the 450 partly very small local national insurance offices.[1] I have access only to the figures for the rate of delegation during the period 1975–1980 when the number of single cases in the National Insurance Administration was reduced by an average of approximately 60%.[2] The figures for this 5-year period give an impression of a delegation process which has been taking place since 1970 and which is still taking place.[3]

I emphasized that delegation had to be seen in conjunction with the instructions given by central authorities. In the Norwegian National Insurance Service there are especially two methods of control to consider: firstly, traditional instructions and guidelines concerning interpretation of rules, and secondly, use of on–line computer systems. I shall first say something about the written internal instructions and guidelines.

As in all other legislation, the National Insurance Act with directives contains rules about which there can be questions of interpretation. To make national uniformity possible in this area, the National Insurance Administration has therefore developed a system of centrally laid down instructions and guidelines which take a stand on a number of interpretation questions. A loose-leaf system with a total of approximately 170 circulars (about 2600 A5 pages) is distributed to all local offices and is updated by the National Insurance Administration.

It stands to reason that such a paper-mill demands both good discipline and overview in order for it to be taken notice of and function as intended. The special thing with such instructions is that, in addition, they are kept on the shelf and are only activated by the desire of the employee. In a work situation under pressure where demands on time and efficiency are emphasized, there is therefore a danger that use will be more limited than the number of difficult cases and the existing interpretation problems should indicate.

The possibility that delegation of authority could weaken the central control of the local administration worried the central authorities when the general decentralization and delegation policy was formed in the 1970s. In

1. About half of the local national insurance offices have between 1 and 5 employees and about 90% have fewer than 20 employees.
2. See Habberstad: Organization of the National Insurance Service, June 1981, page 44.
3. Even though there have been great variations from benefit area to benefit area, the figures illustrate the extensive changes which the local national insurance offices have been through.

the government's long-term programme of 1980,[1] it was stated in this connection that information technology makes possible easier access to information in the local environments and therefore weakens the arguments for centralized administrative solutions. At the same time it is maintained that the same technology offers the possibility of increased control and coordination such that delegation does not necessarily have to lead to the creation of new, local, self-governed units.

The on-line computer systems in the Norwegian National Insurance Service are a good example of how information technology can be used as a tool of control of the organs to which authority is delegated.[2] Instructions and guidelines which are a built-in function of the two data systems of the Service are of a totally different nature than the traditional instruction and guideline systems I have mentioned. The two most important functions of the system are registration of case information and calculation of benefits and tax. Where registration of information in individual cases is concerned, the system functions in the first instance as a reminder list of which details can be included in the case-handling. Next, the system indicates which details are mandatory and which can be obtained voluntarily. In addition there are certain marginal values which the registered figures cannot exceed, and certain lists of allowed values for representation of special types of facts. Some details are filled out beforehand by the system which transfers information from one routine to another. Moreover, the automatic calculation of benefits can only be activated when mandatory values are filled out properly.

The computer system is therefore – in contrast to circulars – not a system which is activated by the individual employee when that individual is faced with a problem, but a tool she has to use to be able to do the job at all. The instructions and guidelines which are built into the computer system in the form of allowed values, indication of relevant facts, etc., are therefore something the employees will be confronted with in any case, and also represent partly the centrally laid down rules which they cannot ignore.

Instructions and Quality of Service

If the importance that instructions can have for the quality of service is to be evaluated, the question will in the first instance be what the relationship is between the demand for quality of service and the demand for national conformity in the application of the rules by the National Insurance Administration. I am of the opinion that one must differentiate between the legal–political and legal-application aspects of this question. On the one side one is of course free to think that from the national insurance political aspect the best solution would be if each local national insurance office were given

1. Parliamentary Bill No. 79, 1980–81, page 78.
2. In addition to use of information technology to instruct and guide the external system, various reporting functions have been established which facilitate a better overview for the National Insurance Administration, and thereby a strengthened potential for steering the local national insurance offices. These tools of control, however, will not be discussed here.

great freedom in the decision process. A service evaluation of the legal application undertaken by the local offices must take place within the limits set by the law at all times. When legislation prepares for national conformity, it implies that a strong central control which leads to uniform practice as a basis has a positive effect on the quality of service. In my opinion it is clear that the Norwegian national insurance legislation does not aim at giving any room for local latitude. In the National Insurance Service, regard for the quality of service will demand uniformity in interpretation regardless of where the insured lives in the country.

As I have pointed out previously, today's computer system instructs and guides the individual terminal operator. The systems establish, in addition, work routines which are the same for all offices and which therefore increase the probability of like results regardless of which local office is involved. All the same there are things in the work situation which have been created by the computer systems in the Service which in my opinion will necessitate a probable modification of this positive basis.

With the system solutions chosen, the division of work between people and machine lessens the possibility for the case-handler to learn and understand the legal rules which steer the results of her work. As an example, the system gives instructions on which information is relevant and mandatory, but does not give any guidance on what importance stipulation of the various factual details has for the final result. The case-handler can by all means be an expert of making minor decisions with regard to whether the factual conditions are fulfilled or not, but she will have difficulty – without special measures – in gaining any particular insight into legal questions and knowledge of the overlying structures in the set of regulations she works with. In general, instructions and guidance given by computer programs correspond to correct results and deal with general cases. In addition they are so self-instructing that good knowledge of the rules is not normally demanded in order to carry out case-handling in simple cases. The systems do not, however, give any support for solving particular problems. A more active use of traditional problem-oriented instructions and guidelines is therefore desirable to ensure a correct result in the problematical cases as well.

In my opinion there is a danger that with today's computer routines the difficult cases will act as obstacles in otherwise well-oiled decison processes, both because the use of them breaks with the effective case procedure and because the traditional instructions and guidelines which are required in order to take a stand as regards the problems are very difficult to access. The result can both be that the case-handler simply chooses to ignore the problematical aspects of cases, or that she makes an intuitive choice instead of conferring with the relevant legal sources.

The influence that information technology in the Norwegian National Insurance Service has had on the question of the quality of case-handling in the sense of regard for a correct result, points in other words not only in one direction. I think it is probable that the computer systems have a positive effect in the large majority of cases in that they first and foremost weed out elementary errors and defects, pure omissions and errors in calculation. On a more advanced level, where legal insight is demanded, the systems give no insight and support, and at the same time the effective routines that the computer-based, case-handling creates, can elevate the threshold against the use of manual problem-oriented instructions and guidelines.

For the sake of good order I emphasize that in the Norwegian part of the project I have only found *indications* of a development such as I have described here. My interpretations of the employees' possibilities to view the decision process they are a part of is first and foremost based on knowledge of system solutions, the employees' work situation and not least the employees' knowledge of the rules regulating award of benefits. Of course, these grounds are not sufficient to make a final decision in the matter.

Information Technology and the Decentralized Organizational Structure

As mentioned, information technology has an influence on the possibilities of issuing instructions parallel to delegation of authority. This can, therefore, be said to have been an important support for the implementation of the changed division of work between the central and the local administrative units in the administration of the Norwegian National Insurance organ. At the same time, however, the on-line computer systems in the Service have had an effect on other important conditions for delegation of authority, and have contributed in addition to changing the content of the services that the local units offer the public. In this part of the discussion I will show how the computer systems in the organ at the same time can be said to have *weakened* the arguments for today's decentralized administrative solutions.

In 1982 there were approximately 150 service units in the National Insurance organ – called "attached offices" – in addition to the 450 local national insurance offices. The attached offices are national insurance offices which have lost their independent status because of the fusing of the municipalities in the 1950s and 1960s. The running of them is partly maintained and the offices, as far as organization goes, are subordinate to the national insurance offices in the new large municipalities. The attached offices have therefore never been visible on official statistics of the number of national insurance offices. Neither were the attached offices mentioned when Parliament deliberated appropriations for computer equipment for the national insurance offices, and thus they were never given any such equipment.[1] The transactions registered manually by an attached office must therefore be transferred later to the national insurance office's computer system, something which entails extra work.

Introduction of on-line computer systems to the national insurance offices was carried out on the condition that – through natural departures – half of the goal of rationalization is withdrawn, i.e., 400 positions.[2] At the same time as the introduction of data and the withdrawal of positions, all the local national insurance offices in addition went through a reorganizational

1. Later five outside offices with almost full capacity were given computer equipment.
2. See Parliamentary Bill No. 116, 1983–1984.

process.[1] These circumstances partly created a very difficult work situation at many offices. A large number of local offices with responsibility for the running of attached offices were therefore forced to gather resources and applied to the National Insurance Administration for permission to close the attached offices. During the last few years more than *half* (or approximately 80) of the attached offices have been closed, most of them as a direct result of the circumstances I have mentioned. Introduction of the on-line systems in the National Insurance organ have, in other words, led to a *less decentralized organ*.

One of the reasons that there has always been a local office in each municipality is that many payments of benefits have always taken place in the form of cash payments by the office. Even though payments of long-term benefits have taken place by giro for many years, many payments of short-term benefits and refunds of expenses still take place by the public visiting the office and receiving the payments in cash.[2] As technological progress has made it possible since the 1950s to transfer long-term benefits by giro, so information technology makes it appropriate to transfer short-term benefits and refunds in the same way. The National Insurance Administration has thus recently begun the development towards such non-cash transfer (or "publicless") local offices.[3]

The Norwegian National Insurance organ also started to use information technology to inform recipients of benefits about their entitlements under national insurance without previous request. This is done by different groups of addressees being picked out with the aid of personal details which are accessible in the national insurance computer-registers. This personal information makes it possible to define smaller groups of addressees in order to dispatch a certain degree of "tailor-made" information.

The developments towards the so-called non-cash transfer offices and such active information measures make it appear less necessary for people to visit the national insurance offices. This has occurred at a time when the organ, because of a lasting rationalization pressure, also uses other methods to deal with the volume of case-handling. At many offices, a public-free day a week has been introduced.

As we see, the data systems have strengthened the central control of the local administration and thereby made it less critical to delegate authority to the local offices, while, at the same time, the same technology has contributed to a reduction of the local units, that is to say, made the structure of the organ *less* decentralized. In addition the use of information technology in the organ has made it less necessary for the public to visit the local offices, and has thereby probably weakened the basis for today's decentralized structure. In the following I will present a more in-depth treatment of this latter problem.

1. Reorganization and introduction of data routines were carried out in parallel to each other in the project "service, productivity and work environment" (the SPA project), which was completed at the turn of the year 1986/87.
2. This concerns 50% of all recipients of sick benefits and the majority of those receiving refunds of expenses which are covered by national insurance.
3. The National Insurance organ has over a lengthy period of time requested the local offices to start to reduce cash payments. Molde and Lunner local national insurance office, as a trial project starting in the spring of 1987, has stopped cash payments completely.

Quality of Service and the Importance of Direct Contact with the Public

I mentioned examples which show that the Norwegian National Insurance organ – within today's ramifications – does not give priority to direct contact with the public. To make the point, one can say that the Norwegian National Insurance Service uses information technology to prevent the public from visiting the local national insurance offices. By anticipating and carrying out certain tasks which the public usually visit the office for, the Service can pre-empt the situation such that the local offices reach out to the public instead of the public coming to the offices.

One could ask if this is not an example of the best type of service, because it does not anticipate any particular effort on the part of the insured and lays the work on the Service instead of the public. To a certain extent this has had a positive effect on the quality of service. When the answer still contains reservations it is because one-sided efforts regarding such measures would in my opinion create imbalances in relation to other service aspects.

In the first instance I think that it is unwise to base assumptions of the public's needs on completely rational methods of observation. One should, for example, be reserved in believing that the people who today come to the local offices to receive cash payments, have only this rational errand and that it is therefore only a payment function which is affected when the local offices change to giro payments. In my opinion there are grounds to believe that many people who come primarily to receive cash payments also ask questions about other national insurance circumstances: they ask for themselves, for a neighbour, a relative or they take a brochure. Some questions will affect things which fall under the national insurance organ's area of responsibility, others will concern benefits under the social welfare system or other public services. We know little or nothing about how important other such errands are to the people who visit the offices. In my opinion, one should therefore be careful about introducing changes in the services offered without having investigated such circumstances further.

The justifications used by the Service for transferring benefits to giro payments are service and efficiency. In the regard for efficiency lies a consideration that the public visiting the offices take up time and this time can better be used on other things. Of course, it can be reasonable to give priority to quicker case-handling. Efficiency and shorter case-handling time, however, have always been central aims in the National Insurance Service. The danger now is that when the time factor is included and given priority as a service aim, the work for improved service will to a large extent coincide with the work for improved efficiency. In this way the work for better efficiency can be continued under the more popular name "service" without any change being made in the priorities. The time aspects of service will in my opinion normally be sufficiently taken care of through rationalization work. I am of the opinion, therefore, that giving quick case-handling priority over using resources for direct contact with the public, leads to a distorted and one-sided focus on time as an aim of service. In my opinion it is therefore necessary to direct attention towards the aspects of quality of service which are not directly linked to time and efficiency.

The computer-based active information measures which the Service wishes to concentrate on will in my opinion only partly have positive effects if no supplementary measures are concentrated on at the same time. There are two things which characterize most of such information material. Firstly, it represents only an *extract* of the rules and is therefore incomplete. Secondly, it represents a simplification of the rules which regulate the area and is for that reason also insufficient. Information material containing a popularization of the rules will never give a completely correct legal picture, and therefore will not give sufficient information to the whole group of recipients. The more extensive and complicated the legislation is, the more difficult it will be to attain a sufficient legal level. On the condition that dissemination of this material is only the first step in an information campaign launched by an organ, such information is anyway positive. The condition is, however, that actively disseminated information is combined with an offer of individual and concrete guidance. In the opposite case, such information activity will have the effect of guidance for some whilst others will be *misguided* and thus risk loss of rights.

I am also of the opinion that for information to be of a sufficient standard at the local information level, it demands concentration on direct contact with the public. Such a demand makes it necessary to have qualified employees in the national insurance offices who can give guidance of sufficient quality. An important condition for sufficient level of competence of the employees is that they participate in the decision-making processes and make use of the aids which give them insight into the legal material about which they will render guidance. And here we are back to the question of instructions and their ability to give insight into legal questions. If the National Insurance organ tries to keep the public at arm's length by the organ being active itself but at the same time not making direct contact with the public possible, there are further grounds to put a question mark by the basis for the whole of the present decentralized organizational structure. What then do we want with local offices operating near the public if the public does not have to visit the offices? Is it to save long-distance telephone calls? The necessity of direct contact with the public would seem therefore to be a condition for maintaining the principle of a local national insurance office in each municipality.

Conclusion

In order to bind the parts of this discussion closer together, some of the factual contexts can be linked together in this way. A sufficient level of information work demands direct contact with the public, direct contact with the public demands decentralization, decentralized guidance demands sufficient legal competence which can best be obtained by practical experience, something which assumes delegation of authority. Execution of delegated authority to a sufficient degree in addition demands instructions and guidance which contribute to increased legal insight.

As a brief summary I would put forward two clear formulations connected to on-line computer systems in the Norwegian National Insurance Service.

First, information technology is in use in the Norwegian National Insurance Service in order to make decentralization and closeness to the public possible, while at the same time being applied in ways that *lessen* the contact with the same public. Second, the applications of information technology which are chosen give improved quality of service in cases which from a legal standpoint are not problematical, and unchanged or worsened quality for atypical and difficult cases, both in regard to case-handling and information work.

I think that in the future it will be important to direct attention towards the aspects of the quality of service which are not directly linked to time and efficiency. Here it is important to see that the Norwegian National Insurance Service has not utilized the information technology potential to assure other aspects of quality. Also, they have hardly maintained a carefully weighed attitude to the relationship between the quality of service and the application of computer systems chosen.

Today we lack a method of evaluating many important aspects of service. I am of the opinion therefore that it is important to develop criteria for the non-time-related aspects of the quality of service thereby being able to define aims for, and to evaluate public-oriented activities. This to a large extent will be a condition for Norwegian authorities to be willing to assign priority to this work.

Acknowledgement. This article is based on: Dag Wiese Schartum (1987) The introduction of computers in the Norwegian local insurance offices. Corepoints and context. Complex 9/87. Norwegian University Press, Oslo. The work is funded by the Stiftung Volkswagenwerk, West Germany.

Applying Expert Systems Technology: Division of Labour and Division of Knowledge

O. Östberg

There is an abundance of promises to expert systems with user-friendly and intelligent interfaces providing cloned expertise for augmented job performance. A closer look reveals that very few systems are in operation, and that there is a serious gap between claims and reality. Basically, "knowledge engineering" is a modern form of "work study engineering", and yet job and organizational design issues are rarely addressed in the literature on designing expert systems. This serious gap is discussed.

Introduction

When launched in the Autumn of 1981, the Japanese project to develop fifth generation computer systems (FGCS) was targeted to provide parallel computing machines with an intelligence approaching that of humans. Feigenbaum and McCorduck (1983) found the project to be a real competitive threat and challenge to the US, and saw present work on expert systems (ES) as only modest pilot projects of the forthcoming FGCS technology. Artificial Intelligence (AI) projects in Europe and the US are now in turn seeking to match the Japanese work.

A bootstrap for the US development work was the $600 million strategic computing project launched in 1983, and the announcement that AI/ES technology would be a requisite for Department of Defense (DoD) contract bids beginning in the late 1980s. It has been projected that an amazing one hundred million lines of software code will be needed in the realization of the US Strategic Defense Initiative project ("Star Wars"), a substantial part of which will be of an AI/ES nature.

In the name of *The human frontier science program,* Japan has since started on the road towards sixth generation computer systems and the connecting point between computers and biological functions ("bio chips"). On 1 April 1987, it was officially launched in the form of an appeal from the ad hoc London wise men's conference to the seven summit nations and the commission of the European Community.

But this time the US was not caught sleeping, and in parallel the US Air Force Office of Scientific Research announced their new *Neural computational program*, to support research on advanced computing techniques inspired by the organization and function of living neural networks. These "new connectionist" researchers believe that it is possible to get a computer to learn and grow more intelligent by wiring up its circuits in the same way as brains are wired (brains are "parallel machines").

Software engineering in general ties up an enormous amount of resources. It has been estimated that the US software costs amounted to 2% of the GNP in 1980, reached a probable 8.5% in 1985, and are expected to total 13% in 1990 (Ramamoorthy et al. 1984). The growth will go hand-in-hand with educational efforts by individuals, organizations and society. For the Federal Republic of Germany it is estimated that by 1990: (i) 5% of the workforce will need a professional education in computer science, (ii) 15% will need an extensive training in a special field of information technology in addition to their own professional knowledge, and (iii) a further 50% will need some simple training enabling them to use equipment of information technology (Bullinger 1985).

To the extent that AI/ES represents a new paradigm, adopting and adapting this new technology at a company level will be a major undertaking. For a company such as Hewlett-Packard, this paradigm shift means facing the problem of training several thousands of software engineers to become conversant with the new AI/ES culture for software development, manufacturing and office automation (Rifkin 1985). Obviously, such a reorientation will also have an impact on jobs and work organization.

The over-all purpose of ES is knowledge transfer with regard to a defined task domain. The key person in this process is the knowledge engineer. The present review is a continuation of that of Östberg (1986), and will discuss the fact that knowledge engineering involves the registration and atomization of mental work in a mode similar to that of work study engineering with regard to manual work.

New Paradigm or More of the Same?

When the FGCS project was announced, Japanese scientists repeated the US optimism of the early 1970s. It is note-worthy, however, that an assessment of the social impacts of future FGCS applications was carried out at the outset of the project (Karatsu 1984). The study painted a picture of a not-altogether-positive revolution, and concluded that there was in fact a risk for a "two culture" society, with one part being left behind and alienated by the FGCS "high-road" technology.

Elaborating on the "high-road" theme of truly rule-based programming and dedicated machines for symbolic information processing, Nilsson (1985) concluded that AI/ES is revolutionary and has a potential for achieving a massive reduction in the amount of human labour, and that, as a consequence, we should convince our leaders that they should give up the idea of full employment.

The notion of revolution and paradigm shift is refuted by the "low-road" theme, which holds that there is an oversell of ES and unwarranted extrapolation from today's very narrow laboratory products to the looming brave new FGCS. Another reason for toning down the wording is that the distinction between ES and traditional systems becomes blurred when ES products are integrated with and made operational in existing computer systems. Once we have understood the problems and see how these AI programs work, then we will not think of it as AI any more.

A critic of long-standing is H. L. Dreyfus who has vigorously opposed the AI scientists' claims that computers are gradually becoming capable of exhibiting human intelligence. While not retracting his basic criticism, he recently acknowledged the existence of ES programs which "in their narrow areas ... perform with impressive competence" (Dreyfus and Dreyfus 1986a).

The ES literature is confused by the tendency for scientists to act as business agents – which some of them *are* – and discuss "high-road" laboratory work mixed with "low-road" industrial applications. Independent of what "road" is chosen, if job and organization design mistakes from the old paradigm are repeated, the new AI/ES paradigm may still be "more of the same" from an end-user perspective (Amick and Östberg 1987).

The "high-road" AI thesis stresses *knowledge, control,* and *heuristic search,* to enable computer systems to perform tasks at an experts' level of competence (Bibel 1985). The "low-road" AI thesis stresses *data, algorithms,* and *functions* to enable computers to perform routine tasks within a finite problem space. The connection between these two roads is that they may both lead to products called expert systems by using the same type of development tools and programming techniques.

An expert system is in fact not definable by its structure, but rather by its role as the final step in the transmission of codified job knowledge from a defined domain. The domain data in the form of "knowledge"[1] gathered from experts, manuals, or otherwise, is translated into a formalized image, which is then delivered to the end-user. If the image presented to the end-user contains no holes or uncertainties, then it is a "low-road" ES very similar to traditional computer systems.

Codifying Domain Data

Industrial engineering (IE) is concerned with all aspects of collecting, refining, representing, processing and analysing production data. The methods apply to industry as well as administration and health care, and range all the way from the "low-road" IE of clocking the performance of manual workers (work study) to the "high-road" IE of mathematical perturbation analysis of automatic production lines (operations research).

The industrial robot is of particular interest to industrial engineers because of its manifestation and symbolization of codified worker skills. For example,

---

1. Knowledge is written within inverted commas because knowledge is a human entity which cannot reside within a computer.

using a playback robot with continuous path control, the motions of a skilled spray painter can be transferred to a computer program. After a subsequent fine-tuning of the motion pattern of the spray gun and the amount of paint sprayed at various positions, the robot becomes a *de facto* spray painting expert by out-performing the human in repetitive painting jobs. Using the robot time measurement (RTM) technique pioneered by Paul and Nof (1979), the performance of the robot can then be compared to that of other spray-painting robots and humans. The performance of humans is assessed by means of traditional method time measurement (MTM) techniques.

According to a large-scale investigation in Japanese industry, the prime benefits of robots is that their introduction forces management to "shape up" in terms of streamlining the production and encode worker skills to pave the way for full automation (JMA 1983). Full automation can only be achieved through the use of ES for supervisory control (Hwang and Salvendy 1984; Hayes and Wright 1986) and through the development of more intelligent robots.

The close connection between industrial robots and ES is underscored by the way AI research and development is usually structured (OTA 1987), tht is, into (i) expert systems, (ii) robotics systems and factory automation, (iii) pattern recognition (vision for robots), (iv) natural language understanding, and (v) computer-aided instruction. And just as robotics speeded up job codification in Japanese industry, so will US firms involvement in ES "lead to the collection and codification of a wide range of company expertise" (Ernst and Djha 1986).

Knowledge engineers' ES continue and supplement where industrial engineers' MTM analysis stopped. This may be illustrated by the following statements:

There is no sense in one (underwriter) guy having all the knowledge when we can de-brainwash him and put his thinking into our machine so that somebody in the field can benefit from what he knows. And should one of those experts quit or get fired in the future, the company is not out in the cold (. . .) The guy fresh off the street will use the system . . ." (Shamoon 1985).

"Instead of building a better underwriting system with AI techniques, Metropolitan is using an expert system to change the underwriting system's rules and to determine the impacts of the rule changes – it's a fantastic tool for doing that." (Raimondi 1985).

"In the future artificial intelligence should simulate easily replaceable people. For example, there are a lot of people in the customer-service area (bank tellers, travel agents, airline reservation clerks) who don't do their job very well." (Shank 1987).

These statements on how ES may be applied in the financial office should be compared with the examples in Tables 16.1 and 16.2.

Table 16.1 Examples of job element codes in KLAR–K, an MTM analysis system for offices.

Job element	Code					
Mental calculation basic value	3	121	000000	11200	0009	2
Wait 0.5 sec for answer in terminal	3	811	118000	11000	0000	9
Proofread line of 11–16 text characters	4	522	000000	11210	3000	2
Calculate number with pocket calculator	4	125	125740	11120	000K	3
Receive data with terminal IBM 2740	5	316	118311	11100	000K	1
File document in locklever binder	6	900	510400	21100	320K	1

Table 16.2. Steps and outputs when using the MLA, which is an expert system for Mortgage Loan Evaluation marketed by Arthur Andersen & Co. (After Smith 1987).

1. Prompted by MLA, a clerical worker or an underwriter enters the client's name, credit rating, finances, property address, etc

2. MLA processes the initial data, and calls attention to areas that may require additional data input or subjective analysis

3. The clerical worker or underwriter performs the additional tasks as required by MLA

4. MLA applies the existing Federal guidelines for mortgage loans, as well as the particular policies being enforced within the lending institution. This may involve some 200 factors

5. MLA generates a semi-final report and states the major impediments to this loan

6. The clerical worker or underwriter decides whether or not to approve the loan, and documents the decision in the MLA

7. MLA closes the case by issuing a Loan Evaluation Report for the lending institution's permanent loan file

Table 16.1 is a list of selected codes used in KLAR–K, which is an internationally renowned MTM system for office work in general and banks in particular. It shows that work-study engineering already has codified the physical acts of office workers in minute detail. Table 16.2 exemplifies how far knowledge engineering has come towards the codification of the mental acts of office workers. It shows a loan evaluation process utilizing an ES called mortgage loan analyzer (MLA). Arthur Andersen & Co., the creator and supplier of MLA, claims that it is superior to the rate scoring systems currently used by many lending institutions in the US.

A worst-case scenario from Table 16.1 would be a "moving belt" office where every single work element has been regimented. A scenario presenting itself in Table 16.2 is very similar to the general, not-so-good ES scenario shown in Fig. 16.1. Combined with the three quotations, these two worst-case scenarios do not bode well for ES end-users.

Fig.16.1 represents one mode of utilizing an ES. Whether or not a particular operational mode is suitable, from an end-user perspective, depends on frequency of use, task proficiency of the user, job design, work organization,

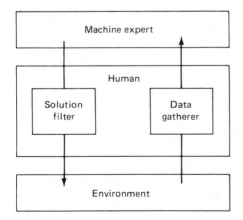

Fig. 16.1. A hypothetical system for knowledge communication where the human has been reduced to a facilitator of the machine–environment interaction. (After Woods 1986).

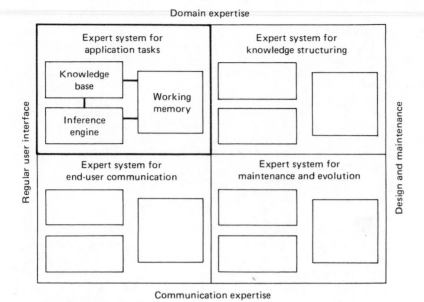

Fig. 16.2.   A hypothetical "full" expert system consisting of the traditional application system, handling the problem space of the tasks to be performed, supported by intelligent front-end systems for design, operation and maintenance.

and economic, technical and social degrees of freedom in the production system. The following modes can be discerned:

Transactional: The ES takes over all responsibilities and performs the task through a human facilitator

Interactive: The human performs the task with the help of the ES and is in charge during the dialogue

Commentary: The human performs the task independently and only uses the ES when in need of a "second opinion".

Teaching: The ES teaches the human until he or she has reached task proficiency, or serves as a manual for the infrequent task performer

Supervisory: The ES is a passive supervisor and only calls attention to "illegal" human actions or actions likely to interfere with developments in other areas of the system of which the task domain is a part

Experiences From Applied Expert Systems

Most ES reported in the research literature are of an interactive or commentary type ("high-road" emulation of experts' heuristic knowledge). The trend in business journals is to look for transactional or teaching applications ("low-road" algorithms of specified task functions). Very few ES are actually in routine operation.

In 1984, no more than 10 ES were reported to be maintained in working order in the US (Hayes-Roth 1984a). Two years later, Buchanan's (1986) world-wide count of working, non-military ES resulted in a "max list" of 61 applications; excluding the "low-road" applications, his "min list" has only one single entry. Many more ES have been designed, but by-and-large these are first-generation exercises. For example, within the Boeing Co. alone, in 1985 over 200 prototype systems have been designed with the help of a particular knowledge engineering tool (Boose 1985). To the extent such that systems are reported in the literature at all, the reports have been described as resembling a bicycle beginner's jubilant cry: "Look Ma – No hands!".

A closer look at Buchanan's list gives an even more disheartening picture. Some disheartening examples are:

DENDRAL searches chemical structure libraries for substructures. The "high-road" version is not being used. What is used, however, is an algorithmic version (traditional computing) for analysis of mass spectrometer data (Dreyfus and Dreyfus 1986b)

LA varieties of ES (see Table 16.2). Three such systems are mentioned in Buchanan's list of 1986, but visits to two of the sites revealed that they had not been implemented at the end of 1987

POMME gives advice to farmers on apple orchards, including pest management, drought control, pesticide selection and treatment of winter injuries. The initiators demanded that the final delivery system be IBM PC machines. The system is currently being converted to the MS-DOS environment, and no field testing is expected until 1988 at the earliest

CATS diagnoses problems in diesel-electric locomotives. This system is one of the flagships in the ES circus. Pictures and descriptions appear in textbooks and scientific and business journals alike. The truth is, that the prototype did not survive without the permanent support of the researchers who developed it, and it no longer exists

MYCIN addresses the problem of diagnosing and treating infectious blood diseases, and is another of the ES flagships. It is not mentioned in Buchanan's list, and rightly so. Although it took 40 person years to develop, very little effort was spent on the user dialogue. A single MYCIN "interview" takes 30–40 minutes of typing, which is a major reason why it has never been used/accepted among doctors (Luger and Stubblefield 1987) Despite all that is written about MYCIN, it is not used anywhere in the world

PUFF interprets pulmonary function tests. It was developed at the Pacific Medical Center in San Francisco, has received a lot of attention and praise, but has not been able to leave the development site

There is obviously a serious gap between claims and reality of ES applications. Thousands of articles have been published about development work in progress and about the potential use of ES. Only very few systems are in actual use outside the laboratory environment, and evaluation reports are non-existent. An explanation for the absence of reports on applied "real" ES could be that their use involves very little reportable glamour.

Expert systems in business are not as they are said to be. They bear little similarity to impressive projects found in the literature on AI. They are not inherently complex, demanding, risky and expensive. They are not built by implementors with doctorates and world-ranking expert knowledge. Instead they are as they have to be: simple in form, limited in aims and built by rather ordinary people with local and relative expertise (d'Agapeyeff 1984).

There is sort of an intellectual pecking order here which has science first, engineering second and manufacturing third. And by the time you get to manufacturing there aren't any smart people left. (Rifkin 1985).

Reviewing ES applications in the UK, Berry and Broadbent (1986) found that discipline is needed in the use of ES, that consultative (commentary) modes of ES operations are lacking, that the explanation function of an ES needs considerable improvement, that less-experienced users easily get overlooked, that the user-interface is too textual, that there is a danger of shoe-horning knowledge into ES design shells, that tailor-made ES design is the one and only solution, and that rapid prototyping may actually serve as a stumbling block in the ES design process.

Based on his extensive experience in ES design, McDermott (1986) concluded that current-generation ES occasionally fail irreparably; not because of inadequacies in the knowledge base, but because of inadequacies in the problem-solving method. Irreparable failures occur because the knowledge required for some part of a system's task is incommensurate with its problem-solving method. The principal vulnerability is that each ES uses only a single problem-solving method – a method that may very well be totally inappropriate at some of the boundaries of its task.

Gillett (1987) reported from two years' experience with ES development in the British financial community. With the help of consultants and researchers from academia, some 20 organizations worked on an ES demonstrator for giving advice on the financial health of certain types of companies. It was found that (i) the knowledge representation was rigid and complex, (ii) the user interfaces had to be characterized as very unsatisfactory, (iii) the end-users had been left out in the design process, and (iv) the ES did not seem credible to the end-user. The development consortium managed to draw strength from these disappointments and felt confident about the possibility to turn around for a "victory from the jaws of defeat".

The Flexibility Myth

When an expert system is implemented as a production system, the job of refining and extending the system's knowledge is quite easy. (McDermott 1982)

Current expert systems are typically difficult to change once they are built. Not only does the changing of a knowledge base require a knowledge engineer who is well-grounded in the design of the system and the structure of the knowledge base, most often it is also required that the changes are made by the same knowledge engineer who originally wrote the program. (Frosher and Jacob 1985)

The medical knowledge is forced into an alien format, it is not easily updated, and the requirements of the explanation system impose an intolerable burden on the system builder. (Alvey 1983)

The above statement by McDermott appeared in an article describing the development of an ES called RI. He is reported to have explained the name of the system in these humorous words: Three years ago I wanted to become a knowledge engineer, and now I *are one*. The system was developed for the

Digital Equipment Corp. (DEC), where its expanded and refined successor is nowadays called XCON.

Refining and extending RI into the continuously growing XCON may not be a problem for McDermott, but Whitby (1984) sees a great danger in such statements from the "adapted AI elite". While "addressing" society's concerns, this elite keep doing what it has adapted itself to do. It is dangerous because it distracts society from addressing the concerns. Whitby sees a similar danger from the camps holding utopian views (positive or negative) or referring to AI/ES as principally or morally wrong. These camps distract society by conducting the debate on too long-term or too broad a basis.

XCON is used for configuring computers to customer specifications, and most of the rules are merely technical facts and requirements related to new components used in DEC computers. DEC's first approach to the component description work was to involve the technicians with knowledge about the technical details. Despite McDermott's claim about the easiness of the *updating* the knowledge base, this proved to be unworkable because of the system and programming intricacies (Bachant and McDermott 1985). Furthermore, because of their lack of knowledge about the "reasoning" inside XCON, the technicians could also not participate in improving EXON within a *given* knowledge base.

A permanent group of ES specialists is now in charge of XCON, which is perhaps the main reason for its success. Similar experiences are reported from ACE (Miller 1984), which is AT&T's successful cable maintenance ES and which is supported by a permanent specialist group, and CATS, which was General Electric's locomotive maintenance ES and which was not successful because it did not get the needed specialist support.

For many years, XCON has indeed grown at a rate of several hundred rules per year and the size of its rule base in 1987 reached 12 000. This may be compared to the estimate that some 10 000 rules would suffice to emulate expertise in any profession (Hayes-Roth 1984a), that it is difficult to predict an ES program's behaviour for a program of any interesting size (Luger and Stubblefield 1987), and that systems approaching 8000 rules are out-of-control even for the developers (Ernst and Ojha 1985). The out-of-control problem was the major reason for Parnas' (1985) dramatic decision to withdraw from his work on intelligent software for the US strategic defence system.

When the regular domain workers are excluded from the continuous improvement of the tools/methods used in the work process, then they become alienated from their own knowledge. The *division of labour* between humans and machines has grown into an unwanted *division of knowledge*. This is contrary to a humanistic view of the human's role in a production system. It is also contrary the managerial wisdom expressed in the quality circle movement.

Maintenance is problematic and costly in any type of computer system. Fox (1982) estimated that 60%–80% of all traditional programming effort is expended on maintenance. The ES maintenance needs and problems are probably greater because the maintainer must know both the code to update the function and the domain to update the knowledge base (Sviokla 1986b).

Complex traditional systems pose increased maintenance problems if the program is written in idiosyncratic "spaghetti code". ES programming is even worse. The nature of the programming languages, the work-station based, rapid prototyping technique, and the general development atmosphere, make the ES design process counterproductive to documentation and hence to maintenance (Ernst and Ojha 1986). In combination with a general lack of formal training in ES design, the knowledge engineer is more or less forced to be a "hacker".

Partridge (1986) objected to the notion that the "hacking syndrome" is endemic to the development atmosphere and will disappear when AI/ES reaches maturity. Rather than a developmental nuisance, he found the problem to be more fundamental and inherent in the current paradigm of no clear problem specification and no clear-cut correct or incorrect answers. To this can be added the necessity for any "intelligent" program to show at least rudiments of self-modification and adapt to individual users (a very difficult problem), and the fact that AI/ES extends the possibilities for computerization in society. When Partridge summed these factors he found "all the ingredients for a super software crisis".

A crisis inhibitor would be to add a special structuring ES (Sandewall 1978) covering both the knowledge acquisition (Boose 1985) and the knowledge representation (McDermott 1986). This super shell for ES development would guide the design process towards maintenance-friendly systems. An intelligent front-end for evolution/maintenance would enable the end-user to take an active part in the continuous upgrading of the ES, and help the ES to grow and "learn".

The Explanation Problem

In a subsequent article Partridge (1987) pointed out that the explanation problem associated with ES technology is a manifestation of the ingredients for a potential software crisis, that is, that the technology is inherently limited to the relatively static and relatively context-free domain of abstract technical expertise. Partridge thus says that ES developers should concentrate on (the mundane) "low-road" applications and stay away from (the glamorous) "high-road" applications. The explanation problem is difficult enough in "low-road" applications.

ES textbooks usually argue that the separation of the knowledge base from the inference engine makes an ES easy to upgrade. This was questioned in the discussion above. For similar reasons this separation does not remove the explanation problem. Current systems can usually list the chain of rules activated in a decision. Such a trace is at best a surface explanation; it does not qualify as an explanation in the sense of providing a justification or rationale for the decision.

"Just as one can follow a recipe and bake a cake without ever knowing why the flour or baking powder is there, so too an expert system can deliver impressive performance without any representation of the reasoning underlying its rules or methods" (Swartout, 1983). If maintenance is of primary concern for management (with consequences for the end-users), then explanation is of primary a concern for the end-users (with consequences for management).

By means of ES operating in a transactional mode, management may be able to enforce a certain policy and hereby reduce the *managerial* uncertainty about the working behaviour of the domain workers (end-users). The domain workers are prompted and the system checks entered-answers for reasonableness and consistency and verifies entered data to make sure they do not contradict organizational rules or information entered elsewhere in the system (compare Fig. 16.1). From a narrow-minded management perspective, in this ES bureaucracy there is no need to provide explanations of the ES decisions to the domain workers.

It is an altogether different situation for the domain workers. They must deal with uncertainty in their jobs. They must cope with the differences between the knowlege (information) needed for task execution and the knowledge (information) available to them. To apply ES technology to the domain means applying technology to a situation where there is uncertainty. To reduce uncertainty, the ES will have to transfer knowledge and provide interpretable information to the domain workers. Otherwise the *division of labour* between humans and machines grows into an unwanted *division of knowledge*. This is why explanation is a necessity in ES applications, and this is why Zuboff (1985) coined the twin concept "automate/informate".

The manual worker can understand the automation of physical functions through the perception of the automate's visible, concrete behaviour. Automation of abstract functions cannot be understood by the knowledge worker unless he is provided with a relevant model for interpretation. The ES needs to model the end-user in order to be able to adapt the explanation to the end-user's mode of thinking and level of competence. The end-user needs to model the ES in order to be in charge and capable of using it as a tool; it is not possible to communicate with a black box, a black box is not a tool. Thus the end-user and the ES need to outmodel each other, which means that each must be more complex than the other (Gaines & Shaw 1986).

Closely linked to the explanation problem is the dialogue problem. Implicit in the design of a dialogue for a human–computer interaction is that the designer employ a model of the end-user in the computer (better still: a system for continuous modelling of the end-user). Young (1984) summarized the dialogue problem by saying that every ES has to contain knowledge about the task domain and about how to communicate task matters with the end-user.

Researchers at IBM have concluded that every ES needs to be at least an "amateur" in psychology and communication (Thomas 1984). This stresses that the human–computer dialogue takes place with some sort of "persona" on the part of the computer. Card (1984) advocated that the task machine should be combined with a user discourse machine in the form of a dialogue ES. He also noted that when a machine starts exhibiting persona and base its output on an individual model of the end-user, then we can no longer talk about the machine being a tool for the user.

The review so far has pointed to a series of problems related to the difficulties of computer-mediated knowledge transfer. The ES designer somehow captures and stores knowledge about a task performance in a selected application domain. To make this new body of knowledge "living" and available to domain workers is very difficult if the goal is to design a joint cognitive system where the human and the computer are colleagues rather than a master/slave system. Merely providing intelligence regarding the application task is not enough. Three more ES units are needed (see Fig. 16.2).

ES Amplification of the Organizational Culture

McDermott (1986) wrote on "making expert systems explicit", and the present review is on making explicit the consequences and options of expert systems applications.

Like any tool, computer artefacts can be used and abused. New technology *per se* does not change skill levels, job discretion or stressors. Bad conditions remain bad and good conditions remain good (Frese and Zapf 1987). There will also be situations where a change may be for the better but where the change is experienced as a threat.

Mowshowitz (1984) saw a potential for ES to be used to amplify the organizational culture of the school of scientific management, which he found to be alive in the factory and growing stronger in the office. The trade mark of scientific management is division of labour. This is a rationalization concept used all over the world, and much labour–management bargaining deals with various ways of regulating its forms and ramifications. A new dimension will be added in that ES applications will extend the division of labour also to include division of knowledge. Mowshowitz believed that this will be manifested in the form of a bimodal distribution. One peak of the distribution will be highly skilled managerial, technical and professional jobs, the other will be unskilled service jobs.

Based on experience with the ACE system, polarization was also judged at AT&T to be a likely effect of ES taking over the middle ground of certain technical workers:

In the case of ACE, and, one suspects, most similar cases, the individuals displaced from a purely analytical function are those with the most experience both in personnel supervision, and in the actual execution of physical repair. . . . This picture, however, leaves no room for those with intermediate skills or else envisions them functioning, at least during a transition, as apprentices to machines which perform (better than they) much of the intellectual task they may well have found the most interesting part of their jobs. (Marcus 1984).

The experiences of ES applications at DEC is that it has provided the company with a set of labour-saving tools for problems that can be solved by the processing of knowledge.

With AI, quite a bit of routine work can be handed over to the computer, and human beings can concentrate on problems requiring greater creativity, allowing them to fulfill more of their potential. *And with each advance in the art of AI the border between routine and creative work can move out further into what was previously the creative territory.*" (Scown, 1985; emphasis added).

Kraft (1984) reported that DEC's introduction of XCON was accompanied by some technicians being worried about losing their jobs. DEC's solution "is to deal with the psychological aspects of the change to new technology and to train them meticulously". XCON now handles 97% of the configuration function earlier handled by technical editors, which saves the company $3.2 million per year in labour costs (Sviokla 1986a).

Mumford (1987a, b) was called in to help DEC with the needed training and change psychology in connection with the introduction of XSEL, which is an ES designed to give the local sales personnel access to some of the information in XCON. An ES application, she said, should assist and not displace the human being who associates with it. It is a business concern and also an ethical process to ensure that an ES acts as an automated expert which adds to human knowledge like a good teacher. This was clearly not the case with XCON, which, said Mumford, was a system designed to replace the technical editors. There seems to be some ethical doubt with regard to the implementation of XCON.

Speller and Brandon (1986) pointed out another ethical issue. According to the Code of Ethics of the American Society of Mechanical Engineers, an engineer using an ES runs the risk of exhibiting improper behaviour unless the ES can clarify its reasoning in a manner directly intelligible to the engineer.

Regardless of the ethical aspects, a humanistic use of human resources is good business. Discussing the thrust for ES to be used in maintenance applications in the military system, Coppola (1984) emphasized that short-term temptations should should not be allowed to interfere with the more important long-term gains. Declining skill levels in maintenance personnel promote a temptation to follow a "smart machine-dumb man" philosophy. However, if a human is subject to direction by a machine (compare Fig. 16.1) which does not credit him or her with capability, then (i) any capability he or she has is wasted, (ii) he or she will not improve in capability, and (iii) he or she will not find satisfaction with the job. These factors are not only demeaning for the human, they can create a dangerous working climate. AI applications to maintenance should for this reason, argued Coppola, to the greatest extent possible be designed to adapt to the skill of the end-user and serve as a means to improve his or her skills.

For a human it may be *intimidating* that an ES is *imitating* his or her intellectual skills (Kowalski 1984; Hayes-Roth 1984b). The following case may exemplify what may be in store for some professionals:

One expert who gladly gave himself and his specialized knowledge over to a knowledge engineer suffered a severe blow to his ego on discovering that the expertise he'd gleaned over the years, and was very well paid and honored for, could be expressed in a few hundred heuristics. At first he was depressed. Eventually he departed his field, a chastened and moving figure in his bereavement (Feignebaum & McCorduck 1983).

Concluding Advice to System Designers

Remember that you are not designing a computer system, but are putting a process in place in a user organisation. (Bobrow & Stefik 1985)

Acknowledgement. During the preparation of this review, the author was a Visiting Professor at the Department of Industrial Engineering, University of Wisconsin-Madison, USA. Financial support was obtained from Teldok, Sweden. The views expressed are those of the author.

References and Further Reading

Alvey P (1983) The problems of designing a medical expert system. Expert Systems '83, pp. 30–42 Cambridge University Press, Cambridge.

Amick BC, III, Östberg O (1987) Office automation, occupational stress and health: A literature analysis with specific attention to Expert Systems. Office: Technology and People 3: 191–209

Bachant J, McDermott J (1985) RI revisited: four years in the trenches. AI Magazine 5(3): 21–32

Berry DC, Broadbent DE (1986) Expert systems and the Man–Machine Interface. Department of Psychology, University of Oxford, (ALV/PRJ/MMI/027)

Bibel W (1985 Artificial intelligence in Europe. In Bibel W, Petkoff B (eds), *Artificial Intelligence: Methodology, Systems, Applications*, pp. 3–10, Elsevier Science, Amsterdam.

Bobrow DG, Stefik M (1985) Knowledge-based programming. Alvey News (Uk), No 13: 13–14.

Boose JH (1985) A knowledge acquisition program for expert systems based on personal construct psychology. Int. J Man–Machine Studies 23: 495–525

Buchana B (1986) Expert systems: working systems under the research literature Expert Systems 3: 32–51

Bullinger H-J, (1985) Technology trend – a challenge to research and industry. *Proceedings of 2nd International Conference on Human Factors in Manufacturing and 4th IAO Conference.* pp. 21–35

Card SK (1984) Human factors and the intelligent interface. *Proceedings of Symposium on Combining Human and Artificial intelligence*, Human factors Society Metropolitan Chapter, New York, November 15, 1984. (pp. 4–23).

Coppola A (1984) Artificial intelligence applications to maintenance. Artificial intelligence in Maintenance. (AD-AI45 349), pp. 23–44. Denver Research Institute, Denver, Colorado

d'Agapeyeff A (1984) Making a start: a review from British industry, in *Expert Systems*, pp. 3–13 Pergamon Infotech, Maidenhead, UK (State of the Art Report 12:7)

Dreyfus HL, Dreyfus SE (1986a) Mind over Machine: The Power of Human Intuition and Expertise in the Era of Computers Free Press, New York

Dreyfus HL, Dreyfus SE (1986b) Competent systems: the only future for inference-making computers. Future Generations Computer Systems 2: 233–244

Ernst ML, Ojha, H (1986) Business applications of artificial intelligence knowledge based expert systems. Future Generations Computer Systems 2: 173–185

Feigenbaum EA, McCorduck P (1983) The Fifth Generation, Reading, Addison-Wesley, MA

Fox JM (1982) Software and its Development. Prentice-Hall, Englewood Cliffs, NJ

Frese M, Zapf D (1987) Introducing new technology hardly changes skill level, job discretion or stressors. (In German). Zeitschrift für Arbeitswissenschaft 41: 7–14

Frosher JN, Jacob RJK (1985) Designing expert systems for ease of change. Proceedings of IEEE Symposium on Expert Systems in Government, pp. 246–251. IEEE, Washington DC

Gillett P (1987) Victory from the jaws of defeat. Alvey Conference Report (UK), p. 20 Cambridge University Press, Cambridge

Gaines BR, Shaw MLG (1986) Foundations of dialog engineering: the development of human-computer interaction (ii) Int J Man–Machine Studies, 24: 101–123

Hayes C, Wright P (1986) Automated planning in the machining domain In Lu SC-Y Komanduri R (eds) *Knowledge-Based Expert Systems for Manufacturing*, pp. 221–232. American Society of Mechanical Engineers, New York.

Hayes-Roth F (1984a) Knowledge-based expert systems – the state of the art in the US In *Expert Systems* pp. 49–62 Pergamon Infotech, Maidenhead, UK (State of the Art Report 12:7)

Hayes-Roth F (1984b) The machine as a partner of the new professional. IEEE Spectrum 21(6), 28–31

Hwang S-L, Salvendy G (1984) Human supervisory performance in flexible manufacturing systems. *Proceedings of the Human Factors Society 28th Annual Meeting*, 1984. (Pp. 664–669)

JMA (1983) Robotics and the Manager (Investigaton report from the Japanese Managment Association; English edition). Fuji Corporation, Tokyo

Karatsu H (1984) Aplicable fields and social impacts of advanced computer. ICOT Journal No 2: 2–12

Kowalski R (1984) Software engineering and artificial intelligence in New Generation Computing. Future Generations Computer Systems 1: 39–49

Luger GF, Stubblefield, WA, (1987) Paradigm dependent human factors issues in expert system design. Proceedings of Expert Systems in Telecommunications. Human Factors Society Metropolitan Chapter, New York

McDermott J (1982) R1: A rule-based configurer of computer systems. Artificial Intelligence, 19: 39–88

McDermott J (1986) Making expert systems explicit, pp 539–544. In Kugler H-J (ed), Information Processing. Elsevier Science, Amsterdam.

Marcus M (1984) AI in 2010: the Impact on individuals of Just Another Important Technology. Office of Technology Assessment, US Congress, Washington DC. (9 November, Draft Report)

Miller FD (1984) Introducing an expert system into the workplace. Proceedings of Symposium on Combining Human and Artificial Intelligence, pp. 41–51. Human FActors Society Metropolitan Chapter, New York.

Mowshowitz A (1984) The Future with AI: Freedom and Community? Office of Technology Assessment, US Congress, Washington, DC (9 November, Draft Report)

Mumford E (1987a) Managing complexity – the design and implementation of expert systems. (Unpublished). Manchester Business School, Manchester, UK.

Mumford E (1987b) The successful design of expert systems – are means more important than ends? (Unpublished). Manchester Business School, Manchester, UK.

Nilsson, N (1985) Artificial intelligence, employment, and income. Human Systems Management 5: 123–135

Östberg O (1986) Expert systems in a social environment – human factors concerns. Proceedings of the Human Factors Society 30th Annual Meeting (pp. 739–743)

OTA (1987) Federal Funding for Artificial Intelligence Research and Development. Office of Technology Assessment, US Congress, Washington, DC. (Staff Paper)

Parnas DL (1985) Software aspects of strategic defense systems. Am Sci. 73: 432–440

Partridge D (1986) Will AI lead to a super software crisis? in Gill KLS (Ed), Artificial Intelligence for Society. Wiley, Chichester, UK (pp. 31–39)

Partridge D (1987) The scope and limitations of first generation expert systems. Future Generations Computer Systems, 3: 1–10.

Paul RP, Nof, SY (1979) Work measurement – a comparison between robot and human task performance. Int. J. Prod. Res. 17: 277–303

Raimondi D (1985) Insurer supporting commercially viable AI programming. Computerworld, 19 (21): 12–13

Ramamoorthy CV, Prakash A, Tsai W-T, Usuda P (1984) Softward engineering: problems and perspective. Computer 17(10): 191–209

Rifkin G (ed), (1985) Toward the Fifth Generation. Computerworld, Update 3–24, 6 May

Sandewall E (1978) Programming in an interactive environment: the 'LISP' experience. Computing Surveys 10: 35–71

Scown, SE (1985) The Artificial Intelligence Experience: An Introduction. Digital Equipment Corporation, Maynard, MA

Shank RC, quoted in Sanger, DE (1987) Computer fails as job-killer. The New York Times, Career section 5–6 11 October

Smith C (1987) Arthur Andersen & Co. creates expert system mortgage loan analyzer for residential mortgages. Artificial Intelligence Letters (Texas Instruments), 3: 2–5

Speller GJ, Brandon JA (1986) Ethical dilemmas constraining the use of Expert Systems. Behaviour and Information Technology. 5: 141–143

Sviokla JJ (1986a) Business implications of knowledge-based systems (1). Data Base 17(4): 5–16

Sviokla JJ (1986b) Business implications of knowledge-based systems. (11). Data Base 18(1): 5–16

Swartout WR (1983) XPLAIN; a system for creating and explaining expert consulting programs. Artificial Intelligence 21: 285–325

Thomas JC (1984) Artificial intelligence and human factors. Proceedings of Symposium on Combining Human and Artificial Intelligence, Human Factors Society Metropolitan Chapter, New York 15 November, 1984. pp. 54–66.

Whitby B (1984) AI: some immediate dangers. In Yazdani M, Narayanan A (Eds) Artificial intelligence: human effects. Ellis Horwood, Chichester, UK pp. 235–245

Woods DD (1986) Paradigms for intelligent decision support. In Hollnagel E, Mancini G, Woods DD, (eds), Intelligent decision support in process environments. Springer-Verlag, Berlin; pp 153–173

Young RM (1984) Human interface aspects of expert systems. In Fox J (ed) Expert Systems. Pergamon Infotech, Maidenhead, UK, pp. 101–111 (State of the Art Report 12:7)

Zuboff S (1985) Automate/informate: the two faces of intelligent technology. Organizational Dynamics, Autumn 1985, 4–18.

Subject Index